KW-041-643

To my parents

WITHDR

British Sociological Association Industrial Studies 2

The Sociology of the Workplace

British Sociological Association Industrial Studies

1   Man and Organization
    edited by John Child

The Sociology of the Workplace

An Interdisciplinary Approach

Edited by Malcolm Warner

London   George Allen & Unwin Ltd
Ruskin House   Museum Street

First published in 1973

This book is copyright under the Berne Convention. All
rights are reserved. Apart from any fair dealing for the
purpose of private study, research, criticism or review, as
permitted under the Copyright Act, 1956, no part of this
publication may be reproduced, stored in a retrieval system,
or transmitted, in any form or by any means, electronic,
electrical, chemical, mechanical, optical, photocopying,
recording or otherwise, without the prior permission of the
copyright owner. Enquiries should be addressed to the
publishers.

© George Allen & Unwin Ltd 1973

ISBN 0 04 301062 8 hardback
    0 04 301063 6 paper

PLYMOUTH POLYTECHNIC LIBRARY

ACC. NO.	60007-1
CLASS NO.	~~301.55~~ ~~WAR~~ 306.36 Soc

-0. SEP. 1977

Calrd 004 3010628

Printed in Great Britain
in 11 point Times Roman type
by Unwin Brothers Limited
The Gresham Press
Old Woking Surrey

Contents

If I'm designed yon lordling's slave
By Nature's law designed –
Why was an independent wish
E'er planted in my mind?
If not, why am I subject to
His cruelty or scorn?
Or why has man the will and power
To make his fellow mourn?

Robert Burns

The Contributors

PETER ABELL

is Director of Research and Reader in the Industrial Sociology
Unit, Imperial College, University of London. He previously
lectured in Sociology at the University of Essex. He is author
of *Model Building in Sociology* (1971), and co-author of *Inward
Investment in the United Kingdom* (1972).

CELIA DAVIES

is a lecturer in the Industrial Sociology Unit, Imperial College.
Her research covers professional organizations with special
reference to hospitals. She graduated in Sociology from the
University of Hull.

SANDRA DAWSON

is Senior Research Officer, Industrial Sociology Unit, Imperial
College, working on aspects of in-prison work experience. She
graduated in Sociology and History from the University of
Keele.

EDWARD OWEN EVANS

is on the teaching staff of Ashorne Hill College. He has
industrial experience in engineering and chemical and zinc
manufacture, and was Senior Research Associate in Industrial
Relations at St Edmund Hall, Oxford. He is joint author
with A. I. Marsh and P. Garcia of *Workplace Industrial
Relations in Engineering* (1971).

JOHN ELDRIDGE

holds the Chair of Sociology at the University of Glasgow. He
was until recently Professor of Sociology at the University of
Bradford, and before that was Senior Lecturer in Sociology at
York. He is the author of *Industrial Disputes*, and the editor of
Max Weber: the Interpretation of Social Society.

ARTHUR FRANCIS

is Research Officer in the Industrial Sociology Unit, working on problems of professionals in organizations with special reference to hospitals. He graduated in Engineering from Imperial College, London.

ANDREW W. GOTTSCHALK

teaches Social Psychology and Industrial Relations in the Department of Adult Education, University of Nottingham. He is co-author of *British Industrial Relations: an Annotated Bibliography* (1969), and co-author and editor of *Bargaining for Change: Productivity Bargaining and Industrial Relations* (1972).

DAN GOWLER

is Senior Lecturer in Industrial Anthropology at Manchester Business School. He graduated in Economics and Social Anthropology at Cambridge on a mature student state scholarship, having previously spent fifteen years in industry, most of that time with an oil company. For the last five years he has worked with Professor Tom Lupton, researching on manpower planning, wage payment systems, the movement of earnings at plant level, and organizational design.

EARL HOPPER

is a lecturer at the London School of Economics, currently completing studies in Social Mobility, Relative Deprivation, and Anomie. He is editor of *Readings in the Theory of Educational Systems*, and author of various articles on the sociology of education and industrial sociology.

KAREN LEGGE

is lecturer in Organizational Behaviour at Manchester Business School. Her publications include articles and essays in the general areas of labour economics and industrial sociology with particular reference to the operation of wage payment systems and internal labour markets.

GERALD MARS

is Senior Lecturer in Industrial Sociology and Industrial
Relations at Enfield College of Technology. He was previously
a research fellow at the Newfoundland Institute of Social and
Economic Research, and a visiting lecturer at the University of
Alberta in Canada.

DAVID MATHEW

is Research Assistant at the Industrial Sociology Unit,
Imperial College, and is currently researching communication
in organizations.

STANLEY PARKER

is working on industrial projects in the Social Survey Division
of the Office of Population Censuses and Surveys. His views in
this article are expressed in a personal capacity.

ADAM PEARCE

is a research student in Sociology at the London School of
Economics and has been collaborating with Earl Hopper on
sociological research.

KEITH E. THURLEY

is Senior Lecturer in Industrial Sociology at the London School
of Economics. He was previously Assistant Labour Officer
with Courtaulds Ltd and Visiting Assistant Professor at the
International Christian University in Tokyo.

MALCOLM WARNER

is Senior Research Officer, Organizational Behaviour Research
Group, London Graduate School of Business Studies. He was
previously Visiting Fellow in the Sociology Department,
Columbia University and a Research Associate in the NSF project
on 'Opposition in Organizations'. He is co-author of *The Data
Bank Society* (1970).

Introduction

This volume is intended to be *interdisciplinary* in nature. We have approached the study of the workplace from the standpoint of industrial sociology, industrial relations, industrial anthropology, and other related disciplines. In addition, we have attempted to pursue a different approach from the earlier volume *Man and organization*, edited by John Child, looking at a broader range of subjects. By taking this view, we hope to reveal the extent to which contributions are being made which shed light on the complex nature of workplace activities not just in departments of sociology, but in several others in universities and other research institutions. The policy of the BSA Industrial Sociology Section has been to open it doors to a number of speakers from different fields of study and disciplines, with this aim in mind, and a number of the papers in this volume were originally presented to that audience. The discussion here presented, we hope, will interest not only those involved in teaching and research but also the third year undergraduate and graduate student. A special effort has been made to invite a number of papers summarizing the state of play in a field of study such as bargaining, for example, as well as more specialised pieces of research. The collection may also be of use to those interested in the practical application of social science in industry, and here the case studies we have included may be of interest.

The research carried out for the Donovan Commission by the Social Survey suggested that there is still a great deal we can learn about industrial relations at workplace level. For example, the survey discussed the shop steward's role, but did not reveal the 'spokesman' function he carries out. As his relationship to the steward is problematic, Stanley Parker has developed this in his attempt to apply concepts within a theoretical framework to further research into workplace industrial relations. He suggests two models: one of clusters of the variables involved, and the other a 'path' model of responses to change in the system (an industrial relations 'episode'). The first, 'macro' model he believes ought to assist us to map out more effectively the system and to encourage further research on the network of interrelationships of structure, behaviour, and attitudes. The second, 'micro' model follows through a specific sequence of events, and attempts to show how decisions made at certain points (including structural characteristics such as whether there is adequate machinery of consultation) can affect the outcome of a particular proposal for change by management or employees' representatives.

The need for a more systematic study of bargaining behaviour at plant level is emphasized by Andrew Gottschalk. In a long paper he summarizes the research to date, drawing on industrial relations and psychology, and to some degree, economics. There is also an attempt to fit the analysis into the context of organizational theory. This paper will be of considerable use in suggesting lines for further research, and illustrating the potentiality of an interdisciplinary approach to the industrial sociologist interested in conflict resolution in the workplace.

'Cheap at twice the price?' is the question posed by a researcher who has examined, in case-study detail, the work of shop stewards in the engineering industry. Here Ted Evans has examined the role of the shop steward as seen by managers, and it explores the minutiae of shop floor institutions and practices in a way which offers an insightful case study of the position in a specific industrial setting. In uniting the survey approach with an eye for detail, Evans covers 432 factories and nearly 9,000 shop stewards without losing the 'feel' of the situation. There is also an attempt to answer some of the questions related to the discussion as to whether managers operate with a unitary or pluralistic view of the enterprise.

The study of the 'regressive spiral' in the labour market by Dan Gowler and Karen Legge, explores the 'vicious circles' that push labour not only out of, but also into, the organization. They attempt to analyse the effects of employees' perceptions of the effort-reward relationships on absenteeism and labour turnover. Their approach looks at occupational role *integration* as well as *differentiation* as a way of dealing with the problem of institutionalization.

The first of two papers by sociologists at Imperial College, London, deals with the importance of technology as a variable in sociological explanation, and particularly focusses on the 'task analysis' approach of the late Professor Joan Woodward who originally set up the Industrial Sociology Unit at that institution. Celia Davies, Sandra Dawson, and Arthur Francis conclude that adopting a technological deterministic approach does not allow prediction of all behaviour, nor does taking an 'action perspective' mean that knowledge of technology can be said to be no predictor at all. They argue for the building of more complex models.

The contribution of mathematical sociology to industrial studies has thus far been limited; however the recent appointment of Peter Abell to head the Unit in Industrial Sociology at Imperial College promises to remedy this state of affairs. In a paper with David Mathew, Abell attempts to argue that organizational tasks, or rather 'task decomposition structures' as the authors call them, are not sufficient to explain features of organizational structure. The paper represents a very concise attempt to lay bare the logical structure of the 'task analysis framework', and to suggest ways of critically refining the concept as a variant of functional analysis.

The relative importance of the technology variable is further discussed in the paper by Keith Thurley on 'Computers and supervisors'. The whole question of the effect of automation on workplace roles is analysed, and Thurley's conclusions have implications for anyone in the managerial role, including supervisors and foremen. The implications for research on the work of the shop steward are important, although not elaborated by the author, but the literature on supervisory roles is well summarized, and the determinants of supervisory behaviour examined on a comparative basis, dealing with the British and Japanese experiences, using empirical data. This paper will be useful for those interested in the sociology of supervision, as well as the technological determinism thesis.

Gerald Mars's study of deviancy in the workplace is a very interesting analysis of pilferage in a hotel, based on the approach of an industrial anthropologist. Having formerly worked on research on a similar problem in the Newfoundland docks, Mars has developed a theoretical framework encompassing the two rather dissimilar locations, and which may be suggestive for social scientists interested in the problem in, say, a factory shop floor setting. Mars concludes by suggesting that further research will involve participant observation as pioneered by anthropologists, 'a path many industrial sociologists still appear loth to tread'.

The paper by Earl Hopper and Adam Pearce deals with relative deprivation, occupational status, and occupational 'situs'; the last of these being a 'little known and neglected concept', and dealing with whether work is, say, indoors or outdoors, or involves contact with jobs versus contact with people. They deal with the personal and interpersonal aspects of participation in a job, and develop a theory to show why feelings of relative deprivation vary with situs classifications. They set out an array of interrelated propositions which are of special interest to the industrial sociologist, using the bureaucratic structures of authority as the independent variable.

The degree to which theories of the labour movement may only be valid for a limited number of settings is discussed in the penultimate contribution, by the editor of this volume. Entitled 'Industrial conflict revisited', it suggests that many writers have underestimated the degree of endemic conflict in industrial societies, and particularly offers a critique of the work of Kerr, Sturmthal, and others, criticizing the organizational maturity thesis, and concluding that the reliance on economic variables alone will not provide adequate understanding for those interested in the sociology of conflict. The paper attempts to present some of the questions relating to conflict, which in earlier papers were illustrated in a plant-level setting, in a broader societal context.

As an Epilogue, John Eldridge has provided an overview of the present state of cross-classification and theoretical craftsmanship in industrial sociology, and the possible directions it might take in the coming years. His paper attempts to deal with problems of the 'sociological imagination', and its relation to industrial life.

The set of papers in this volume, we believe, shows the diversity of research and methods of social study which exist in British academic institutions today, whether universities, business schools, polytechnics, and so on. The volume also represents a forum for those with parallel but distinct approaches to the sociological dimensions of workplace activity, relations, and organization. Most of the scholars who have contributed to this volume are young, involved in empirical research, and active members of the profession. If the diversity of readership matches that of the contributors, then the goal of this inter-disciplinary effort will have been achieved. Finally, I should like to thank all my contributors for their support in the collection of these chapters, my colleagues in the Research Group for their interest, and particularly Betty Leigh for her continuous assistance in the final production of this volume.

Malcolm Warner
Organizational Behaviour
Research Group
London Graduate School of
Business Studies

Summer 1972

1 Research into Workplace Industrial Relations: Progress and Prospects

S. R. PARKER*

In this chapter I propose to review the progress that has been made in researching into different aspects of industrial relations at workplace level. My review starts with an assessment of some of the main findings of the survey carried out for the Royal Commission on Trade Unions and Employers' Associations (the 'Donovan Commission') and goes on to note some of the possible topics for further survey research. I then turn to the contribution of case studies in gaining a deeper understanding of a single situation or relatively few situations. Finally I propose two models to help guide future research into workplace industrial relations in a systematic way: a general model of the variables involved, and a 'path' model tracing the various paths that can be taken in handling a particular industrial relations episode.

THE DONOVAN SURVEY

In 1968 the report of the first large-scale national survey of workplace industrial relations was published.[1] This inquiry was carried out by the Government Social Survey (now part of the Office of Population Censuses and Surveys) for the Donovan Commission. Representative samples of all the main types of people involved in workplace industrial relations were interviewed: works managers, personnel officers, foremen, shop stewards, union full-time officers, union members, non-

* The views expressed here are those of the author and do not represent the views of the Office of Population Censuses and Surveys.

unionists, and employers' association officials.[2] Altogether over 3,500 interviews were carried out during 1966.

The full report contains a large amount of factual information and the Royal Commission Research Paper 10 added some interpretation of these results. The survey was intended to give the Commission members background information likely to be useful to them in coming to some of their conclusions. It was largely a fact-finding rather than a hypothesis-testing exercise, because little prior information was available and the question had to cover a wide variety of topics on which information was desired. Some analytical work was done on the results of the survey (notably to suggest types of shop steward and their correlates[3]). The main value of the results, however, was to enable some broad descriptive conclusions to be drawn about workplace industrial relations, backed up by a mass of survey data and interpreted in the light of previous smaller-scale research and the experience of the industrial relations experts who were involved in the Commission's work.

Without attempting an exhaustive review of all the findings,[4] I should like to discuss briefly a few of what seem to me to be the more important topic areas:

1. *The extent of workplace bargaining.* This is probably the single most important and most often quoted topic covered by the survey. It relates to the significant role that shop stewards were shown to play in conducting negotiations with local managements on a wide variety of issues affecting the interests of their members. Besides enabling a more accurate estimate of the total number of shop stewards to be made, the survey revealed details of stewards' bargaining activities with different levels of management. Five out of six stewards in the sample discussed *and settled* at least some issues with management. Three-quarters had settled some aspect of working conditions as standard practice and just over half had settled some wage issues. The widespread existence of pressure to increase the range of issues negotiated with management was clear: nearly half of the stewards said there were issues which they wanted to settle with management but which the latter regarded as their own right to decide.

2. *The growth of informal practices alongside formal procedures.* The role of shop stewards in formal grievance procedures is

usually supposed to be that of taking complaints or claims raised by members to the first level of supervision (foreman). However, the survey showed that 80 per cent of stewards said their members brought problems to them without first approaching their foreman. Furthermore, nearly half of the stewards said they sometimes bypassed the foreman to approach the next stage of management above, and nearly three-quarters said they had 'unofficial' ways of approaching management. Yet these informal practices did not seem to be accompanied by any widespread lack of formal procedures. Four out of five stewards said there was a nationally agreed procedure for settling disputes that arose at local level. A third of managers in federated plants said that the use of procedure *within their plant* had increased in recent years (only 3 per cent said it had decreased). Informal practices would seem to have supplemented formal procedures rather than to have replaced them.

3. *Favourable evaluation of stewards.* The stereotype of a shop steward as a militant trouble-maker and a scourge of management was shown by the survey to be quite false. There was no question that most stewards represented the interests of their members conscientiously and on occasions forcefully, but their role in doing so was widely accepted by all parties to industrial relations. In the words of the report, they were seen as 'more of a lubricant than an irritant'. Not only were stewards generally regarded as *less* militant than their members, but 70 per cent of managers preferred to deal with a steward if he and a full-time union officer were competent to settle an issue. Moreover, stewards generally saw themselves as playing a positive role in the production system: 68 per cent thought they were helping management 'quite a lot' to solve its problems and run the firm more efficiently (only 6 per cent thought they were not helping at all).

4. *Favourable evaluation of 'the system'.* Rather than ask a very general question about the degree of satisfaction that the various parties to industrial relations felt about the operation of 'the system' at workplace level, the researchers built up indices of such satisfaction from the answers to specific questions. Since the indices included different items for stewards, managers, foremen, etc. it was not possible to make an exact comparison.

21

However, the general picture was one of majority satisfaction with items such as the procedure for dealing with grievances and claims and the efficiency and reasonableness of 'opposite numbers'. Perhaps it is significant that union officers were rather less satisfied with questions of procedure and 'access' than the other parties (the officers' experience of a number of different workplaces may have led them to judge the worst by the standards of the best). The general picture of satisfaction should not, however, divert attention from the existence of minority dissatisfaction with specific aspects of the system in specific workplaces.

5. *Dissatisfaction with management efficiency and manpower utilization.* If one takes a narrow view of 'industrial relations' the question of management efficiency is relevant only in so far as it concerns efficiency in handling industrial relations and the question of manpower utilization is not relevant at all. But the survey findings indicate that a wider view is desirable. Large minorities of informants were dissatisfied with these two questions – generally much large minorities than were dissatisfied with points concerning the working of the industrial relations system itself. Nearly a third of the stewards and more than a third of the union officers thought that management was either 'not very efficient' or 'inefficient'. One clue to the relationship between perceived management efficiency and industrial relations was the finding that 40 per cent of the stewards who were dissatisfied with facilities to deal with members' grievances and claims thought their management was 'inefficient', but only 5 per cent of stewards who were very satisfied with facilities thought this. Four out of ten foremen and employees thought that the work they supervised or did could be better organized. Similar proportions of managers and personnel officers claimed that there were time-wasting and inefficient labour practices in their workplaces.

The above are only a few of the findings of the Donovan survey. I have said nothing about the findings of the survey on a very large number of other specific questions, because I want to leave space to consider what further research questions are posed by the results obtained. It is convenient to discuss the possibilities of further survey research in relation to the five points above:

1. *Workplace bargaining.* Although the Donovan survey obtained information about the range of bargaining between stewards and management, it did so by asking questions about the situation at the time of interview. It would be interesting to know the progress that stewards may be making in gaining the right to negotiate further issues with management, and what type of issues these may be. As associated concerns it would be instructive to examine the circumstances in which the range of bargaining may tend to be increased, as well as the reactions of the parties to any unsuccessful attempts by stewards to encroach on what management see as their decision-making prerogatives.

2. *Informal practices.* There is scope for finding out more about the reasons why workplace bargaining seems to be preferred by the parties involved in industrial relations, and what are seen to be the advantages and disadvantages of this type of bargaining as opposed to bargaining above workplace level. Is it the flexibility and informality of local bargaining which is the attraction, or would unions and/or management prefer to negotiate more workplace agreements? A different aspect of informality is the role of the informal work-group spokesman, to which Goodman and Whittingham[5] drew attention but which was not examined at all in the Donovan survey. In non-union workplaces attention could focus on the degree to which such spokesmen acted as substitute stewards, while in unionized workplaces the possible intervention of the spokesman in the worker-forman-steward relationship seems likely to repay study.

3. *Evaluation of stewards.* The crucial relationship is between the steward and the members he represents. Although this relationship can survive a certain amount of disagreement (which the survey showed was not infrequent), a deeper division of interests could alienate the steward from his members in a way similar to the gulf that sometimes appears between union members in a workplace and the national leadership. As a basis for understanding the possibilities and the limitations of the steward role in other directions, we need to know more about the variations in quality of the member-steward relationship and the circumstances which accompany these variations.

Specifically, to what extent are stewards mere mouthpieces of their members and to what extent are they leaders?

4. *Evaluation of 'the system'*. The Donovan survey asked about degrees of satisfaction with a number of particular features of workplace industrial relations, but it did not go very deeply into *why* there was dissatisfaction in some cases. Also, more positively, there is scope for finding out what are the main kinds of change thought to be needed to improve industrial relations at workplace level. It would not be surprising to discover that a fairly large proportion of all those involved think that better communication between employees and management would help. Other suggestions might not be so easy to predict. It would also be worthwhile to know the relative emphasis that the different parties place on different possible ways of improving industrial relations in their workplaces.

5. *Efficiency*. There were many indications from the Donovan survey that a more intensive study of the mutual influence of the industrial relations system and the production system would yield positive results. Efficiency or inefficiency – particularly of middle and top management, who have more scope for decision making than other groups – may well be a characteristic that pervades both industrial relations and production systems in a given workplace. The implications of such a finding for policies designed to secure improvement in either or both spheres would be far-reaching.

Again, the list of topics proposed for further research is not exhaustive, though I hope it includes some subjects that are generally agreed to be worth researching. One important methodological point should be mentioned in connection with any possible future survey of workplace industrial relations involving a number of different workplaces. It was pointed out in a section on the samples in the full report of the Donovan survey that 'the ideal method of obtaining information about workplace relations would have been to interview all those involved in a number of randomly selected workplaces'. Unfortunately it was not possible to use this method, and several separate representative samples had to be drawn. While the method of interviewing people who deal with each other in the same workplaces is not without its own sampling problems, it would clearly allow more to be learned about the way in which the different parties perceive each other's roles and react to the same environment.

I have concentrated so far on discussing the Donovan survey and the possibilities of further workplace surveys along similar lines. But there is, of course, another kind of research – that confined to a single case or a very small number of cases. Except in so far as they may allow samples of particular types of people to be taken within one work unit, case studies do not permit statistical analysis to be made of their findings. But they do enable more to be understood 'in depth' about a particular situation. The two methods of sample surveys and case studies really complement each other, because each adds a dimension to the possibilities of data analysis afforded by the other.

A scrutiny of existing case studies carried out in the field of industrial relations (plus those case studies which have had industrial relations as a subsidiary rather than a main research aim) might enable us to formulate hypotheses testable either in further case studies or in surveys. To illustrate some of the possibilities I shall take two examples, one from officially sponsored and one from academic research.

Among the reports of the Commission on Industrial Relations on particular references made to them is one on British Home Stores Ltd.[6] The report is mainly concerned with the industrial relations institutions and procedures of BHS as a whole, but the reference arose out of events at one of the company's stores and in the course of the inquiry the Commission thought it appropriate to make some general assessment of the industrial relations situation in the multiple retail trade as a whole. Thus the findings of the report have implications for at least three levels of industrial relations – the workplace, the company, and the industry.

I shall not attempt to summarize either the findings or the recommendations of the report. Instead I want to draw attention to one feature of the report which seems to me to have important implications for both the design and interpretation of future research. This feature is the influence that an individual or small group of individuals can have on the 'structure' of a situation. With regard to trade union recognition and influence, the report notes that 'The energy and keenness of collectors of individual branches is important; one divisional officer mentioned two stores in which a very high rate of membership had dwindled to almost nothing when the collector left the store. . . . The personality of the local manager appears to have been a factor in the decision of employees in certain areas to join or refrain from joining the union.'

It would be wrong to conclude from such observations as these that 'all industrial relations is basically human relations' and that all problems would be solved if the right individuals were placed in the right key positions. But it would be equally wrong to deny that at least some individuals have scope to play their industrial roles differently or to exercise personal – sometimes even charismatic – influence on the course of events. To recognize the scope that there may be for individual differences to affect the conduct and outcome of industrial relations is not to seek an explanation of particular industrial relations phenomena in terms of the 'personalities' involved. It is rather to pose the research question: to what extent may differences in the climate of industrial relations – if not in specific procedures and activities – be explained in terms of the way in which certain key figures on both the management and union sides play their respective roles? This is obviously a question for intensive case study rather than extensive survey. It also underlines the importance of having a social psychologist on any multi-disciplinary team engaged in industrial relations research.

Mention of social psychology brings me to the second example I want to quote of case study research that could prove instructive in the planning of further inquiries. A few years ago Chadwick-Jones investigated the effect on working life in a steel plant of a change from hand-rolling to automated production.[7] After the change, management organization became more specialized, formal, and in many ways more remote. The relative functional importance of process workers and maintenance craftsmen shifted to the advantage of the latter. Appreciation of physically lighter work was outweighed by dissatisfaction at the loss of job autonomy on the part of the cohesive, largely self-selected, interdependent task groups which had existed in the hand-rolling plant. The study did not include a comparison of the state of industrial relations before and after the change, and this is perhaps one of the least satisfactory aspects of the report. But the author said enough about industrial relations in the old plant to make it clear that the technical changes were most unlikely to have left industrial relations unaffected in the new plant. The tone of industrial relations was said to have been militant in the old plant, yet 'antagonism and opposition to management actions expressed in union meetings was rarely brought to the point of a strike'. The changed relationship with management suggests that overt militancy may be a poor measure of the quality of industrial relations, judging by the remark of one operative: 'Before you could give your opinion on anything and you could always approach the foreman or go right to the top. Here it goes up and up . . . until it's squashed!'

My point in discussing these two case studies (as examples of others which could also have been discussed) is that technology, management, and supervisory practices, the scope for differences in individual role playing, and industrial relations are probably all interconnected in ways which we have yet fully to explore. Indeed, the variables I have mentioned so far are only part of the complex network of variables which may eventually form part of our understanding of workplace industrial relations systems and activities. At this point, then, I propose to widen the discussion to a more theoretical consideration of the use of explanatory models.

A GENERAL MODEL

In Figure 1 is set out a model of variables which it is reasonable to suppose have a measurable influence on part or the whole of the system of workplace industrial relations. The arrows show the directions in which various types of influence are believed to operate. The model is an attempt partly to describe what is already known in general terms about the operation of industrial relations at workplace level, and partly to suggest hypothetical relationships which may be tested by further research.

The model consists of five clusters of variables. These clusters are intentionally few in number in order to make the whole model easier to comprehend. Thus the cluster 'organization/ production variables' may be broken down into two clusters such as 'administrative and supervisory organization' (size, number of management levels, shape of management hierarchy, etc.) and 'production technology' (industry, technology, productive efficiency, etc.). Each cluster contains variables of the same general type, implying that in most cases the value of one variable in a cluster will be correlated with a value of another variable in the same cluster (thus, for example, there is evidence from the Donovan survey that the chemicals industry, continuous-flow technology, and large size of establishment are intercorrelated). The directional arrows a–g between the clusters indicate the probable direction of causation, both between a variable in one cluster and a variable in another cluster and between one cluster in general and another cluster. Again, for simplicity's sake certain other possible directional arrows are omitted: for example, influences outside the establishment are also likely to affect some aspects of development of the industrial relations system.

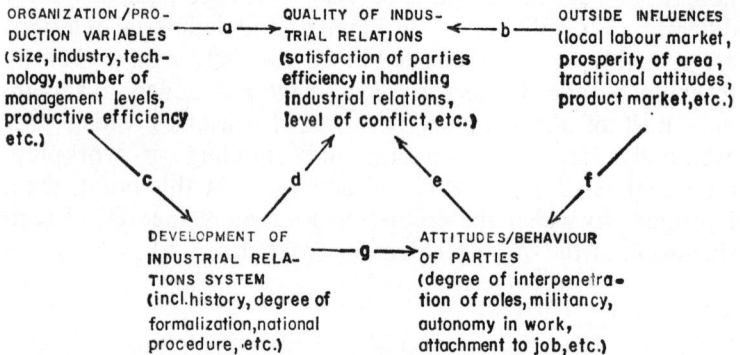

Figure 1

General model of scope of workplace industrial relations

The list of variables shown can easily be extended. The meaning of most of them should be clear, but a few explanatory remarks about some of them may help. *Quality of industrial relations* is probably the most contentious cluster, both in terms of its constituent items and of who judges the quality. This may be said to be varying degrees of good or bad, but an important question is: good or bad for whom? Ideally, a state of good industrial relations exists when all the parties involved judge it to be good, both from their own point of view and from that of the other parties involved. In practice, however, there may be a state of affairs where the management think industrial relations are good while the workers think they are bad, or even where workers and management succeed in achieving relations satisfactory to both parties but at a price judged to be unacceptable from a wider, 'public' point of view.

The *level of conflict* is inserted as a variable contributing to the quality of industrial relations. This is not to imply any necessary causal connection between the absence of conflict and good industrial relations. The absence of conflict may be a sign, not of positive agreement between management and workers about ends to be achieved or means to achieve them, but disengagement or alienation of one or both sides from the problems of the other or of the whole enterprise. On the other hand, a *certain level* of conflict may be accompanied by a generally stimulating atmosphere, conducing both to the rapid resolution of problems and to productive efficiency. The positive functions of conflict in general[8] and of strikes in particular[9] have been suggested, and it would clearly be of value to know more about the optimal level of conflict associated with good industrial relations and productive efficiency.

Degree of interpenetration of roles is proposed as a variable worth including under attitudes and behaviour of the parties. The subject of 'involvement at work' has become popular recently, and it seems quite likely that it is related to quality of industrial relations. There could be a direct relationship between involvement at work and quality of industrial relations, or an indirect one via the effect of worker involvement in decreasing certain forms of militancy. The hypothesis may be tested by asking about attitudes to worker involvement and relating these to measures of the quality of industrial relations. It may also be possible to measure the degree to which the structure of roles in a workplace shows interpenetration, a high degree being exemplified by the observation that 'The shop stewards talk like managers and the managers talk like shop stewards.'

It would be possible to produce a very large number of testable hypotheses starting from the general model I have outlined or a modified version of it. Proving these hypotheses to be true or false by case studies or surveys could add considerably to our knowledge of the working of the industrial relations system, or help solve the problems of one or more of the parties, or both. It would take too long to list even the hypotheses implicit in the present version of the model: instead I shall give one example of each of the inter-cluster relationships:

 a. In workplaces where there is a relatively high degree of productive efficiency there is more often general satisfaction of all the parties with industrial relations.
 b. In workplaces in areas where there are a number of different industries competing for labour there is felt to be more management efficiency in handling industrial relations.
 c. In larger workplaces the industrial relations system is more often formalized.
 d. Where the industrial relations system is more developed at local *and* national levels there is more often a moderate level of conflict.
 e. Where there is a greater interpenetration of roles the level and quality of conflict are perceived as being more tolerable.
 f. Workplaces in areas where occupational mobility is traditionally low have more workers who (feel they) have autonomy in their work.
 g. Where the industrial relations system is more developed locally shop stewards will more often stand in a leadership (rather than mouthpiece) role to their members.

These hypotheses have been chosen to illustrate the wide variety of possibilities. Different strategies of inquiry to test these hypotheses are possible. Thus a comparatively low-budget inquiry, taking the form of a fairly searching series of field or case studies, may choose to concentrate on variables in only some of the clusters, limiting the scope of the inquiry by subject matter. A higher-budget (probably sponsored) inquiry might consist of, or include, a large-scale survey, obtaining mainly quantified data and limiting the scope of questions by their implications for choice among alternative administrative policies. There is, of course, no rigid dividing line in terms of research strategy between these different approaches or possible permutations of them. In all cases the questions need to be framed in the light of having some provisional but at least loosely structured ideas about the set of research problems. Theoretical 'explanations' thought up afterwards to account for answers obtained are always open to the suspicion that some other questions would have yielded answers that would have 'proved' some other theory.

A 'PATH' MODEL

A general model such as the one outlined above is useful both in drawing attention to relevant variables and in showing the probable pattern of linkages among them. It is not a static model and allows for changes in the state of the system, but its overall emphasis is on relations between elements in a structure. This type of model needs to be supplemented by one that has a rather different, though complementary, purpose: that of depicting the various paths than can be taken in handling

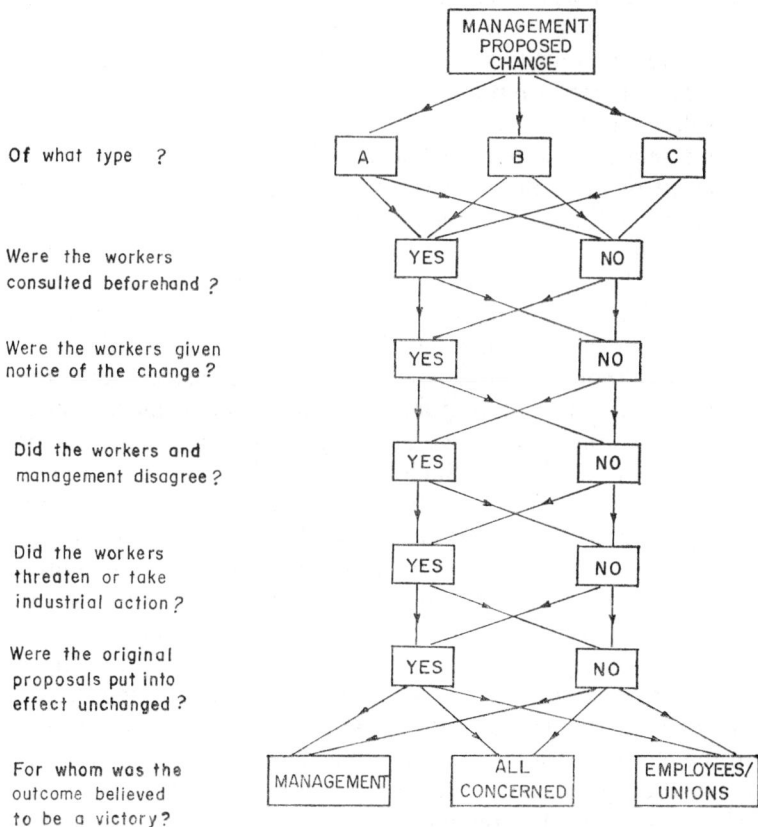

Figure 2

Example of path model of response to management proposal for change a particular industrial relations 'episode'. Whereas a general model enables hypotheses to be formulated, a 'path' model enables more specific predictions to be made about the probable outcome of taking certain types of decision along the path.

The type of model proposed in Figure 2 is one in which the probability of a given path through the episode is determined by the choice between alternative 'decisions' at successive stages. These 'decisions' are perhaps better understood as resultants of a prior chain of action and reaction between the parties to industrial relations and limited by the specific environment, rather than seen as the exercise of free choice by individuals. (Thus industrial relations in a given workplace at a given time may be described as good, not because anyone has decided that they shall be good, but because a variety of circumstances, behaviour, and attitudes has resulted in their becoming good.) It is convenient to represent the model graphically in the form of a flow chart.

In a sequential model such as this it is necessary to start with an event or piece of behaviour which is presumed to lead to a succession of problems which have to be resolved and eventually to a result. Each of the decisions about problems along the way has the effect of narrowing the range of choice at subsequent decision points. Changes affecting workplace relations usually stem either from a decision of management or of unions or other representatives of employees. Consider first the sequence of types of response resulting from a management proposal to make a change affecting the operation of part or whole of the workplace. Such a change might be, for example, a productivity agreement, the introduction of new machinery in one section, or moving the whole plant to a new location.

In Figure 2 various possible types of response to this initial proposal are set out.[10] It is not suggested that all of the subsequent 'decision' points always have to be faced after a proposed change, or that every possible variable that might have an effect in such a situation is included. Indeed, the choice of particular 'decision' points considered worth putting in the chart is to a large extent influenced by a view of what is considered significant, both in research and operational terms. The flow depicted in the model can be set out in the form of a number of propositions and alternatives, simplified for the sake of clarity.

Starting from the initial management proposal for change, the first question to ask is what type of change is being proposed. It is quite likely that the methods of dealing with, and the reactions to, a change such as the introduction of new plant or machinery will be different in some ways from those connected with a proposal for a new system of wage payment. Research is needed to find out whether certain kinds of change fall into groups so far as typical paths are concerned, so that we might draw parallels and make predictions in the light of this knowledge.

The next question to ask is whether the workers affected were consulted by the management before the change was due to take place. To be effective, prior consultation usually needs to be undertaken in a spirit of wanting to find out how the change is likely to be received and of willingness to modify or even scrap the proposed change if opposition is seen to be justified. The kind of consultation described by those 'consulted' as 'Yes, we were consulted – they told us what they were going to do' may, because of its apparent hypocrisy, be worse than no pretence of consultation at all.

The question of consultation is closely bound up with that of advance notice. In most cases – except those in which a period of uncertainty is felt to be more upsetting than living in ignorance of bad news (as with redundancy) – it is usually better that people are given advance notice so that they can adjust in attitude or behaviour or both to the change. A further crucial question is whether there is disagreement between the workers and management about the proposed change. There may be initial disagreement but, as a result of negotiations, subsequent agreement. In the event of disagreement, a lot will depend on whether the management regard the particular change as within their own prerogative to determine – if so, they will probably adopt a harder line towards opposition than if they accept that the proposed change is a subject for negotiation.

The question of disagreement leads on to whether the workers affected threaten or take some kind of industrial action in protest about the change. This is obviously more likely to happen where management do not grant employees the right to have a say in the decision. Conflicting ideas about the implementation of the change may lead to the next stage of

C

33

modifying the original proposals – this could also happen as a result of consultation and negotiation about details in an atmosphere of broad agreement.

Finally, some measure of how the outcome of the change was received would appear to be useful. One possible measure of this is whether the episode as a whole is thought to have improved industrial relations, worsened them, or made no difference. An episode seen to be well handled and with a satisfactory outcome for all concerned probably leads to a better climate for the handling of future episodes, whereas a badly handled episode may well sour a previously good climate or make a bad one even worse. The measure proposed in the chart is of whether the outcome of the episode is believed to be a victory for management, for the employees' side, or for all concerned. Hopefully there are few episodes resulting in no one being thought to have gained anything.

The provisional nature of this model should be stressed. It provides a guide to the sort of sequence of events that may take place following a management proposal for change of some kind. Research into actual episodes may show that the paths and variables in the present model are not usually the crucial ones in explaining the difference between 'good' and 'bad' ways of handling change.

Certain modifications in the model are required to trace a typical set of paths resulting from a change proposed by the unions or the workers. A wage claim or a demand for union recognition would be among the kinds of change that could be analysed using the model. The question of consultation might concern the union communicating both with the management and with its own members. Unlike the cases of management-proposed change, militant action would only follow *failure* to implement the change.

The above models of consequences of management- and union-proposed change could be adapted for episodes in non-union workplaces. The model shown is in fact applicable both to union and non-union situations, and a model with more decision points (for example, to include the possible roles of shop stewards and union full-time officers) would be needed to compare union episodes only. We have relatively little systematic knowledge about industrial relations in non-union workplaces or about 'employee relations' in white collar workplaces. Accounts of non-union firms which encourage worker participation in management[11] or co-partnership[12] tell us something about the structure of communication and consultation in a few firms, but there is still a lot to be learned in a systematic way about actual practices over the whole range of industry. As a rule the work group in an office is smaller than in manufacturing industry, and management of the work entails less impersonal discipline. A comparative study of workplace relations which attempted to draw parallels between union and non-union, manual and non-manual situations could contribute to a better understanding of the probable outcome of alternative arrangements for employee representation and of alternative ways of handling industrial relations episodes.

NOTES

1 W. E. J. McCarthy and S. R. Parker, *Shop stewards and workshop relations*, Research Paper no. 10, Royal Commission on Trade Unions and Employers' Associations, HM;O, 1968; for the full report see *Workplace industrial relations*, Government Social Survey, 1968.

2 A separate report on the survey of employers' association officials was published as Royal Commission Research Paper no. 7, Part 2.

3 S. R. Parker and J. M. Bynner, 'Correlational analysis of data obtained from a survey of shop stewards', *Human Relations*, November 1970.

4 For a review of the Social Survey report see R. M. Blackburn, *British Journal of Sociology*, December 1969; and of the Donovan research more generally H. A. Turner, 'The Royal Commission's research papers', *British Journal of Industrial Relations*, November 1968.

5 J. F. B. Goodman and T. G. Whittingham, *Shop stewards in British Industry*, McGraw-Hill, 1969.

6 Report No. 24, Cmnd. 4791, HMSO, October 1971.

7 J. Chadwick-Jones, *Automation and behaviour*, Wiley, 1969.

8 L. Coser, *Continuities in the study of social conflict*, Free Press, 1967.

9 A. Kornhauser *et al.*, *Industrial conflict*, McGraw-Hill, 1954.

10 The sequence here is a modified version of one given in S. R. Parker and M. H. Scott, 'Developing models of workplace industrial relations', *British Journal of Industrial Relations*, July 1971.

11 F. H. Blum, *Work and community*, Routledge, 1968, on the Scott Bader Commonwealth.

12 A. Flanders *et al.*, *Experiment in industrial democracy*, Faber, 1968, on the John Lewis Partnership.

2 A Behavioural Analysis of Bargaining*

ANDREW W. GOTTSCHALK

An interest in and concern with the pattern of British work-place industrial relations has now emerged as one of the major research topics during the last decade. There exists a growing literature on practically every aspect of plant industrial relations with the exception of systematic study of bargaining behaviour. The purpose of this chapter is to draw together some of the previous researches, begin the process of evaluation, and finally to suggest certain new lines along which future studies might well develop with considerable theoretical and practical profit. Initially we will examine the range of definitions of bargaining behaviour that exist and seek to identify some of the most important agreed characteristics. This will have prepared the ground for an appraisal of the research work conducted in three disciplines, namely economics, industrial relations, and psychology, although the emphasis will be focussed on the latter two subjects. The chapter will conclude with some suggestions as to the lines along which future research might develop with the aim of relating bargaining behaviour to the organizational context within which it occurs.

The study of bargaining behaviour has been hampered because of the interplay of two factors. A practical reason for the paucity of research lies in the phenomena being studied. Most, if not all, negotiations take place in private. Successes and failures are kept hidden from prying eyes with the result that legends abound and researchers are often resented by both parties. The other reason for the previous neglect may

* This chapter contains in a revised form parts of two papers, the first being 'A behavioural science approach to the study of industrial relations', presented to the Industrial Sociology Group of the British Sociological Association in June 1970, and the second being 'Bargaining behaviour', a paper presented to a staff seminar of the Social Science Research Council's Industrial Relations Research Unit, the University of Warwick, in February 1972.

in part have been caused by the fact that the study of bargaining has not yet coalesced into a discipline conducted within a single integrated theoretical framework.[1] The consequence of this situation is that one is confronted by a series of researches which appear to have studied a collection of wholly unrelated phenomena rather than different components of the same thing, which is in itself the result of the application of highly specialized analytical techniques by individual researches. A number of approaches can be clearly identified. The first is that of the economist who attempts to analyse the components of wages and the concept of bargaining power. The second, a sociological approach, attempts to explain negotiations in terms of the application by institutions of power in the conflict over the allocation of limited resources. This very tempting approach has not yet produced a consensus definition of what 'power' is! The third approach concentrates on social psychological factors drawing in particular upon research on small group behaviour and studies of interpersonal conflict. The fourth approach seeks to explain bargaining in terms of games theory which may not be as strange to the negotiators as it often is to outsiders, because of the game-like unreality in which negotiations take place according to rules which appear to have no reference to either the parties' positions or the outcome.

Bargaining behaviour has been studied at a variety of levels which must be separated for the purpose of analysis but these have in the past, in practice, often merged into one another. The first level is person to person, where research has focussed upon such topics as language, social skills, the use of threats, and the characteristics of the negotiators in terms of status and experience. The second level concerns intra- and inter-group behaviour. Here researchers have studied the handling of information by group members, group risk taking, decision making, and the development of inter-group hostilities. The third level deals with the organizational characteristics of bargaining. It has involved the examination of the relationship between institutional procedures and the level at which agreements are reached, the influence of bargaining on interdepartmental relationships, and the distribution of power in the organization. To compound this problem of levels it must be organization.

To compound this problem of levels there must be added

that a further three approaches which although separated in the past are also related analytically. The first has been concerned with the settlement point or outcome of the negotiations. The second has focussed upon the concession process and the third has dealt with attempts by the parties to change some of the parameters of the situation. Studies which have focussed upon outcomes generally begin with a series of givens about the environment, for example, the preferences of the parties, the benefits to be distributed, and the maximum payoff to each party. Most economic models of duopoly and oligopoly are of this character. Studies concerned with the process of concession have emphasized bargaining behaviour and the multitude of variable which influence its evolution to such an extent that virtually no general predictions can be made about outcomes. The work of Walton and McKersie which will subsequently be discussed in more detail exemplifies this research strategy. An over-concentration upon the process may however do little to help develop an understanding of the long-run pattern of bargaining outcomes because the relationship between the two parties invariably continues beyond the particular bargaining period being studied. The third approach to bargaining has focussed upon the attempt by negotiators to change some of the basic parameters of the situation. To a great extent the costs and benefits of negotiations are themselves subject to choice rather than being given by the environment. To attempt to identify the cost of disagreement, for example, one must take into account both the current demands of the parties and the circumstances in which they negotiate. What emerges so far is a pattern of research along two related dimensions, one concerned with 'size', e.g. the individual, the group, and the organization, the second being concerned with 'levels', e.g. parameters, process, and outcomes.

The reader may already have realized that the terms 'bargaining' and 'negotiation' tend to be used almost interchangeably. When a distinction does arise, the term bargaining will refer to the process of demand formation and revision which provides the basic mechanism whereby the parties seek to come towards an agreement. The term 'negotiation' will refer to the situation within which bargaining occurs. The key concepts included in the definition of a formal negotiation are: that it refers to an occasion where one or more representatives of two or more parties interact in an explicit attempt to reach a jointly acceptable position over one or more divisive issues.[2] Such occasions are distinguishable from informal negotiations in which individuals either discuss topics on which they happen to disagree or alternatively where each person comes to terms entirely on his, or her, own behalf. Negotiations are concerned with the voluntary process of distributing the proceeds of cooperation. They arise whenever the allocation of gains between the parties to an agreement are subject to their own choice rather than predetermined by circumstances which lie outside the control of the actors.[3] It is also implied that both parties stand to benefit by reaching an agreement and that the moves made during the process are made voluntarily. Negotiating as defined here is always characterized by some form of communication no matter how imperfect. The divisive characteristic of negotiations emphasizes that one is concerned with the distribution of values. If there were no value distribution there would be no bargaining.[4] The benefits, or payoffs, which accrue to either party tend to be lower until both sides have accepted the terms of an agreement. Intermediate payoffs before an agreement is reached may be of symbolic value but if overemphasized they may result in a failure to reach a jointly acceptable position. The bargaining process, although emphasized as being a distributive device, also has a productive characteristic. It is productive in that it can be used to discover possibilities for an agreement which were not previously recognized. Another important characteristic of the bargaining process is that it is fundamentally time-dependent. If it did not matter when the parties agreed, it would not matter whether or not they agreed at all.[5] American writers are much more used to emphasizing the time element because of the existence of fixed term contracts. In the British situation the time factor must not however be neglected because it operates in a different way. The functioning of the disputes procedure in the engineering industry provides an illustration of how the failure to maintain adequate time boundaries between stages may have had a bad effect upon industrial relations in the industry. Certainly many shop stewards feel they have 'lost' a case if it is not settled at the plant within known time limits. The economic constraints in which bargaining in industrial relations take place must not be totally ignored. Stevens's definition of bargaining as a 'social control technique for reflecting and transporting the basic power relationships which underlie the conflict of interest inherent in an industrial relations system'[6] is a good example of the potential hazard to be avoided.

Although this chapter will focus on a behavioural approach to the study of bargaining it is appropriate to start by reviewing the research findings of the labour economist as he has been working in this field for longer than most sociologists and psychologists. The model of negotiating behaviour suggested by Zeuthen[7] is that of a two-person situation, in the context of wage negotiations, in which the possibility of conflict (in the form of a strike or lockout) is taken as the motivation for making concessions. Zeuthen assumes that conflict will yield a known payoff to each party and that these utility values remain unchanged throughout the bargaining process being dependent upon neither time nor the demands made by the parties. The nature of the concessions made (how much and by whom) is specified but no explanation of why they are made is offered. The loser is the party who displays a willingness to accept a lower level of risk which in itself could easily be used as a solution criterion without regard to the process at all. As Coddington[8] has noted, no matter how naive and implausible its behaviour assumptions, we are provided with some form of answer to a number of questions about outcomes, process, and parameters. Hicks's[9] theoretical treatment of wage negotiations is based on a model using two functions; the first an 'employer's concession curve' which related the wage which an employer would be willing to pay in order to avoid a strike to the expected length of the strike. The second is the 'resistance curve' which gives the wage which the union would accept rather than call a strike also expressed as a function of the expected length of the strike. The functions have opposite slopes and their point of intersection gives, according to the Hicks model, the maximum possible wage. Two important ideas are contained in this model; the first being the importance of the amount of time which a negotiator expects to lapse before agreement is reached and the magnitude of the payoff demand. The second is the suggestion that a strike or lockout reflects a mistake, it being the consequence of an error in the parties' attempt to estimate the opponents' concession curve[10].

A concern with the specification of the outcome rather than the process is a characteristic of game theoretic models. Within this conceptual framework, the American economist Nash has undertaken some work which is of considerable interest. He considered as relevant only that data about the utilities which each alternative point of agreement would provide to the parties and came to the conclusion that the only function which could describe the outcome of the bargaining process was one which maximized the product of the parties' utilities. Although Zeuthen's and Nash's theories rest on quite different reasoning they both predict an identical outcome.[11] The former rests on a theory of individual decision-making regarding the process of concession making, the latter identifies a set of conditions which a joint outcome is supposed to satisfy.[12]

Two of the more recent contributions that have been made to the growing literature on bargaining behaviour, by economists, are of great interest because they are formulated in terms that take into account the dynamic nature of the process. Mabry[13] suggests a model based on net gain which evaluates benefit levels in disutility or utility functions (i.e. pain or pleasure) or in terms of costs and revenue functions. A net gain or net yield function assesses the positive and negative attributes associated with particular levels of benefit. Each party to the negotiations makes an estimate of these functions, both for their own side and for their opponent. During the course of the negotiation, as information is exchanged, as an awareness of the parameters develops, and as new tactics and strategies are employed, the estimates of the utility functions change. As a result of the pressures generated the parties are forced to alter their positions towards the zone of agreement. Bargaining power is measured by the ratio of change in the net gain or the net yield functions of the parties. 'The conditions for settlement are that both parties must believe, at the benefit level under consideration (which has been successively approximated) that no other benefit level will give each of the parties a positive net yield (or net gain) and that no party can alter the functions to his advantage through bargaining tactics.'[14]

Coddington's study of bargaining behaviour is one of the most significant pieces of work to emerge in recent years in the United Kingdom. Its importance lies in the strenuous attempts that are made to avoid oversimplification. His starting point is

Parsons's observation concerning social action, 'that it does not consist only of ad hoc 'responses' to particular situational 'stimuli' but that the actor develops a system of 'expectations' relative to the various objects of the situation. These may be structured only relative to his own-need dispositions and the probabilities of gratification or deprivation contingent on the various alternatives of action which he may undertake. But in the case of interaction with social objects a further dimension is added. Part of the ego's expectation, in many cases the most crucial part, consists in probable reaction of alter to ego's possible action, a reaction which comes to be anticipated in advance and thus affect ego's own choice.'[15] Coddington quite firmly states that his work should be 'seen as an attempt to explore this property of social action within a particular economic context'.[16] The bargaining process is approached from the point of view of individual decision-making. The decision-making model is of the simple utility maximization type rather than of the game theoretic variety. The interdependence of maximizing processes is developed by means of a theory of expectations and their adjustment. 'The dynamics of the model then consist simply of a repetition of these cycles until such time (if any) as agreement is reached.'[17] In Coddington's model the decisions of the bargainer are based upon his perception of his own utilities which are influenced by his expectations regarding his opponent's behaviour. A determinate solution is indicated as is the process by which the negotiations move towards a solution. Coddington himself recognizes the fact that the assumptions of his model are rarely valid in practice but we have nevertheless obtained through his work greater insights into the nature of bargaining. The value of his contribution will re-emerge at various points in this chapter.

The experimental work of Siegel and Fouraker[18] on bilateral monopoly and duopoly provides an important link between the researches of economists and psychologists on bargaining behaviour. As they themselves note, 'the bare structure of the situations has the essential characteristics of many social conflict situations. In one sense a situation of bilateral monopoly appeals to the mutual interests of the participants, and would seem to ask for harmonious co-operation between them. In another, the interests of the participants are exactly in opposition, and acrimonious competition would seem to be the behaviour norm. Social scientists are particularly concerned with the system of decisions whereby such conflicts are resolved.'[19] Their studies concerned those situations in which a single (unique) buyer confronted a single (unique) seller. The subjects were asked to agree upon the price/quantity combination at which goods were exchanged. Each player of the bargaining pair was given a table on which were printed his 'profits' associated with certain combinations. Bargaining was conducted by means of 'bids' written on slips of paper which were delivered by intermediaries in order to avoid personal contact between the subjects. Siegel and Fouraker studied not only the actual agreement point but also the outcomes under various controlled conditions. Amongst the variables they studied were: the effects of complete versus incomplete information, variations in the structure of the payoffs, and variations in the level of aspiration. The results suggested that there existed a tendency for bargainers to negotiate contracts that are Pareto optimal and that increase in the amount of relevant information available strengthened the tendency towards Pareto optimal agreements. Increases in the amount of information tended to lead to a more equal division of the joint payoffs. In conditions where both parties had complete information they tended to be more modest in their initial demands than in those situations where they had incomplete information. Subsequently Johnson and Cohen[20] replicated and elaborated these experiments exploring the interrelationships of socio-cultural and economic variables. They found that career aspirations were apparent as a significant factor bearing upon bargaining behaviour. Forman and Cohen[21] then studied how the availability of threats affected bargaining efficiency in a game similar to that originally devised by Siegel and Fouraker. Their game did however contain certain changes. The subjects involved bargained on four issues, each consisting of four alternatives. Communication was limited to sequences of offers and counter-offers and subjects had no knowledge of their opponents' profit table. Their findings supported the proposition that the availability of threats reduced bargaining efficiency: the greater the number of threats the larger the number of bids required to reach an agreement. The pioneering work of Siegel and Fouraker has served to encourage other social psychologists to begin a systematic study of bargaining behaviour. This is now one of the 'growth areas' in experimental social psychology but before an evaluation of these research findings can be made we must first examine the models of the bargaining process which have originated primarily from 'industrial relations'.

STUDIES OF BARGAINING BEHAVIOUR IN INDUSTRIAL RELATIONS

Ann Douglas[22] has developed a three-stage model of the bargaining process based on data obtained from the United States' government mediation agency. Her studies were concerned with the attempts of mediators to resolve deadlocked union-management negotiations. The distinguishing characteristic of those situations in which the mediator's intervention led to a settlement was that in the sessions at the bargaining table there was 'movement, orderly and progressive in nature'.[23] The negotiations showed an orderly progression through three stages. By implication, this orderly progression was regarded as essential (i.e. a necessary condition) so that a settlement could be reached. The first stage consisted of 'a thorough and exhaustive determination of the outer limits of the range in which they [the parties] will have to do business with each other'.[24] The behaviour of the negotiators could be seen to emphasize the representative role which they had to take. Judges working 'blindly' from unlabelled and unedited transcripts could accurately identify speakers on the basis of their party (i.e. union, management, or mediator) and their 'bargaining role'. Speeches during this, the first stage, were exceptionally long, in contrast to those which followed, and it appeared that in successful groups the negotiators 'strive for a convincing demonstration that they are impossibly at loggerheads'. In the second stage the negotiators were concerned to reconnoitre the bargaining range. This involved searching earnestly in the background for any signs of tacit agreement without 'in any wise penalising their respective parties for any of their exploits'.[25] This second period was characterized by interparty and interpersonal exchange. Behaviourally, interparty exchange was signalled by official statements of position which ostensibly committed the party (or parties) concerned to some future action congruent with that position. Interpersonal exchange, on the other hand, involved unofficial behaviours which did not commit the party (or parties) in question, and which indicated the most promising areas of the bargaining range in which agreement might be reached. Speeches were shorter and did not appear to be so well rehearsed. Judges working 'blindly' from transcripts which were unlabelled and unedited found it much less easy to identify speakers on the basis of party and bargaining role. The third and final stage of the negotiations was concerned with precipitating the decision-making crisis. As Douglas noted, 'the design in bargaining is to force the opponent into making a decision'.[26] During this final period the distinctions between the parties once again became more obvious.

The model which has just been described may appear to state the obvious: namely that this complex social process has a beginning, a middle, and an end. It contains however a number of subtleties which should not be overlooked. It allows for the fact that negotiators' behaviour reflects both individual, group, and organizational characteristics. Secondly, it recognizes different levels of analysis, i.e. the parameters, the process, and the outcomes. Finally, it draws our attention firmly to the timing element. 'So far as the actions of the parties are concerned, the main imperative is that the movements of the two sides be synchronised to take on the phases of the bargaining sequence concurrently.'[27]

Probably the most significant and challenging study of bargaining behaviour that has emerged within the last decade is that of Walton and McKersie.[28] This work analyses the process whereby agreement is reached in bargaining between organizations which are taken to be management and the trade unions. They suggest that formal negotiations 'are comprised of four systems of activity, each with its own function for the interacting parties, its own internal logics and its own identifiable set of instrumental aids or tactics'.[29] The subprocesses are distributive, integrative, and intra-organizational bargaining and attitudinal structuring.

Distributive bargaining deals with the division of a fixed volume of resources between the parties. It comprises 'competitive behaviours that are intended to influence the division of limited resources'. Each party tries to hide his own aims while unmasking those of his opponent and seeks to commit himself to positions as favourable to himself and hence as unfavourable to his opponent as is possible. Integrative bargaining occurs when the parties strive jointly to increase the volume of resources available to them both. This calls for openness about one's aims and a constant willingness to examine possible new solutions: to quote the authors, 'problem-solving behaviour and other activities which identify, enlarge and act upon the common interests of the parties'.

Attitudinal structuring and intra-organizational bargaining are subsidiary to the main activity of determining and distributing rewards (although the attitude of the opponent to oneself has a value in its own right and can therefore be regarded as a reward itself). The attitudinal structuring subprocess aims 'to influence the attitudes of the participants toward each other and to affect the basic bonds which relate the two parties they represent'. The final process, that of intra-organizational bargaining, functions to achieve an internal consensus within a party.

Formal negotiating situations involve 'mixed motives' and these in practice pose 'dilemmas' for the actors because the four subprocesses are interrelated. For instance, the processes of distributive and integrative bargaining are 'manifestly dissimilar in form and require different attitudes and approaches on the part of the decision makers'. Successful problem solving requires accurate information about 'the motives, needs, and preferences of others and about the present state of the situation'.[30] Both parties would have to attempt to avoid consequences that would produce new or additional difficulties for the other. Distributive bargaining, if it is to be pursued successfully, may involve assessing the other party's minimum terms; modifying these minimum terms in a direction favourable to oneself; and finally committing oneself to a position nearer the other's minimum. As Walton and McKersie note, 'In brief, problem solving is tentative, exploratory, and involves open communication processes whereas bargaining involves adamant, directive and controlled information processes.'[31] Negotiators have to decide whether or not to engage in (or attempt to engage in) integrative bargaining. This involves a choice between problem solving (P.S.) or *status quo* (S.Q.) strategies. A problem-solving strategy may allow the parties to increase the sum to be divided but it also exposes the party which initiated this strategy to receiving only a very marginal

gain. The negotiators' second decision involves the determination of utilities. The more one aims for, the higher the risk of a
costly no-agreement. Essentially one is here concerned to choose
between a 'hard' (H) or 'soft' (S) approach to distributive
bargaining. Consequently, if one only considers distributive and
integrative bargaining there are four strategic possibilities,
namely (1) P.S. + S, (2) P.S. + H, (3) S.Q. + S, (4) S.Q. + H. Each
of these four possibilities poses dilemmas. The first exposes one
party to the risk of exploitation in the distributive phase. The
second faces the problems that arise squarely but is difficult to
implement particularly as a result of the distortions introduced
by competition. The third strategy appears to have little in its
favour but it 'may however be the most effective defensive
strategy when Party has advance information that Opponent
will be very difficult to deal with'.[32] The fourth and final
strategy ignores any potential for increasing the sum available
for distribution. It must however be noted that in distributive
bargaining the sum is never completely fixed, for should the
parties fail to reach an agreement then both lose because of the
costs incurred during the negotiating process. The game theory
roots become obvious as do the echoes of Mabry's net gain
model. The contrast between the approaches of Douglas and
Walton and McKersie may be considerable. The former's work
has a simplicity not found in the latter's taxonomic model
which at most is a list of types of behaviour grouped by functions.

Two British writers, Anthony and Crichton,[33] appear to
provide us with the opportunity for a synthesis which is of
particular value on two counts; first, because of the clarity of
language with which it is presented, and secondly, because it is
grounded in research conducted within the United Kingdom.
They write, 'It may be useful, although an over-simplification,
to regard distributive bargaining as taking place in three
stages: the preparation for bargaining . . . the actual process of
negotiations and, finally, their termination . . . The first and
third stages are the ones most capable of rational analysis.'[34]
The preparatory stage involves the determining of negotiating
objectives which may be influenced by what Anthony and
Crichton describe as 'aspirational rigidity',[35] this being the
result of an established negotiating relationship in which control often rests within a comparatively small group of negotiators. As Walton and McKersie suggest, 'the resistance points of

parties will tend to be compatible if each party has a relatively accurate picture of the other's utilities . . . When there are well established traditions and role requirements for each of the negotiators and when specific pressures bearing on them are generally known, the negotiators tend to enter bargaining with more or less consistent expectations about each other's utility function.'[36] Determining the bargaining agenda for the actual negotiations is an important step in the preparatory stage because it is here that the negotiator can minimize his tactical dilemma by establishing 'separate agendas assigned to different committees'.[37] This procedure was often adopted in plant productivity bargaining.[38] Where this could not be achieved dilemmas based on the fact that information necessary for successful problem solving might be detrimental to success-ful distributive bargaining would only be completely resolved if the bargaining phase had actually been completed before the problem-solving phase. An important feature of the preparatory stage, which appears to have escaped comment, except by Anthony and Crichton, concerns the items or non-targets which are continually left out for a number of reasons. One of the distinguishing characteristics of plant productivity agree-ments was the number of new agenda items included, in particu-lar those dealing with 'fringe benefits'.

The movement of the two parties away from their unaccept-able initial positions into a range of acceptable preferences and finally to an agreement is the result of the interactions of two sets of factors – situational conditions and process con-ditions.[39] The former concerns the parameters within which the negotiations take place, the latter being the influences which the parties can bring to bear on one another within the negotia-tions. These two factors do not operate as independent deter-minants. 'It is not necessary for the objective conditions to change; it is only necessary for the perception of the conditions to change in order for a negotiator to alter his position.'[40] The completion of the process stage usually results in agree-ment. We have been provided with a restatement of Codding-ton's model but from within a different subject discipline and in a different 'language'. Anthony and Crichton are, however, unhelpful in providing an answer to more detailed questions about the agreement itself. They write, 'How this agreement is arrived at is a mystery which no discussion of situational and process conditions or of tactics really helps to solve.'[41] The validity of this claim must be questioned. The economist has already provided some insights and as we will argue subsequently so has the social psychologist.[42] Anthony and Crichton appear to contradict themselves when they subsequently note, 'A more frequent reason for a breakdown ... is a sudden change in the strategy of one of the parties, which results in the expectations of its opponents becoming mistaken.'[43] The implication for the study of tactics is clear! This may occur when a soft line management is replaced by hard liners.

The other important contribution of Anthony and Crichton lies in their restatement of one of the Walton and McKersie subprocesses, namely intra-organizational bargaining. Their discussion of this subprocess, for which they use the expression 'internal adjustment', is based on empirical research conducted amongst personnel managers in the United Kingdom.[44] This may go some way towards checking against the charge of cultural specificity which could otherwise be directed towards Walton and McKersie's book. Negotiations take place within an organizational context and because of this the negotiators are representatives and are therefore rarely free agents. There exists a two-way pattern of influence which is how Anthony and Crichton define 'internal adjustment'. Its importance, they argue, is particularly great in the case of the personnel specialist who has a negotiating role because 'it illuminates the distinction between short- and long-term objectives, between tactics and strategy'.[45] From their questionnaire addressed to British personnel specialists they formed the impression that there exist two levels of bargaining, the one between the company negotiator and the unions and the other between the negotiator and the senior management. There emerged a pattern of aspirational rigidity on the part of the negotiator and of aspirational optimism from senior management. The same pattern holds true on the trade union side. The author has often heard newly elected shop stewards comment unfavourably about their convener's aspirational rigidity which they suspect merges into a collusive relationship with the management's chief negotiator, usually a personnel specialist. One of the practical results of this situation may be that those who determine strategic goals should not be responsible for the conduct of the negotiations. An indication of the difficulties which may

D

49

arise can be found in the 1971 negotiations between the Ford Motor Company and the unions representing their manual employees. A significant shift in the internal policies of one of the larger unions towards closer involvement between full-time officials and plant representatives, in formulating the claim and evaluating the progress made in negotiations, did much to overcome the problem of aspirational rigidity on the part of one side. But it also lengthened the subsequent conflict because the management representatives were faced with a new situation which required the learning of new responses. The shape of the changed bargaining programme reflected the relative weight, importance, and status of the parties within their own organization. The same situation may arise in workplace bargaining as can be seen from the following instance.

In a Midland organization negotiating a plant productivity agreement it was widely known, to both managers and trade union representatives, that the senior manager on the site was the driving force behind the company's involvement in the bargaining process. Being a relative newcomer and leading the management negotiating team the manager had himself to cope with both the aspirational rigidity previously present and his own aspirational optimism. This conflict was resolved in what was for the organization a perfectly acceptable way. The senior manager referred to the clearly developed and highly internalized set of organizational values. The development of productivity bargaining required a re-analysis of the division of authority between the plant and head office. From the centre he was seen as being the negotiator with aspirational rigidities whose ideas needed careful scrutiny. In the plant his constant travels to head office were known and were regarded as being appropriate because they signalled quite clearly his aspirational optimism. His behaviour could also be reconciled to the known organizational values; they were regarded as being tradition orientated and did therefore not constitute a threat. The negotiations were completed and a variety of changes ensued. Within the negotiating relationship a certain degree of aspirational rigidity subsequently tended to re-emerge. The senior manager was promoted and his successor was concerned primarily with the implementation of the productivity agreement. This almost induced aspirational rigidity. These negotiations provide us with a very good example of boundary role conflict.[46] The negotiator feels himself pulled in at least two directions. In the case of the example mentioned above the senior manager had also to cope with demands from his own middle management and supervisors who felt threatened by the productivity agreement. The aspirational optimism of their senior manager was most unwelcome to them. They had learnt to cope with the previous pattern of industrial relations in which problems were not solved, they were administered.

Walton and McKersie list a number of tactics which may be associated with successful intra-organizational bargaining[47] but their account is of only limited value because it emphasizes how the negotiator copes with intra-group conflict. It tells us little about how pressure is exerted on the negotiator. Anthony and Crichton feel that one of the most serious aspects of intra-organizational bargaining in British companies concerns the means whereby senior managers exert pressure on the company's negotiator.[48] Their survey suggests that there exists a 'penumbria of imprecision within which the negotiator is expected to reach a settlement', which suggests 'the existence of a control zone or a range of acceptable preferences between the aspirational rigidity of the negotiator . . . and the aspirational optimism of management . . .'[49] Perhaps the concern echoed by Anthony and Crichton is slightly misplaced. The personnel specialist, if he is the management negotiator, is a member of a group whose behaviour is bound to be subject to certain controls. The ability of the specialists to cope with this situation depends to a very great extent on the relative success they have enjoyed in initiating and following power maintenance strategies.[50] The four main strategies that might be used are (1) norms which deny the competence of outsiders, (2) protective myths, (3) norms of secrecy, and (4) protection of their knowledge through controls on entry.[51] It should be added that successful negotiations might take place were both negotiators unhindered by group pressures and demands but whether or not this would result in agreements which could be implemented is a more debatable point.

SOCIAL PSYCHOLOGICAL STUDIES OF BARGAINING BEHAVIOUR

We have so far been concerned with studies of bargaining behaviour undertaken by economists and industrial relations specialists. With the exception of the work of Siegel and

Fouraker the researches of the social psychologists have not yet been discussed. It is now necessary to examine what is in social psychology a growing body of research findings. These studies have proceeded along both of the dimensions previously identified: those concerning size, i.e. the individual, the group, and the organization, and the levels, i.e. the parameters, the process, and the outcomes.

The greatest obstacle to the study of negotiating behaviour has been the difficulty of recording and analysing the interaction between the negotiators. Most of the earlier attempts to provide us with a detailed description of negotiating behaviour used Bales's Interaction Process Analysis Categories or some fairly straightforward modifications thereof.[52] Bales distinguished, first of all, between those actions which bring nearer the solution of a group's problems (these he called contributions in the task area) and those actions which did not facilitate the solution of the problem. The latter he called contributions in the socio-emotional area. The task-related contributions took the form of questions or attempted answers and these in turn involved three consecutive problems which arose in the course of decision making, namely communication, evaluation, and control. Contributions in the socio-emotional area were classified according to a similar pattern: problems of decision, tension reduction, and reintegration. The use of Interaction Process Analysis can best be illustrated by reference to the study of problem-solving groups.[53] The interaction which occurs in all such groups, irrespective of whether they are successful or not, is to some extent orderly and progressive in nature. As Bales and Strodtbeck note, 'We have presented a hypothesis which states that under these specified conditions the process tends to move through time from a relative emphasis upon problems of orientation, to problems of evaluation, and subsequently to problems of control; and that concurrent with these transitions, the relative frequencies of both negative and positive reactions tend to increase.'[54] A formal negotiating situation as we defined it earlier is *not* the same as a problem-solving situation. The distinction which Walton and McKersie make between integrative and distributive bargaining concerns the sum, whether it is fixed or variable. They suggest that integrative bargaining may utilize problem-solving strategies but that it is of itself not a problem-solving situation. Care must therefore be taken in generalizing Bales's results to other negotiating situations. Landsberger[55] used the Interaction Process Analysis to study the negotiations arising out of disputes referred to a United States mediation agency. He reported on the link between the categorization of behaviour in certain of the socio-emotional categories and the success of the mediation in producing a settlement or at least a return to work. The negotiations moved through an identifiable series of phases as described by Bales and Strodtbeck. The greater their conformity to this idealized pattern the more successful the parties were in finding a solution of their problem. Landsberger, from his observations, noted that it was especially important that 'antagonism' was not shown in the initial third of the meeting. Echoes of Ann Douglas's work can be heard here; when determining the bargaining range the exchanges are characterized by interparty hostility *not* interpersonal hostility.

More recently McGrath[56] has studied simulated negotiations using process analysis methods. He concluded that 'effective negotiation outcomes appear to be associated with certain patterns of interaction in the negotiating session'. In his analysis two crucial features emerge in the negotiating process, the first being the display of positive or negative effect and the second being the display of structuring or controlling activities. Successful and unsuccessful groups differed in the amount and the timing of these displays of positive and negative effect. Successful groups displayed less negative effect than did the unsuccessful ones. Their communications were more of an 'effectively neutral kind' but they did not show more positive effect than unsuccessful groups. The successful groups displayed during the final phase a rise in positive effect and in effectively neutral communication as well as a drop in negative effect. Unsuccessful groups displayed entirely the opposite pattern of behaviour. During the final phase there was a rise in negative effect and a drop, or at least a levelling off, in positive or neutral communication. The pattern of group interaction and length of communications differed between successful and unsuccessful groups. The former interacted more and their communications were generally shorter in length than those of the latter.

One of the difficulties in the use of Bales's Interaction Process Analysis for the study of negotiating behaviour is that it was never intended for such a task. It cannot cope with some of the essential characteristics of negotiating: that the actors represent parties, the interdependence of the parties, and the range of behaviour which the negotiator may select. In negotiations the search for an agreement requires that the exchange of information and opinion between the parties shall be thorough. The analysis of problem-solving groups emphasizes individual contributions. Stephenson[57] has written, 'Concessions, threats, settlement points, procedures are not separately represented by Bales, for they are the stuff of negotiating, not problem solving groups.' A system for the description of negotiating behaviour must therefore reflect the full scope of the exchanges between the parties.

The Conference Process Analysis which is being developed by Morley and Stephenson[58] sets out to describe interaction during negotiations and meet the objections to earlier work which have been discussed above. This system 'invites one to suppose that members of a negotiating team each have *resources* for exchange with members of the opposing team, and with each other. An *outcome* refers to all proposals which set a limit to the final agreement. A *procedure* defines the way in which the conference shall be conducted. The *threat* category contains all references to conditional statements of hostile intent. *Acknowledgments* recognise or praise the contribution of a party or participant, including oneself. *Provocation* includes a multitude of sins, principally derogatory statements, including those against oneself. *Description* covers all the other facts and opinions. The fate of resources is recorded by the *mode* dimension. Resources are introduced by being *offered* or *sought*. Subsequently, they may be *accepted* or *rejected*, and *yielded* or *withheld*. Thus, each *act* in a negotiation is classified initially according to its *resource* and *mode*. A third dimension – *referent* – indicates to whom the information conveyed by the act refers, whether to self, one's party or to the opposing side. Two remaining dimensions are employed in the Conference Process Analysis which encourage its use in the analysis of strategies and tactics. The *time* dimension indicates when the events referred to in the act occurred or were expected to occur. The *source* dimension specifies whether or not an act is a direct response to an act initiated by some other person. There are detailed rules for dividing negotiations into acts, and for coding the different dimensions.'[59] This system for describing interaction in negotiations is still being developed but even in its present form it makes a significant methodological contribution. It copes with the representational element, it allows calculation of the amount and quality of exchange between the sides, and it facilitates the recording of responses to particular offers, thus enabling an analysis of strategy and tactics to be undertaken.

The attempts to analyse negotiating behaviour which have been described are in the mainstream of one of the major research areas in modern social psychology: namely the study of small group behaviour. This has meant that the researches, often conducted in the experimental laboratory, have not only used highly sophisticated paradigms but that their findings have also been integrated into a larger corpus of knowledge. This has helped the social psychologist to avoid some of the grossest charges of methodological obscurantism, although some dangers still remain. McGrath,[60] for example, has argued that the design for experimental simulation of formal negotiations should meet the following five criteria. First, the subjects should be genuine representatives of a party. Secondly, the issues being debated should be of importance. Thirdly, that a conflict of interest should occur between the parties independently of the experimental setting. Fourthly, that full verbal communication must be allowed for and that the issues must be sufficiently complex to allow genuine debate to take place. Finally, that 'the issues must be of sufficient complexity that there is more than a single, unitary dimension of payoff', the aim being to 'study the negotiation of issues which are actually divisive issues for the people involved and the groups they represent. They are not artificial or simulated issues. What is "non-real", artifically created, is the actual negotiation – the confrontation of the opposed parties in an attempt to resolve the issue.'[61]

The exacting standards which McGrath laid down for simulations have in general not been met by other researchers. The difficulty of finding suitable subjects has been a major obstacle. Consequently 'simulation games' and 'games' have featured almost exclusively as research tools. The simulation game resembles a simulation in that it allows full verbal communication and that the payoff is not restricted to being a unitary one. The subjects are briefed, being given background information about their roles and an account of some of the parameters within which the bargaining takes place. Usually the brief also contains some information about the previous conduct of the relationship between the two parties so that the subjects can 'get the feel' of the bargaining situation. [62] The pattern of communications is not in any way constrained. In fact, it is the communications and the resulting pattern of interaction over the divisive issue which constitute the game and which are being studied.

The majority of the research on bargaining has been concerned with informal negotiating situations, i.e. those where the parties are not representatives. The subjects have usually been asked to play a 'mechanical game', for example the Prisoner's Dilemma game,[63] the Deutsch and Krauss trucking game,[64] and the Siegel and Fouraker buyer-selling game.[65] The use of games, and of the prisoner's dilemma in particular, is a research problem which has traversed traditional subject disciplines to engage the attention of economists, mathematicians, and psychologists alike. For the latter there exists an intriguing problem – the optimum behaviour prescribed by the rational dictates of game theory is not the behaviour in which people typically engage. Within the context of such games the effects of a wide range of variables on bargaining efficiency[66] have been studied, such as: the availability and use of threats, the characteristics of the payoff matrix defining the type of game, the strategy of the other player, and information about the other's profits. It was concluded that the availability of threats reduces bargaining efficiency in a variable sum bargaining game [67] which may be taken to confirm some of Walton and McKersie's statements about the characteristics of integrative bargaining and the dilemmas raised by negotiators in the choosing of a hard or soft problem-solving strategy.[68] Smith in a study of reward structure and information found that fully informed players cooperated more than did less informed players, although information did not appear to affect play in any dramatic way.[69] Transmission of almost any kind of information appears to be helpful.[70] Uniformed bargainers use their opponent's bids to set their own goals, whilst informed bargainers use them to assess the reasonableness of the opponent's goals.[71] All these and the many other similar findings require further replication and validation so that we may begin to develop a theoretical framework for the study of bargaining behaviour.

The methodology of game theory is in many respects very attractive; replication is easy and endless variations can be made in the form of the matrix. Difficulties of recording the participants' behaviour are virtually non-existent. Yet in spite of these advantages a number of problems have yet to be resolved. Many of the experiments appear to be culturally specific and the dependent variables ambiguous. The utility of the outcomes should not be assumed to be constant. One of the most important ways in which research on the prisoner's dilemma, for example, differs from typical human interaction is in the constraints imposed: the participants are not allowed to communicate with each other; their impact upon one another is limited to a choice between two crude behavioural alternatives which may have little meaning to them. These bargaining studies differ sharply from most other social situations in that they drastically restrict the range of behavioural options available. In those instances where multiple options are available to the parties the exchange process may be totally different in character from that which offers only a choice between cooperation and exploitation. Exploitive behaviour as we know is in reality often heavily disguised by a range of subtle manoeuvres. For example, the exploiter may engage in behaviours that are of a low cost to himself but which go a long way towards reducing the possibility that his truly exploitive behaviour will be perceived as such. Such trade-offs are not allowed for in the basic two-option bargaining problems as at present developed. In retrospect the use of games has been of some value in at least three different ways. They have stimulated the development of more sophisticated methods; in particular the use of simulations. Secondly, despite their poor predictive power, they have remained a valuable source of ideas by providing clues which have been of use to the observer of negotiations. Finally, they have allowed investigators to test hypotheses based upon data collected from observations.

So far we have considered two of the contributions of the social psychologist to the study of bargaining behaviour. The first concerned the attempt to analyse the negotiating process and the second dealt with some broader methodological considerations which have to be kept in mind in experimental studies. We will now turn to what is one of the largest substantive areas in social psychology, namely the study of

57

behaviour in small groups, to examine some of the findings which may provide further insights into bargaining behaviour. The definition of a group which will be used is that it comprises any number of people who interact with one another, are psychologically aware of one another, and regard themselves as constituting a group. These three criteria of interaction, identification, and awareness are all of importance in a discussion of bargaining behaviour. The use of these criteria was implied, to a great extent implicitly, in Coddington's study, and explicitly in the three industrial relations approaches described earlier in this chapter.

From studies of inter-group relations a number of findings emerge which are of direct relevance to the study of negotiating behaviour. The more competitive the relationship between two groups the more difficult it will be to obtain agreement on a particular issue; the less acceptable will be the solution to any one party and the less creative will be the solution. These effects stem from three factors: first, the increased commitment of the negotiators to their parties' goals; secondly, from the increased mutual misunderstanding between negotiators, and thirdly, from the negotiators' increased fear of rejection by their parties in the event of 'failure' which heightened competition between the groups may entail. The level of competition may be de-escalated if steps are taken to decrease the commitment of the negotiators to their own parties' goals, to increase their understanding of the other party's position, and to strengthen the individual negotiator's freedom of manoeuvre. Unfortunately competition is very easy to begin, but difficult to end. A partial solution to this problem is suggested by Blake, Mouton, and Slomn[72] who derived 'an educational-laboratory approach to the resolution of conflict'. Management and union representatives met for a two-day period 'to confront the conflict between them. The differences uncovered by the two groups were presented in detail . . . Through self-analysis and an exchange of views, management and the union moved slowly towards a better understanding of the relationship between them.' The result of this experience 'will become evident when new issues and different problems arise in the relationship. At that time, the parties will be able to apply themselves in a more problem solving manner.'[73] The restructuring of a competitive relationship may be also achieved by the initiation of a 'superordinate goal'.[74] Yet in the context of a bargaining relationship this may be very difficult to achieve. It also begs the question as to whether and how conflict and competition should be restructured. Much of it may have a symbolic value for both parties. The aspirational rigidity of the negotiators indicates the existence and functioning of an accommodation process[75] which allows interaction between the union and management groups on the basis of their separate achievement norms. 'Such norms may be modified in the course of negotiations because of pressures or changing perceptions. Since the norms are not ordinarily single points but rather range from a minimum point of what a party will accept if it feels it must, to a maximum point of what it believes is warranted (or that the market will bear), there is room for a considerable range within which agreement may occur.'[76] The interaction of the two parties is considerably oversimplified if described only in terms of 'conflict' and 'co-operation'. Managements and trade unions continue to secure agreements upon both procedural and substantive issues in collective bargaining at the workplace precisely because the norms are not 'single points' but 'ranges'. In a negotiating situation the result of a particular level of conflict may according to Walton and McKersie influence the extent to which either party resorts to integrative bargaining strategies. 'Essentially the competitive and manipulative elements of bargaining tend to produce greater defensiveness, which in turn has . . . consequences adverse to effective problem solving.'[77]

So far the emphasis in our assessment of the effect of conflict has been upon the bargaining process and its outcomes. It may however be more appropriate to consider the problems of conflict associated with implementing the outcome or agreement. In the context of plant productivity bargaining the author has noticed that the negotiators were often so exhausted by the process that virtually no attention was given to the problem of implementing and maintaining the agreement.[78] Management-union conflict does not simply disappear with the signing of a particular document. The focus of the conflict, however, shifts away from the conference room back to the shop floor. In one or two companies where productivity agreements had been negotiated the actual language of the agreement appeared to create new conflicts of interpretation. The negotiators, partially as a result of their own aspirational rigidity and in part as a consequence of the demands to 'show results', had drafted an agreement which presented their audience with a serious problem of comprehension. The communication of a particular outcome, no matter how welcome it may be to specific groups, does not of itself guarantee to reduce the level of conflict.

Research on the various aspects of leadership behaviour has been one of the recurring themes in the study of group behaviour and is of considerable relevance to any study of bargaining behaviour. A functional analysis of the leadership role has resulted in the identification of two main task areas,[79] the first being a goal-orientated and the second a maintenance function. Thibaut and Kelley have indicated the activities which might be included in a maintenance function: '(1) perceiving and assessing the reward-cost position of the various members (2) allocating the rewards to the various members (3) synchronizing reward allocations with cost peaks (4) smoothing out fluctuations . . . so that regular payoffs are provided (5) creating new rewards (6) cutting costs by reducing anxieties (7) cutting costs by improved communication (8) lowering both the comparison level and the comparison level for alternatives for the various members, for example, by censoring favourable information about available alternatives'.[80] The implications of this list are quite startling. It suggests for example that aspirational rigidity may reflect the exercise of a leadership style orientated towards a maintenance function within the parties' own group. In the context of workplace bargaining the last item on the list, i.e. the censoring of favourable alternatives, is a charge which is frequently levelled at shop stewards by individual managers. They bitterly criticize the steward for such action although it would appear that it could be justified in terms of a maintenance task orientation. Shop stewards, it has been suggested by Goodman and Whittingham, should not be regarded as work-group leaders but as leaders at work groups.[81] If this is the case then the strategy of censoring information could also be defended, in particular in those situations where they experience competition from a rival union for membership.

The study of leadership behaviour has also been fruitfully pursued in terms of interpersonal processes, in particular the perceptions and expectations of followers. The observed attributes and actions of the leader have a discernible role in creating the impressions which contribute to his legitimacy. In many situations it is the leader's perception of his own legitimacy that has a direct impact upon his willingness to assert influence. The source of a leader's authority is particularly important, whether he is elected or appointed, especially under conditions of strain. Hollander and Julian[82] have concluded that 'the members' support for the elected leader depended both on his initially perceived competence for the role of spokesman and a successful outcome of his activity on behalf of the group; on the other hand, support for the appointed leader appeared to depend on either the perception of his competence or a successful outcome . . . elections build higher demands on the leadership role'.[83] Within those situations where it is appropriate to have an elected leader, as for example a shop steward, the 'incumbent of the role senses the idiosyncracy credits at his disposal and can expend them through deviations from the group'.[84] The practical implications are both clear and significant. The shop steward as an elected leader of work groups may have more freedom in a negotiating situation than his management opposite number who has been appointed and does not therefore have any idiosyncracy credits at his disposal.

At the workplace negotiations can proceed at various status levels. The union negotiators may be shop stewards, senior stewards, or conveners and district officials. The management role may be taken by supervisors, line managers, and personnel specialists. Comparatively little research has, to date, focussed on how negotiations among individuals in leadership positions differ from negotiations between individuals with delegated authority. At one extreme may be the messenger who only delivers prepared statements and set positions and who acts merely as an intermediary, and at the other end of the scale we may have a representative who can initiate proposals, develop counter-proposals, conclude agreements, or break off negotiations at his own discretion. Hermann and Kogan[85] have suggested that the role, of leader or delegate, influences both the strategy adopted and the level of risk accepted. Delegates aimed at compromise settlements whereas leaders were willing to choose one party's position. As a result of this it was found that delegates showed little change from their initial positions whereas leaders showed significant change towards a potentially more risky outcome. Leaders were more concerned with the ongoing negotiating process in contrast to the delegates for whom the conduct of the previous negotiations was of greater importance. Delegates, in this study, did not take longer to reach a consensus nor did the negotiations result in a deadlock more frequently than leaders. In contrast with leaders, delegates took extreme amounts of time to negotiate a settlement – either a very long or a very short time. These findings about leaders as negotiators, and in particular the shift to risk which may take place, can in part be accounted for by 'idiosyncracy credits'. In practice at the workplace, shop stewards will adopt leader roles and only as the negotiations become more protracted through previous failures to arrive at a settlement will they assume delegate roles. It is probably more appropriate to see the district official when involved in local negotiations as a delegate. The situation becomes more complicated on the management side. Line managers as appointees may have few 'idiosyncracy credits' to draw on and thus be forced, partially as a result of policy decisions and partially for personal reasons, to adopt delegate roles. Negotiations between leader and delegate may break down more easily because of the different levels of risk the actors are prepared to accept and because one party is concerned with the ongoing negotiations whereas the other has focused his attention on the previous bargaining pattern.

One point that has been raised in the previous paragraph merits further discussion. It has been suggested that a characteristic of leader negotiators was a willingness to reach riskier outcomes. The literature on group decision making and the shift to risk has now taken on considerable proportions. In a detailed review of these studies Dion, Barron, and Miller[86] concluded that 'as a single explanation of the risky-shift, the cultural-value interpretation fares best'.[87] They also pointed out that future research needed to be focussed on the characteristics of real or naturally existing groups because few of the actual characteristics of decision-making groups that exist in organizations paralleled those studied in the laboratory. Bearing this cautionary note in mind, two studies remain of interest. The first is a study by Harnett[88] and his colleagues which investigated the effects of risk-taking propensity on bargaining behaviour under varying conditions of information. Risk-taking propensity failed to explain the subjects' bargaining successes but it did influence their initial demands and their willingness to yield from that level. The amount of information available influenced the degree of risk: the less there was available the greater was the impact of a risk-taking propensity on bargaining behaviour. The more recent study of Lamm and Kogan[89] indicates that a high level of commitment by an elected representative to a particular position may in the context of inter-group negotiations prevent the processes underlying the risky-shift from operating. Representatives reached their decisions through averaging.

A principle of bargaining which appears to have widespread acceptance, irrespective of the level of the negotiations, is that of unanimity.[90] Each party must present and maintain a united front before its opponents if it is not to allow its adversary the advantage of exploiting the internal conflicts that lie just below the surface. Practitioners, in particular, stress the dangers of presenting anything other than a 'united front'. The consequence of this situation may be that it has encouraged each party to adopt strategies and postures associated with what Rapoport refers to as a 'game'[91] rather than allow the exchange of genuinely held views, i.e. what Rapoport calls a 'debate'.[92] Evan and MacDougall have suggested that this emphasis on unanimity may, when employed by both parties in industrial relations, have one of two outcomes – 'it leads to either mutual compromise or to a victory of one of the parties'.[93] The adoption of the opposite principle, one based on dissent, may if employed bilaterally increase the probability that the conflict will be resolved but that a creative or integrative solution may emerge. When these ideas were tested experimentally it was found that two two-man teams representing management and trade unions which exhibited bilateral dissensus were more likely to reach an agreement than teams exhibiting bilateral consensus and that the outcomes under these conditions were more likely to be classifiable as creative or integrative. It would appear that the practitioners' fears are an overstatement. Certainly from those negotiations which the author has observed the existence of dissensus is taken for granted and depending upon the previous bargaining relationship may or may not be ignored.

Before starting to examine some of the studies of bargaining which focus on the individual it is appropriate to draw together some of the threads. It may therefore be useful to borrow an idea first suggested by Ross[94] and subsequently developed by Fox[95] and apply it to the study of bargaining behaviour. They suggest that it is appropriate to regard the firm as a pluralistic system, a coalition of interests that in some respects are divergent. This pluralistic frame of reference can be contrasted with a view which stresses unity and communality of interest, the 'unitary' system. All the previously cited research underscores this plurality. The major difficulty may be that whereas it is almost natural for trade union representatives to accept plurality, for the management negotiators it may be more difficult. The more senior the status of the magement negotiator the greater will be the conflict he as an individual experiences between the unitary and pluralistic frames of reference. A lower-level participant may communicate his acceptance of pluralism by joining a trade union. A more senior employee may behave as if he accepts pluralism by adopting power maintenance strategies but he may still have to accept, and express, where appropriate, the unitary frame of reference subscribed to by his peer group. The effect of this on bargaining behaviour can only be assumed although it may in part be coped with and modified by the 'aspirational rigidity' which is said to exist amongst those who might be termed as 'professional negotiators'.

One of the most neglected areas of bargaining behaviour concerns the social performance of the participants in the actual negotiating situation. This could be more systematically studied if one were to regard the situation as one of 'focussed interaction'[96] and agree that the behaviour of the people involved could be described as being in some way organized and skilled.[97] I am using the term 'skilled' in exactly the same way as one might describe the behaviour needed in driving a car, a skill being defined as organized and coordinated activity, in relation to an object or situation, that involves a series of sensory, central, and motor mechanisms. The characteristic of a skilled performance is that the behaviour is correctly adapted to the occasion. The interaction of people, be they negotiators or friends, is affected by all aspects of behaviour including physical proximity, posture, orientation, language and speech, patterns of looking at the other person, body movements, and facial expressions.[98] The negotiator must, quite clearly, modify his behaviour to ensure that his voice, choice of words, gestures, and level of involvement in what he is saying are appropriate for the situation. If only as a reminder the reader is drawn to Ann Douglas's observations about differences between the first period when the parties are defining the bargaining range and the second when they are exploring the bargaining range. Argyle has suggested that in analysing social performance we can distinguish 'at the level of general orientation how individuals may adopt a distinctive pattern of activities . . . the level of general method or subplans . . . an opening "greeting" phrase . . . at the level of knacks and dexterities we deal with such things as sequences of acts of communication'.[99] In examining the social performance of one participant one must not overlook the fact that it takes place within an encounter (i.e. a negotiating situation) and that the behaviour of one individual is interrelated with that of another. Negotiators have usually obtained agreement about the purpose of the encounter, what Goffman calls a 'working consensus'.[100] In some encounters, for example the 'works conference' in the engineering industry where local managers meet local trade union officials, the form is highly structured and the participants know their parts. The working consensus appears to be ready-made, yet this situation does not always exist. For example, in one plant where a productivity agreement had been negotiated a new domestic disputes procedure was agreed upon. It met in the same room as a now defunct consultative committee with each person sitting in 'his own seat'. The participants told the author that their early difficulties might have been lessened had a new venue been found. Both the management and trade union representatives 'transferred' their previously acquired skills to the new meeting without recognizing that a new task existed. The participants moved very gradually away from their stereotyped patterns of response towards new techniques to see how the other party behaved. Quite frequently the author heard comments about the new situation as one shop steward remarked, 'Look don't come that consultative stuff now. I am here for my members. I want answers I can take back, not your problems.'

An analysis of the structure of the social performance in a

negotiating situation must take into account both the 'standing features' and the 'dynamic features'.[101] The former consists of such components as posture, distance, and orientation which change little throughout a given encounter. The latter, which comprise utterances, movements, and patterns of looking, are as the term implies subject to change according to the kind of encounter being considered. Movement may serve to clarify or emphasize aspects of messages transmitted; patterns of looking and movement may regulate the 'pace of the action' and facial expressions and levels of eye contact may regulate the emotional content of the relationship. Given that virtually no systematic experimental work has as yet been undertaken, the only confirmatory evidence that exists are the recollections and anecdotes of negotiators, a situation which should not, I believe, remain unchanged for long.[102]

Negotiating involves communication no matter how imperfect. Argyle and Kendon conclude their review of social performance with an observation that 'perhaps surprisingly, remarkably little is known about the role of language and speech'.[103] A systematic study of negotiating must take into account our general knowledge about the sociology of language. Between negotiators at the plant level there exist very clear differences in the length and quality of their previous educational experience.[104] This gap may be of less significance amongst very experienced management and union negotiators because of their frequent formal and informal contact with one another. In some instances both negotiators develop, over time, their own common language, using expressions from work study, job evaluation, and technical trade terms, which gives a superficial impression that language is not a barrier. In one series of negotiations in a Midland firm the local district official of the largest union with members in the plant made strenuous efforts to learn the Company's language, with the result that some of his members became suspicious and attempted to secure his removal. Their complaint was that the official sounded 'too much like a management man'.

There exist a number of studies which go some small way towards filling some of the most glaring gaps in our knowledge of bargaining at a person-to-person level. Krauss[105] examined the effects of structural and attitudinal factors on interpersonal bargaining. He hypothesized that where a conflict existed between the structure of the bargaining relationship and the bargainer's attitudinal orientation the degree of attitudinal anchoring would determine the mode of interpersonal conflict resolution, and consequently the effectiveness of bargaining. The results confirmed this hypothesis. Druckman[106] has studied the effects of personality in a formal negotiating situation and found that where both persons were high scorers on a dogmatism scale[107] they, in contrast to pairs of low scorers, took longer to reach an agreement, were less likely to reach an agreement in a given time, ended bargaining further apart, and had finally a larger number of unresolved issues remaining. As earlier studies would indicate it appears that the need to maintain face affects the bargaining relationship. Brown,[108] in his study, operationalized this willingness to 'cut off one's nose to save one's face' and found that humiliated subjects were more likely to retaliate, with greater severity, than those who though similarly exploited had received favourable feedback. Retaliation occurred although it required sacrificing the available outcomes. The implications for the negotiator are quite clear and observations of formal negotiating sessions suggest that this actually takes place. The accommodation process at an inter-group level, and the aspirational rigidity at a personal level, ensure that neither party 'lose too much face'. Brown also noted that retaliation was suppressed in those situations where the other party knew their costs. In most instances negotiations do take place under conditions of incomplete information,[109] and it is other topics such as the use of threats that have interested social psychologists and therefore been studied by them in some detail.

A threat is generally conceived of as the communication of an intention to do harm to another. The purpose of a threat is to establish, in the threatened party, the expectation that if he performs some undesired act he will suffer some harm. A successful threat is one which does not have to be executed. The experiments of Deutsch and Krauss suggested that the availability of threats resulted in decreased bargaining efficiency[110] (bargaining efficiency being defined as the extent to which players obtain maximum joint profit outcomes). The conception of the relationship of threat to bargaining which was suggested by Deutsch and Krauss in their trucking game was too simple. It assumed that the use of threats would alter the bargainers' perception of their relationship with one another. It is not a gain-cost relation that determines the effect of a threat but the complex relationship involving the bargainers' perception of their social status, their expectations of appropriate behaviour, and their loss of face in yielding to a threat. In the trucking game the use of 'threat' amounted to the use of a gate preventing the other player from taking the shorter, more profitable route – but this was really only a sanction. It did not indicate that unless the other party did such-and-such then (and only then) would sanctions be employed. Between bargainers the threat potential, i.e. the degree to which one party can harm the other, is often distributed unequally. The use of threats may therefore be encouraged or discouraged by the differential threat potential of the bargainers. Hornstein[111] has studied the effects of different magnitudes of threat upon interpersonal bargaining and concludes that some distribution of threat potential increased the likelihood of agreement. His data also supported the notion that threats and aggression tended to lessen the probability of agreement. Guyer and Rapoport[112] have suggested that a threat-appeasement, punishment-capitulation interaction may develop between the two parties. The party which was more likely to carry out their threat was the one which obtained most concessions from the other party. How far this situation, derived from a two-person nonzero-sum game, can be said to obtain to other conditions requires further research. Certainly the author would admit to have grave reservations, in particular because of the danger that 'threats' could be taken out of their context.

In drawing to a close this review of the studies of bargaining behaviour conducted by social psychologists both at the interpersonal and group level a number of points emerge which deserve further consideration. To date the number and range of studies is still comparatively small. The subjects used in the experiments may limit the general validity of some of the studies but this should not be an insurmountable problem. The warning of McGrath about the difference between simulations, simulation games, and games must be constantly kept in mind if only because this may encourage experimentally orientated research workers to avoid the pitfalls of methodological obscurantism. Attempts at synthesis between the work undertaken focusing on the individual and the group must be begun. The closer study of language as used in inter-group negotiations could be of considerable interest. The author has frequently been told by shop stewards that they can identify the difference between negotiating meetings and those of a more consultative nature by the language used by management representatives. As one commented, 'They sound smoother, as if they are selling something. They talk of "we" not "you".' The work begun by Argyle on social skills requires urgent replication in the context of bargaining if only to lay some of the myths that abound. For example, some shop stewards claim to be able to distinguish between genuine and feigned anger yet such a claim has never been systematically examined. Perhaps the greatest weakness of existing researches is that they lack a cogent theoretical underpinning. Both Stephenson[113] and the author feel that exchange theory may provide an initial framework despite some of the criticisms that can be directed at it.[114] Its value may however differ according to whether one is primarily concerned with the negotiating process or the outcomes. Certainly the influence of Homans and some of his ideas can be identified in the conceptualization and development of the Conference Process Analysis which has been described earlier in this section. Exchange theory may have its limitations but in the study of bargaining we may be in what appears to be a paradoxical situation.[115] When questioning shop stewards about their failure to reach a mutually acceptable outcome on a substantive issue in plant level negotiations with local managers, I have often heard explanations offered in terms of a 'lack of fairness'. A theory of inequity in human exchanges may help us to understand the failure to reach an outcome, rather than explain why agreements are reached.[116]

We have so far been concerned with the bargaining process and its outcomes. It is now appropriate to move on to a discussion of the parameters of bargaining and in particular an analysis of the organizational context within which bargaining takes place.

THE ORGANIZATIONAL CONTEXT OF BARGAINING

The largest gap in a systematic study of bargaining behaviour is the absence of studies of the parameters within which the process itself takes place. In the past the parameters have been studied in economic terms: for example, a study of the external and internal labour markets which has sought to identify factors which might explain a particular settlement or series of settlements over time.[117] It must however be recognized that economic parameters are not the only ones which might influence the bargaining process and the outcomes. Bargaining takes place within the context of the organization. Probably the most important contribution of Walton and McKersie has been made by them by default. Their treatment of intra-organizational bargaining is not a study of the parameters. They focus on the problems which the negotiator faces in achieving consensus within his own party, on what they call the 'conflict which occurs within each organization'.[118] It might be more appropriate to describe this as intra-sub-organizational bargaining but despite these limitations the reader is introduced to the term 'organization' which may be counted as a small gain. One searches, for example, through Stevens's study on strategy and collective bargaining negotiations and finds no mention of the organizational context; the book is process and outcome orientated.[119] This neglect of one of the most important areas of research need not be allowed to continue for long.

One might have been able to justify the lack of studies of the bargaining parameters, other than in economic terms, had not the study of organizational behaviour made such considerable advances in the last decade. Perhaps to a greater extent than is true in many other areas, the study of organizations has been of interest to researchers from a wide range of disciplines and each with rather different perspectives. The present state of the field may bear little resemblance to an ordered collection of knowledge but this does not explain the failure of studies of bargaining to take into account the organizational context. Considerable strides have been made in the methods employed in studying behaviour in organizations and it is my intention to identify two approaches which may be of considerable value in a study of the bargaining parameters. The first approach is suggested by the work of Pugh and his colleagues and the second is that of Derber and his co-workers. Before describing their work in more detail it is appropriate to note Homans's cautionary message, 'People who write about methodology often forget that it is a matter of strategy, not of morals. They are neither good nor bad methods but only methods that are more or less effective under particular circumstances in reaching objectives on the way to a distant goal.'[120]

A more systematic approach to the study of the organizational parameters of bargaining may be made possible by the application of the research findings of Pugh and his colleagues in the 'Aston Researches'.[121] The starting point of these researches was the recognition that previous studies had tended to be case studies and had made little systematic attempt to relate work behaviour to its contextual and organizational setting.[122] From a survey of the literature on bureaucracy they developed a conceptual framework for analysing the structure and functioning of organizations in terms of a set of variables (specialization, standardization, formalization, centralization, configuration, and flexibility) which were capable of empirical validation. As they noted, 'by setting up empirically defined scales for these, clear comparisons can be made between organizations . . . the typology will serve as a means of controlling organizational factors when intra-organizational research is attempted'.[123] Subsequently Pugh and his colleagues reported on the applications of their ideas. In the first article[124] they set out to demonstrate the value of a multivariate approach to the analysis of the relationship between the structure and context of an organization. Seven primary concepts, previously identified, were analysed and operationally defined scales were constructed which were used as independent variables in a multivariate regression analysis to predict three underlying dimensions of organization structure. As the authors note, 'the framework is also seen as a means of controlling the organisational factors when individual and group level variables are being studied'.[125] In a second article[126] the Aston research team reported on an empirical taxonomy of structures of work organizations based upon the use of three dimensions of organization structure which they had previously identified, namely: the structuring of activities, concentration of authority, and line control of workflow. A sevenfold classification of organization structures was developed. These were identified as full bureaucracy, nascent full bureaucracy, workflow bureaucracy, nascent workflow bureaucracy, and implicitly structured organizations. 'Each

71

class or cluster of organizations was associated with a typical pattern of contextual variables, from which its occurrence might be predicted.'[127] We thus have two research instruments which if employed jointly could provide quantified data on the organizational parameters within which bargaining takes place. In a subsequent replication Inkson, Pugh, and Hickson[128] reported on the reliability and validity of a short form for the measurement of the previously identified dimensions of organization's context and structure. This may go some considerable way towards meeting the criticism that these Aston measures are too time-consuming to warrant their application. An interview of one hour's duration can hardly be called long! The more recent work of Warner and Donaldson suggests that this basic concept of quantification of organizational dimensions can also be applied with certain modifications to the study of trade unions.[129]

The other parameter of the bargaining process which requires systematic analysis is that of union-management relationship within the organization. The functioning of the industrial relations system at the level of the plant is the backcloth against which negotiations take place. As Walker has noted, 'if the study of industrial relations is to progress beyond the mere historical recording . . . these systems must be characterised in some general way and a taxonomy of systems be developed as a first step . . . it is indeed only through such taxonomic comparisons that we shall come to a full understanding of industrial relations systems by relating their variations to diverse determining influences'.[130] This is almost the same departure point as that of Pugh and his colleagues in their study of organizations. An attempt, similarly, to combine both quantitative and qualitative methodologies in an analysis of the plant level management-union relationship has already been undertaken by Derber and his team of co-workers at the University of Illinois.[131] These studies are quite the most ambitious and thorough attempts that have as yet been made to characterize the dimensions of plant industrial relations systems. Unfortunately this American work has been neglected in the United Kingdom for two main reasons: first, because the application of such quantitative techniques presupposes the existence of large quantities of data about the industrial relations system at all levels, and secondly, because of a lack of interdisciplinary research teams which are essential to such work. This means that the initial task facing British researchers is one of replication but nevertheless the attempt has been made and future work should be made easier.

Within the organization Derber and his colleagues assumed there exist two organized goal-orientated groups, the management and the union, 'each striving toward various goals and each guided in its activities by norms or standards as to (1) acceptable achievements . . . and (2) appropriate tactics . . . The accommodation process was concerned as the interaction between the two groups in which . . . agreement is sought as to the conditions of employment and the conduct of the joint relationship.'[132] The accommodation of the group interests, i.e. those of management and the unions, move through two distinct phases; the first concerns the negotiation (or periodic renegotiation) of the substantive and procedural rules, and the second is 'the process of administering and giving effect to the general rules'.[133] The Illinois researches suggest that the accommodation process, which becomes institutionalized over time, can be described. A comprehensive account would need to cover the following aspects: (1) the parties involved and the functions which they serve in the plant situation; (2) their goals and standards (including the concept of ideology); (3) the structure of the interaction; (4) the manner of the interaction; (5) the environmental conditions within which the interaction takes place; (6) the substantive rules, and (7) the attitudes and satisfactions of the parties. Given that one is concerned to describe a dynamic situation, a change is likely to have repercussions, in proportion to its strength and the reaction of counteracting forces, elsewhere in the plant industrial relations system. Data, on which to conduct the analysis of the union-management relationship, was generated by means of interview schedules completed with the chief management and union spokesmen in the plant. Questions were of two types. A proportion which were common to both interviews concerned 'factual' matters, e.g. questions about safety rules, arbitration, the number of grievances raised, etc. The remaining questions sought to measure the attitudes and perception of the respondents towards the conduct of the joint relationship, e.g. preference for the amount of detail in the contract, the use of pressure in grievance settlements, etc. Using factor analytic techniques seven principal factors were extracted, 'apparently representing some distinctive central tendency . . . which we labelled (*a*) feelings about the joint relationship, (*b*) union influence, (*c*) joint problem solving, (*d*) union aggressiveness, (*e*) size of establishment, (*f*) employment stability and (*g*) self sufficiency'.[134] Factor analysis had clearly suggested that the union-management relationship could not be adequately described by a single all-embracing concept. This conclusion about the description of these parameters is similar to that of Pugh and his colleagues writing about organizational structures. It appears, therefore, that the application of factor analytic techniques to the description of the union-management relationship within the organization may be the first step towards a more systematic approach to the study of plant industrial relations systems.

A closer analysis of the data suggested that three factors, namely leadership feelings about the joint relation, union influence, and joint problem-solving, were the most important. To these was added a fourth factor, 'pressure'. The concentration on these four factors allowed Derber and his colleagues to undertake a comparative description and analysis of the union-management relationship at specific periods in time and then by means of subsequent re-surveys begin an analysis of change over time which would take into account the dynamic process. The earlier surveys have been criticized for not taking into account the time scale,[135] but this is something that the subsequent re-survey of the earlier sample overcame. Our interest in this work is however limited initially to one important consideration – the quantification of the bargaining parameters. The systematic study of union-management relations within their organizational context requires the development of two research instruments which would follow on the pioneering work of the Illinois researchers. The first is likely to be very similar to that used by Derber in their second survey and would measure the parameters at the level of the plant. The second instrument, using the same factor analytic techniques, would be used at a suborganization level, e.g. . . . the departmental manager and the shop steward. The latter would need to be very brief and could be used at the outset of specific negotiations which were being observed. The task to be tackled is large, the payoffs may however be equally great.

To conclude, this paper has been concerned to examine some of the previous studies of bargaining behaviour that have been undertaken. Two dimensions have been identified; one of 'size', e.g. the individual, the group, and the organization, and one of 'levels', e.g. the parameters, the process, and the outcomes. It has been suggested that the systematic study of bargaining behaviour would be facilitated by a concentration of research activity on a number of quite specific problems. These are (1) work on language and social skills at the interpersonal process level, (2) the further development of methods of recording the process at the group level, along the lines of Stephenson's Conference Process Analysis, and (3) the development of instruments for the description and analysis over time of the bargaining parameters at the level of the organization. Here it has been suggested the work of Pugh in England and Derber in the United States provides an indication of the path to be followed. Much still remains to be done even before attempts at model building can proceed.

NOTES

1 An indication of the scope of the literature can be found in my *Bargaining behaviour – a bibliography*, University of Nottingham, Department of Adult Education, 1972.
2 J. E. McGrath, 'A social psychological approach to the study of negotiations', in R. V. Bowers (ed.), *Studies on behaviour in organisations*, Athens, Georgia: University of Georgia Press, 1966.
3 J. A. Cross, *The economics of bargaining*, New York: Basic Books, 1969, p. 4.
4 *Ibid.* p. 7.
5 *Ibid.* pp. 12–13.
6 C. M. Stevens, *Strategy in collective bargaining negotiations*, New York: McGraw-Hill, 1963.
7 F. Zeuthen, *Problems of monopoly and economic warfare*, London: Routledge, 1930, pp. 104–50.
8 A. Coddington, *Theories of the bargaining process*, London: Allen and Unwin, 1968, p. 35.
9 J. R. Hicks, *The theory of wages*, London: Macmillan, 1932, pp. 136–58.
10 Cross, *The economics of bargaining*, p. 33.
11 J. C. Harsaayi, 'Approaches to the bargaining problem before and after the theory of games', *Econometrica*, vol. 24, 1956, pp. 144–53.
12 Coddington, *Theories of the bargaining process*, p. 34.

13 B. D. Mabry, 'The pure theory of bargaining', *Industrial and Labour Relations Review*, vol. 18, 1965, pp. 479–502.

14 *Ibid.* p. 502.

15 T. Parsons, *The social system*, New York: Free Press, 1951, p. 5.

16 Coddington, *Theories of the bargaining process*, p. 1. The economic environment is subsequently defined as 'a theoretical construction which serves to represent, for each actor, the behaviour of all the relevant economic units which are not under his immediate control' (p. 2).

17 *Ibid.* p. 15.

18 S. Siegel and L. Fouraker, *Bargaining and group decision making*, New York: McGraw-Hill, 1960.

19 *Ibid.* p. 1.

20 H. L. Johnson and A. M. Cohen, 'Experiments in behavioural economics; Siegel and Fouraker revisited', *Behavioural Science*, vol. 12, 1967, pp. 353–72.

21 L. A. Fromm and M. D. Cohen, 'Threats and bargaining efficiency', *Behavioural Science*, vol. 14, 1969, pp. 147–53.

22 A. Douglas, 'The peaceful settlement of industrial and inter-group disputes', *Journal of Conflict Resolution*, vol. 1, 1957, pp. 69–81.

23 *Ibid.* p. 70.

24 *Ibid.* p. 73.

25 *Ibid.* p. 78.

26 *Ibid.* pp. 80–1.

27 *Ibid.* p. 81.

28 R. E. Walton and R. B. McKersie, *A behavioural theory of labour negotiations*, New York: McGraw-Hill, 1965.

29 *Ibid.* pp. 4–6.

30 R. E. Walton and R. B. McKersie, 'Behavioural dilemmas in mixed-motive decision making', *Behavioural Science*, vol. 11, 1966, pp. 370–84.

31 *Ibid.* p. 381.

32 *Ibid.* p. 377.

33 P. Anthony and A. Crichton, *Industrial relations and the personnel specialist*, London: Batsford, 1969.

34 *Ibid.* p. 106.

35 *Ibid.* p. 107.

36 Walton and McKersie, *A behavioural theory of labour negotiations*, p. 44.

37 Walton and McKersie, 'Behavioural dilemmas in mixed-motive decision making', p. 381.

38 A. W. Gottschalk, 'The process of plant productivity bargaining', in B. Towers, T. G. Whittingham, and A. W. Gottschalk, *Bargaining for change, productivity bargaining and industrial relations*, London: Allen and Unwin, 1972.

39 Anthony and Crichton, *Industrial relations and the personnel specialist*, p. 113.

40 Walton and McKersie, *A behavioural theory of labour negotiations*, p. 60.

41 Anthony and Crichton, *Industrial relations and the personnel specialist*, p. 116.
42 See for example the work of I. Morley and G. Stephenson, 'Strength of case, communications systems and outcomes of simulated negotiations: some social psychological aspects of bargaining', *Industrial Relations Journal*, vol. 1, 1970, pp. 19–29.
43 Anthony and Crichton, *Industrial relations and the personnel specialist*, p. 119.
44 *Ibid.* pp. 121–32.
45 *Ibid.* p. 121.
46 R. L. Kahn *et al.*, *Organisational stress: studies in role conflict and ambiguity*, New York: Wiley, 1964.
47 Walton and McKersie, *A behavioural theory of labour negotiations*, pp. 310–11.
48 Anthony and Crichton, *Industrial relations and the personnel specialist*, p. 128.
49 *Ibid.* p. 129.
50 A. M. Pettigrew, 'Occupational specialisation as an emergent process', paper presented to the British Sociological Association Industrial Sociology Group, London, October 1971.
51 *Ibid.* p. 36.
52 *Interaction process analysis: a method for the study of small groups*, Cambridge, Mass.: Addison Wesley, 1950.
53 R. F. Bales and F. L. Strodtbeck, 'Phases in group problem solving', *Journal of Abnormal and Social Psychology*, vol. 46, 1951, pp. 485–495, reprinted in D. Cartwright and A. Zander (eds.), *Group dynamics: research and theory*, 3rd edition, London: Tavistock, 1968.
54 *Ibid.* in *Group dynamics: research and theory*, p. 397.
55 H. A. Landsberger, 'Interaction process analysis of the mediation of labour-management disputes', *Journal of Abnormal and Social Psychology*, 1955, vol. 51, pp. 552–9; and H. A. Landsberger, 'Interaction process analysis of professional behaviour: a study of labour mediators in twelve labour-management disputes', *American Sociological Review*, 1955, vol. 20, pp. 566–75.
56 J. E. McGrath, 'A social psychological approach to the study of negotiations', in R. V. Bowers (ed.), *Studies on behaviour in organisations*, Athens, Georgia: University of Georgia Press, 1966.
57 G. M. Stephenson, 'The experimental study of negotiating', paper presented to the Social Psychology Section, British Psychological Society, Durham, September, 1971, p. 7.
58 I. E. Morley and G. M. Stephenson, 'Conference process analysis: the description of behaviour in negotiations', unpublished report, Nottingham University Department of Psychology, 1971.
59 Stephenson, 'The experimental study of negotiating'
60 McGrath, 'A social psychological approach to the study of negotiations', pp. 117–18.
61 *Ibid.* p. 118.
62 See for example R. Loveridge, 'Demarcation dispute at Greens

(Heavy Engineering) Ltd., mimeo, London Graduate School of Business Studies, 1971.

63 A. Rapoport and A. M. Chemmah, *Prisoner's dilemma: a study of conflict and co-operation*, Ann Arbor, Mich.: University of Michigan Press, 1965.

64 M. Deutsch and R. M. Krauss, 'The effect of threat upon interpersonal bargaining', *Journal of Abnormal and Social Psychology*, 1960, vol 61, pp. 168–75.

65 Siegel and Fouraker, *Bargaining and group decision making*.

66 Bargaining efficiency is here taken to mean the extent to which the subjects achieve their maximum joint profits.

67 L. A. Froman and M. D. Cohen, 'Threats and bargaining efficiency', *Behavioural Science*, 1969, vol. 14, pp. 147–53.

68 Walton and McKersie, 'Behavioural dilemmas in mixed-motive decision making', pp. 376–7.

69 W. P. Smith, 'Reward structure and information in the development of co-operation', *Journal of Experimental Social Psychology*, 1968, vol. 4, pp. 199–223.

70 V. Daniels, 'Communication, incentive, and structural variables in interpersonal exchange and negotiations', *Journal of Experimental Social Psychology*, 1967, vol. 3, pp. 47–74.

71 R. M. Leibert *et al.*, 'Effects of information and magnitude of initial offer on interpersonal negotiation', *Journal of Experimental Social Psychology*, 1968, vol. 4, pp. 431–41.

72 R. B. Blake, J. S. Mouton, and R. L. Slomn, 'The union-magagement intergroup laboratory,: Strategy for resolving intergroup conflict, *Journal of Applied Behaviour Science*, 1965, vol. 1, pp. 25–57, reprinted in W. G. Bennis, K. D. Beane, and R. Chin (eds.), *The planning of change*, New York: Holt, Rinehart and Winston, 1969, pp. 176–91.

73 *Ibid.* in *The planning of change*, p. 191.

74 D. W. Johnson and R. J. Lewicki, 'The initiation of superordinate goals', *Journal of Applied Behavioural Science*, 1969, vol. 5, pp. 9–24.

75 M. Derber, W. E. Chalmers, and R. Stagner, 'Uniformities and differences in local union-management relationships', *Industrial and Labour Relations Review*, 1957, vol. 11, pp. 56–71.

76 *Ibid.* p. 57.

77 Walton and McKersie, 'Behavioural dilemmas in mixed-motive decision making', p. 380.

78 A. W. Gottschalk, 'The process of plant productivity bargaining', in B. Towers, T. G. Whittingham, and A. W. Gottschalk, *Bargaining for change, productivity bargaining and industrial relations*, London: Allen and Unwin, 1972.

79 J. W. Thibaut and M. H. Kelley, *The social psychology of groups*, New York: Wiley, 1966.

80 *Ibid.* p. 276.

81 J. F. B. Goodman and T. G. Whittingham, *Shop stewards in British industry*, London: McGraw-Hill, 1969, p. 74.

82 E. P. Hollander and J. W. Julian, 'Studies in leader legitimacy, influence and innovations', in L. Berkowitz (ed.), *Advances in experi-*

mental social psychology, vol. 5, New York: Academic Press, 1970, pp. 33–69.

83 *Ibid.* p. 66.

84 *Ibid.* p. 67.

85 M. G. Hermann and N. Kogan, 'Negotiation in leader and delegate groups', *Journal of Conflict Resolution*, vol. 12, 1968, pp. 332–44.

86 K. L. Dion, R. S. Baron, and N. Miller, 'Why do groups make riskier decisions than individuals', in L. Berkowitz (ed.), *Advances in experimental social psychology*, vol. 5, New York: Academic Press, 1970, pp. 305–77.

87 *Ibid.* p. 370.

88 D. L. Harnett, L. L. Cummings, and G. D. Hughes, 'The influence of risk taking propensity on bargaining behaviour', *Behavioural Science*, vol. 13, 1968, pp. 91–101.

89 H. Lamm and N. Kogan, 'Risk taking in the context of intergroup negotiations'. *Journal of Experimental Social Psychology*, vol. 6, 1970, pp. 351–63.

90 W. M. Evan and J. A. MacDougall, 'Interorganisational conflict: a labour-management bargaining experiment', *Journal of Conflict Resolution*, vol. 11, 1967, pp. 398–413.

91 A. Rapoport, *Fights games and debates*, Ann Arbor, Mich.: University of Michigan Press, 1960, pp. 2–5.

92 *Ibid.* pp. 5–12

93 Evan and MacDougall, 'Interorganisational conflict', p. 399.

94 N. S. Ross, 'Organised labour and management', in E. M. Hugh Jones (ed.), *Human relations and modern management*, Amsterdam: North Holland Publishing Co., 1958; and N. S. Ross, *The democratic firm*, London: Fabian Society Research Series no. 242, 1964.

95 A. Fox, 'Managerial ideology and labour relations', *British Journal of Industrial Relations*, vol. 4, 1966, pp. 366–78; and A. Fox, *Industrial sociology and industrial relations*, Research Paper no. 3, Royal Commission on Trade Unions and Employers Associations, London: HMSO, 1966.

96 E. Goffman, *Behaviour in public places*, New York: Free Press, 1963.

97 This approach to the study of social performance is associated in the United Kingdom primarily with the work of Michael Argyle, cf. *The psychology of interpersonal behaviour*, Harmondsworth: Penguin, 1967; *Social interaction*, London: Methuen, 1969; and M. Argyle and A. Kendon, 'The experimental analysis of social performance' in L. Berkowitz (ed.), *Advances in experimental social psychology*, vol. 3, New York: Academic Press, 1967, pp. 55–98.

98 *Ibid.* p. 56.

99 *Ibid.* p. 59.

100 E. Goffmann, *Presentation of self in everyday life*, London: Allen Lane, 1969.

101 Argyle and Kendon, 'The experimental analysis of social performance', p. 62.

102 An indication of how such studies could proceed can be obtained from K. Ring *et al.*, 'Performance styles in interpersonal behaviour:

an experimental validation of a typology', *Journal of Experimental Social Psychology*, vol. 3, 1967, pp. 140–59.

103 Argyle and Kendon, 'The experimental analysis of social performance', p. 82.

104 Government Social Survey, *Workplace industrial relations*, London: HMSO, 1968, paras. 2.5, 4.9, and 4.10.

105 R. M. Krauss, 'Structural and attitudinal factors in interpersonal bargaining', *Journal of Experimental Social Psychology*, vol. 2, 1966, pp. 42–55.

106 D. Druckman, 'Dogmatism, pre-negotiation experience and simulated group representation as determinants of dyadic behaviour in a bargaining situation', *Journal of Personality*, vol. 6, 1967, pp. 279–90.

107 M. Rokeach, *The open and closed mind*, New York: Basic Books, 1960.

108 B. R. Brown, 'The effects of need to maintain face on interpersonal bargaining', *Journal of Experimental Social Psychology*, vol. 4, 1968, pp. 107–22.

109 H. H. Kelley, L. L. Beckman, and C. S. Fuscher, 'Negotiating the division of a reward under incomplete information', *Journal of Experimental Social Psychology*, vol. 3, 1967, pp. 361–98.

110 M. Deutsch and R. M. Krauss, 'The effect of threat upon interpersonal bargaining', *Journal of Abnormal and Social Psychology*, vol. 61, 1961, pp. 181–9; and M. Deutsch and R. M. Krauss, 'Studies of interpersonal bargaining, *Journal of Conflict Resolution*, vol. 6, 1962, pp. 52–76.

111 M. A. Hornstein, 'The effects of different magnitudes of threat upon interpersonal bargaining', *Journal of Experimental Social Psychology*, vol. 1, 1965, pp. 282–93.

112 M. Guyer and A. Rapoport, 'Threat in a two-person game', *Journal of Experimental Social Psychology*, vol. 6, 1970, pp. 11–25.

113 G. M. Stephenson, 'Intergroup relations and negotiating behaviour', in P. B. Warr (ed.), *Psychology at work*, Harmondsworth: Penguin, 1971, pp. 347–73.

114 R. H. Fryer, personal communication, February 1972.

115 An example of the indirect application of exchange theory to the explanation of the effect of outcomes can be found in H. A. Turner, G. Clack, and G. Roberts, *Labour relations in the motor industry*, London: Allen and Unwin, 1967, pp. 333–9.

116 A valuable review of this topic can be found in J. S. Adams, 'Inequity in social exchange' in L. Berkowitz (ed.), *Advances in experimental social psychology*, vol. 2, New York: Academic Press, 1961, pp. 267–99.

117 D. Robinson (ed.), *Local labour markets and wage structures*, London: Gower Press, 1970.

118 Walton and McKersie, *A behavioural theory of labour negotiations*, p. 281.

119 C. M. Stevens, *Strategy and collective bargaining negotiation*, New York: McGraw-Hill, 1963.

120 G. C. Homans, 'The strategy of industrial sociology', *American Journal of Sociology*, vol. 54, 1954, pp. 330–7.

121 Thus entitled because the work was initiated by a group of researchers based upon the Department of Industrial Administration at the University of Aston in Birmingham.

122 D. S. Pugh *et al.*, 'A conceptual scheme for organisational analysis', *Administrative Science Quarterly*, vol. 8, 1963, pp. 289–315.

123 *Ibid.* p. 315.

124 D. S. Pugh *et al.*, 'The context of organisation structures', *Administrative Science Quarterly*, vol. 14, 1969, pp. 91–114.

125 *Ibid.* p. 112.

126 D. S. Pugh *et al.*, 'An empirical taxonomy of structures of work organisations'. *Administrative Science Quarterly*, vol. 14, 1965, pp. 115–26.

127 *Ibid.* p. 125.

128 J. H. K. Inkson, D. S. Pugh, and D. J. Hickson, 'Organisation context and structure: an abbreviated replication', *Administrative Science Quarterly*, vol. 15, 1970, pp. 318–29.

129 M. Warner and L. Donaldson, *Dimensions of organisation in occupational interest groups: some preliminary findings*, working paper, London Graduate School of Business Studies, Organisational Behaviour Research Group, 1971.

130 K. F. Walker, *Research needs in industrial relations*, 2nd edition, Melbourne: University of Western Australia Press, 1964, p. 12.

131 The research is cogently summarized and presented in M. Derber, W. E. Chalmers, and M. T. Edelman, *Plant union-management relations: from practice to theory*, Urbana, Ill.: University of Illinois, Institute of Labour and Industrial Relations, 1965.

132 Derber, Chalmers, and Stagner, 'Uniformities and differences in local union–management relationships', pp. 56–7.

133 Derber, Chalmers, and Edelman, *Plant union–management relations*, p. 3.

134 *Ibid.* p. 6.

135 Walker, *Research needs in industrial relations*, pp. 22–3.

3 Cheap at Twice the Price ? Shop Stewards and Workshop Relations in Engineering

E. O. EVANS

INTRODUCTION

In recent years, especially since the impetus given to research and the wider dissemination of research findings by the large-scale inquiry of the Donovan Royal Commission, the role of the shop steward has become much better understood. Nowadays in even moderately well informed discussion the old stereotype of the belligerent, irrational, and deaf-to-argument shop floor leader has been replaced by a concept of the shop steward as a rather conciliatory figure. Indeed the description of his function given in the Donovan report as 'more of a lubricant than an irritant'[1] has become something of a cliché.

This improved understanding has emerged very largely from the growing interest in workplace industrial relations following the long period when writers and research workers were concerned to analyse and describe the more visible and accessible institutions and organizations outside the plant. It seems probable that key documents in this growth of understanding were the first research paper produced for the Commission[2] which usefully summarized the knowledge about shop stewards available at the time it was written and the final paper in the research series (no. 10)[3] which presented the most immediately relevant material relating to stewards from the workplace industrial relations inquiry undertaken by the Government Social Survey.

A further example of this shift of research emphasis was the national survey of workshop relations in engineering which was carried out from St Edmund Hall, Oxford by Arthur Marsh, Paul Garcia, and the present writer. Work commenced in September 1968, the survey was carried out between December 1968 and March 1969, and analysis of the data was completed in the summer of 1971. The overall picture of workshop relations which emerged from the replies to our long and detailed postal questionnaire has been published elsewhere,[4] but the material can be examined more specifically for the light it throws on the role of the shop steward in one of our largest and most complex industries. Since our questionnaire was answered by managers it is particularly useful in giving the view of shop stewards as it looks from behind the manager's desk.

Before describing the role of stewards and their activities which was revealed by our study it is important that the nature of this particular survey should be made clear. An extensive inquiry of this kind, addressing itself to workshop practices across a whole industry, is crucially dependent on the *active* cooperation of employers, as distinct from mere toleration of research workers in their plants. Given the limited funds available for the project, field interviews to secure the information were not a feasible proposition and reliance had to be placed instead on getting managers themselves to complete a lengthy and formidable looking questionnaire.

We were fortunate in being able to secure the interest and assistance of the Engineering Employers Federation whose research department gave us constant encouragement throughout.* The Federation gained for us the cooperation of employers by circulating, through their constituent associations, all 4,700 member establishments.[5] The nature and purpose of our projected inquiry was explained to the employers and their cooperation invited. 555 establishments agreed to take part and each one appointed a particular manager to be responsible for contact with the research team. In the outcome 432 establishments actually completed the questionnaire and omissions and ambiguities in the answers were subsequently cleared up by telephone; so that, within the limits of what could be the subject of inquiry even in a lengthy schedule of questions, a fairly complete picture of workshop practices in industrial relations emerged for a collection of units comprising just over

* I should like it to be clearly understood that the interpretations and conclusions presented in this paper are those of the present author only and should not be taken as necessarily in line with the views of the Federation or indeed with the views of anyone else, including my fellow authors of the earlier report.

9 per cent of the establishments in membership of the Federation and employing rather more than 588,000 workers both manual and staff.

When an inquiry is answered by self-selected volunteers it is obvious that what it reveals cannot be regarded as reliably representative of what goes on in the whole population of federated establishments, and all we would claim is that we examined practice in an unusually large range of firms and that these examples were from all regions of the United Kingdom, were of all sizes,* and included representatives from all the major engineering categories in the standard industrial classification. Some of the bias introduced by the selection process we were able to identify by comparing certain characteristics of our survey group with known figures for the industry as a whole. We found that, broadly speaking, our collection of establishments was more unionized than the average, its members had been involved in procedural conferences at works, local, and national level much more frequently than most; it contained many of the newer members of the Federation and appears to be more liable to strike action than is usual in the industry.

The survey did not, nor did we expect it to, reveal anything dramatically new about shop stewards. From the outset we anticipated that much of its value would lie in exploring the minutiae of workshop institutions and practice and in putting quantities on many variables for the first time; a process which, while not wildly exciting, is not to be despised since, in social as in other kinds of exploration, maps of the territory are a prerequisite for making safe journeys and for altering the landscape intelligently.

SHOP STEWARD WORKPLACE ORGANIZATION

The power and influence of shop stewards rests at bottom on systematic union organization in the plant, and the basis of this must always be the extent and continuity of union membership. In the 432 establishments surveyed just under one-third of the managers estimated manual union membership in their establishments to be 100 per cent, another 40 per cent thought

* Following Federation practice we took as the measure of size the total number of manual and staff employees, counting every two part-time workers as one full-time worker.

that over three-quarters of their workers were union members, while the figures submitted by more than one establishment in every ten showed less than half the manual workers in membership of trade unions. In only three cases did we find establishments altogether without union membership. It is perhaps surprising in an industry popularly supposed to be union-dominated that overall only 77 per cent of the manual workers covered by this survey were organized in trade unions, and this is very likely a maximum figure since union membership figures were probably obtained in many cases from the unions themselves and so are subject to at least marginal exaggeration.

Bearing in mind the fact that these establishments were among the more recently joined of the Federation's membership and that firms tend to join employers' associations when they experience labour trouble indicative of union activity, it appears that previous estimates of union density in engineering have been too high.[6] The figures give some indication of the great difficulty that manual unions have in recruiting the last quarter of their potential membership.

Given recognition, union recruitment tends to be most successful where unions can secure the cooperation of employers, whether willing or forced, in imposing a closed shop. We found that full pre-entry closed shops, where workers needed a union card before being employed, existed in only 37 establishments and partial ones, enforced for parts of the plant only, existed in a further 86. In 301 cases, just under 70 per cent of the total, union recruitment was not assisted in this way. We found, as we expected to, that unions had more often secured management cooperation in persuading workers to join unions after engagement and post-entry closed shop existed in 179 cases (41·4 per cent) though again, in one-third of these the arrangement only covered part of the plant and not every worker.

It is not at all surprising that managers are often reluctant to assist the unions in recruiting members since this obviously strengthens the power base from which shop stewards operate. But it is a feature of this study that many managements see advantages in having a well-organized and authoritative system of worker representation in their plants and unions may well have scope to extend the post-entry closed shop in engineering, perhaps in the form of agency shops, since 10 per cent more establishments than have such arrangements at present, reported to us that they saw advantages from having 100 per cent union shops.

Having recruited workers into membership, unions must try to keep them and the maintenance of membership levels is facilitated if contributions can be collected easily and regularly, so that members do not accumulate a burden of arrears and fall out of membership from this cause. Management cooperation can be of considerable assistance to unions in this matter too. The most effective method for the purpose, the check-off system whereby union dues are deducted from wages by the employer, we found to be much less prevalent than the various forms of the closed shop. A check-off scheme operated in only 5 per cent of the 432 establishments. In relatively few cases had the unions approached management for such an arrangement and this may have been partly because managements were known not to favour it. We asked managers whether they would agree to the check-off if asked and just under 50 per cent of them said that they would not. However, in view of the fact that 99 managers replied favourably to the idea it seems that in this area of workplace organization also the unions could make progress if they pressed the matter with more vigour and consistency.* Even without going so far as to give the positive assistance of the check-off, managements can make it easy or difficult for unions in the plant to collect union dues. We found that 71 establishments had a formal arrangement whereby stewards or collectors could do this part of their union work in the plant with management approval, but in the great majority of cases union dues were collected during breaks or very informally during working hours, the contribution of management being, at best, to turn a blind eye to practices which, in many cases, were specifically forbidden in the works rule book.†

Engineering employers and their representatives have been prone to complain about the number of unions with which they have to deal, and complaints have also been made about

* In respect of the AUEW it was not until the rules revision conference of 1970 that the conditions for positive authorization of the check-off were finally spelled out: rule 3(1).
† Works rules very commonly contain a clause forbidding the collection of money on the works premises without prior management approval.

the degree of conflict between unions. Without wishing to deny that unstable relations among unions can be an acute problem where such situations exist, if our survey is at all representative it seems that the degree of multi-unionism in engineering has been exaggerated. The maximum number of unions we found in a plant was 12 and only four plants had so many. The average number of unions was only four. Similarly the degree of conflict between unions over membership seems to have been exaggerated; only 9 per cent of the 432 managers reported serious conflict of this kind between unions at their plants. However it is true that relatively few plants are organized by a single union. We found only 60 single-union plants. A further 78 had only two unions operating and a further 72 had only three. Clearly in multi-union situations inter-union friction is always a potential danger and this emphasizes the need for managements to ensure that adequate procedural arrangements are available to deal with problems as they arise.

Though our inquiry seems to reveal a lower degree of unionization in engineering than was formerly supposed, it does confirm the impression of many observers that the number of shop stewards has increased. It was estimated in 1960 that there might be 30,000 stewards in federated firms[7] and it seems that by the time our survey was conducted the number of stewards had risen to perhaps as many as 40,000. Despite the increase in their numbers stewards are not to be found everywhere. Among the establishments that we studied 25 had no stewards and these firms were not all, as might be supposed, small. About half of them had over 100 employees and three of them over 500. If the size distribution of firms without shop stewards in our survey group represents the situation in the Federation as a whole it could be that as many as 1,500 establishments or 30 per cent of federated units had no shop stewards early in 1969. However, we know that about a quarter of the firms with no stewards at the time of the survey did have stewards at some time in the past, and it seems likely that in some firms fluctuations in the effectiveness of union organization results in stewards operating during some periods and not in others. Even where union organization is rudimentary to the point where no formal stewards have been appointed it is still possible for informal workplace representatives to emerge and we made some inquiry about this possibility. We found

100 establishments with informal stewards though most of them had formal stewards too. It seems that from time to time, even in well-organized plants, the workplace arrangements of particular unions will fall into disrepair, and when this happens someone may fill the breach when representation is needed, acting as an informal steward and being so accepted by the management. Of the 25 firms in our group with no formal stewards, 10 were found to have informal representatives of some kind. Some informality extends also to the make-up of the constituency that many stewards represent in negotiation. Managers in 36 per cent of the establishments reported that in their plants some stewards represented members of other unions as well as their own and in 11 per cent of cases this multi-union representation was reported to be general throughout the plant.

Our 432 establishments reported a total of 8,894 shop stewards, an average of one steward for every 32 union members. Naturally the average number of members represented by a steward varied from union to union. Among the major unions the ETU had the lowest constituency with 28 members per steward and the GMWU the highest with 44; the AEF, the union with the greatest membership investment in engineering, had an average constituency of 30.

Many union rule books are vague about the method by which shop stewards are to be elected and most stewards (when they *are* elected) are probably elected by show of hands at very informal breaktime meetings on the shop floor. We found that facilities for the formal election of stewards, such as the provision of ballot boxes, were provided by very few managements, probably because in most cases they had never been asked for. On the other hand most managers reported that they had been properly informed by the union office about the appointment of stewards in their plants, and the issue of appropriate union credential cards.

The engineering *Procedure Agreement – Manual Workers* gives the unions the undoubted right to have the stewards they themselves desire, but our survey reveals that federated establishments by no means take for granted that they must accept without objection the persons put forward from the shop floor. One-quarter of our managers reported having objected at some time to particular shop steward appointments. The reason most frequently given for objecting was that the shop was adequately represented already, and here managers were clearly attempting to restrain the multiplication of shop steward numbers. In other cases the reasons related to the person's attitudes or his lack of experience; in only one case did a manager report having objected on political grounds. We were very interested, and surprised too, to discover in how many cases where objections had been made, the managers had been able to get the unions to change their minds. In no less than half of the cases the union subsequently agreed to withdraw the credential it had issued to the steward and presumably another person was elected in his place.

How experienced are stewards in engineering? We were particularly interested in this question in the light of the growth of interest in shop steward training in recent years, and we asked a number of questions designed to establish the degree of turnover among shop stewards over the two years prior to our survey (i.e. between 1967 and 1969). These questions were not answered as fully as others, probably because, as field interviews have shown, managerial records are often of poor quality. What does emerge is that the number of resignations each year was considerable. In this collection of plants perhaps four out of every ten stewards had been appointed in the previous two years. No doubt some of these appointments were of people who had been shop stewards in the past, or in other industries, but it is consistent with the overall growth in steward numbers that many recently appointed stewards must have taken up the role for the first time.

In the light of this how many managements have thought it necessary or wise to provide facilities for training their new (or existing) stewards? We asked about this and found that two-thirds of the establishments had released stewards for training courses held outside the plant but during working hours, and one-third had arranged for courses to be held at the plant itself. We asked those who had not given facilities for training whether they would be prepared to give them and an overwhelming majority said that they would, scarcely more than 5 per cent of establishments preferring to have nothing to do with training of this kind. When it is remembered that a decade ago facilities for such training were almost unknown in engineering our findings give a striking impression of the degree to which the acceptability of training for stewards has made headway among engineering managements.

A multiplicity of bodies was reported as involved with the organization of training courses. Outside educational bodies (universities, technical colleges, the Workers' Educational Association, etc.) were most frequently mentioned; however, for those courses held at the plant, companies themselves organized them in 60 per cent of establishments. It has been widely believed hitherto that stewards would not happily accept training unless the management was seen as facilitating rather than running courses themselves; our findings suggest that unions are more tolerant of internal courses run by management than has been supposed.

Although officially the employers in engineering have never recognized the office of convener or senior shop steward it has long been known that informal recognition is common.[8] 77 per cent of these establishments admitted that they recognized, formally or informally, some form of steward with a status superior to the ordinary shop representative, although often managers were reluctant to use the term convener. In the 432 establishments there were altogether 893 senior stewards, taking that term to mean merely a steward with more influence than an ordinary steward. This means that for these firms there was at the time of the survey one senior to every ten ordinary stewards. In fact terminology is a problem because sometimes the terms convener* and senior steward are used synonymously, and some unions have a preference for one term rather than the other, yet again and more importantly the term convener is used to refer to a further upward stage in the shop steward hierarchy at a plant, with below it the level of senior steward and below that again the ordinary stewards. We made no attempt to define the term in our questionnaire, preferring to let the differences in role, if any, emerge from the replies. Among the establishments 83 reported that they had both conveners and seniors, 132 had conveners only, and a further 118 had only senior stewards. These senior posts seem to muliply: 32 establishments reported that they had more than one convener and 76 had more than one senior. What can be said with confidence is that there is a tendency for the union organization in an engineering plant of any size

* The term 'convener' is, in origin, an AEF expression (rule 13 (21)).

to develop a hierarchy or superstructure of shop steward organization, and that each of the major unions in the plant will want to have a senior of its own. It is also clear from our study that these senior men are much more likely to be involved in representing to management the interests of other unions as well as their own.

The tendency of unions in the workplace to generate the office of convener or senior steward so that someone can speak on behalf of substantial groups of workers, and the way in which they typically come to act on behalf of members of unions other than their own, is a resultant of the forces which operate at works level to draw together the members of different unions and their workshop organizations in order to be able to negotiate collectively with a unitary management on that range of issues which affects them all. A further expression of this pressure for organizational solidarity is the prevalence of joint shop stewards committees. In its simplest form a joint shop stewards committee may be just a meeting, regular or irregular, of all the stewards at a plant. Its functions can be to consider any management proposals, especially if these are made in similar form to all unions, to formulate plant wage claims, and generally depending on the degree of sophistication of its leadership the advancement of union policies in the plant as a whole. When plants are large it may consist not of all the stewards but of representatives elected from among them. When organization is good, and relations between unions harmonious, these committees easily become complex, developing elected officers, especially chairman and secretary, and perhaps sub-committees to deal in detail with matters in current negotiation. We came across one case where in a large and important plant the committee had for a long time worked to a set of formal printed standing orders which laid down the rules for election of officers and the conduct of meetings.

In view of their need to negotiate at plant level with a number of unions, it is not surprising that managements have found joint stewards committees to be very useful instruments for the negotiation of matters on which they want to secure uniform regulation. They have proved especially useful as bodies with which managements can negotiate productivity agreements, being useful means for overcoming the fragmentation of the workforce between different unions. We found that stewards

at 295 plants (68 per cent) met in a joint shop stewards committee. In eight out of every ten cases the committee comprised
all the stewards and in the other cases representatives of the
stewards, though in a minority of cases (16 per cent) stewards
of some unions (notably the ETU) were known not to take
part in the committee, probably indicating an insufficient sense
of common interest or conflicting policies. In almost 70 per cent
of establishments with these committees their working was
sufficiently formal for managers to know which union usually
provided the chairman and secretary. The bulk of committees
met in the works, in works time, and in a room provided by
management. Their meetings tended to be held on a regular
basis, the most popular intervals being weekly or monthly.
Three-quarters of the committee were recognized by managements at least in the sense that management met them, usually
on request, but in 37 per cent of cases monthly.

Our study of the ownership pattern among the 432 establishments revealed that the majority of establishments were linked
by ownership into multiplant companies. 213 companies
appeared to be involved in the ownership of 370 establishments.
In a situation of this kind it would seem natural for stewards
to seek to build unofficial links between their own workplace
organizations and those of stewards at other plants owned by
the same company. We inquired about this and managers of
111 establishments representative of 46 (21·6 per cent) of the
213 multi-plant companies replied positively that they were
aware of the existence of unofficial combine committees. It
appears from what managers know of their activities that
these committees rarely try to secure uniformity of wages and
conditions throughout the company. Managers believe that
almost all of them exchange information and that about half
of them seek to coordinate action so as to influence wages and
conditions from time to time.

What facilities are given to shop stewards in these establishments to enable them to carry out their representational duties?
During working hours, when they have to leave their bench,
machine, or assembly line and engage in bargaining with
supervisors, rate fixers, time study men or managers, or
accompany a member into the office on an individual grievance
to support his case – do they lose money? When they need to
discuss workshop problems with their members are they free

to leave their work to do so? If they wish to communicate with the convener or feel the need for his advice can they easily contact him by telephone or by going along to his department?

Aside from the few establishments where the working of the stewards system has been formalized as part of a detailed domestic procedure agreement, the only formal point of reference available as a guide to the facilities a shop steward might expect is clause 11 (3) (*d*) (9) in the *Procedure Agreement – Manual Workers* where stewards are to be 'afforded facilities to deal with questions raised in the shop or portion of the shop in which they are employed', and the principle of recompensing stewards for time lost was urged upon member firms as early as 1918 by the Federation.[9] It follows that facilities tend to be determined informally along with so many other things that are decided at workshop level as a resultant of pressure from stewards themselves and the degree of management resistance.

We found that the earnings of stewards in most establishments were protected against loss while they engaged in negotiation by such arrangements as payment at average earnings, but in nearly 10 per cent of establishments the stewards lost money, though this was less true for conveners and senior stewards. Loss of earnings tended to be made up by shop collections from union members, and managers at 70 establishments reported that they knew of such a practice. The seriousness to stewards of such earnings loss and the cost of maintaining stewards on average earnings while they are not working at their bench or machine depends on the length of time they spend performing their functions.

A number of previous studies have inquired about the average time spent by stewards on union and representational duties. We did not go over this ground again, but we did ask about the time spent by senior stewards of all kinds. We found that, considering the known volume of domestic bargaining in engineering plants, the amounts of time spent on average were surprisingly modest. Only 69 out of the total of 893 senior posts in the steward superstructure were effectively full-time, and, although paid employees of the firm, did no work other than their union duties. These 69 full-time conveners were concentrated in 42 establishments; 27 establishments had one full-time steward each and the remaining 15 plants had more than one, a single plant accounting for no less than five of them. Over two-thirds of the establishments with conveners and eight out of ten of those with senior stewards reported that these officers spent, on average, less than a quarter of their working hours on union duties, and only 27 out of the 215 establishments with conveners said that they spent more than half of their working hours on union work.

With regard to freedom of movement it is clear that managers by no means allow stewards to wander about the place at will, at least not officially; 42 per cent said they gave their conveners complete freedom of movement and 24 per cent gave it to senior stewards. Most managers allowed ordinary stewards to contact members within their own shop but 72 per cent said permission was required, and 16 per cent said it was sometimes refused. Over one-third of the establishments did not allow stewards to contact members outside their own shop; most of the others did allow it with permission but permission was often refused. The other facilities widely provided for stewards included the use of internal plant telephones (rather more than half the establishments), some secretarial help for conveners and seniors (43 establishments), and an office was provided for the convener in 24 cases. All in all the survey suggests that the facilities afforded to stewards, supplemented as they probably are in many cases in ways that managers may be reluctant to acknowledge, are probably adequate but are far from lavish.

THE RANGE OF SHOP STEWARD ACTIVITY

Moving from the static picture of shop steward workplace organization to the dynamics of steward activity, it is proposed to consider in turn the degree to which stewards are involved in maintaining and improving their own union structure at the plant; the degree to which they try to impose, in the workshop, unilateral rules of a traditional kind or, alternatively, offer challenges to rules traditionally regarded as within the sphere of managerial functions; the degree to which they are involved in the negotiation of particular issues in the area of recognized bargaining and consultation; and finally, the degree to which they are becoming involved in new patterns of workplace regulation involving more comprehensive agreements of a formal kind. Looking at this latter kind of activity another way, to what degree does it appear that managers in engineering are attempting to regain control by sharing it?

The steward's role has two major aspects. One is to act as a workplace representative and the other is to build and maintain a union structure at the plant. The growing awareness of the positive role played by shop stewards as managers of discontent and sources of order in the workshop raises important questions about the most effective use of their time and energies. For instance it can be asked to what degree their effective performance as representatives is impaired by the need for them to operate primitive and time-consuming systems of union membership recruitment and maintenance? To what degree were stewards in these 432 establishments found to be preoccupied with such matters? While it does not necessarily follow that their representational work must suffer from such preoccupation, it is probably true that undue difficulty in securing adequate workshop organization absorbs energy and time that can ill be spared if stewards are to become really effective in operating the more sophisticated systems of workplace relations that we need in this country. Clearly, in those 122 establishments (28·2 per cent) where managements were not assisting union recruitment by persuading new employees to join an appropriate union, stewards are likely to have to give membership a good deal of attention. Rather a large number of managers (131) declined to answer questions on this matter, perhaps indicating that stewards were imposing some degree of closed shop but without any willing management assistance in the matter. Even in those firms where management aid was forthcoming, in over one-quarter of the cases it was only given to help recruitment in part of the works. In only 82 establishments (19 per cent) did we find that an agreement or understanding on 100 per cent trade union membership existed for the whole plant which fully legitimated union membership by putting the authority of the employer behind recruitment. Some indication of the burden of persuasive recruitment carried by the steward is given by the fact that over one-third of the establishments in our survey had experienced, in the five years prior to the study, cases of union members refusing to work with non-unionists. In three-quarters of these cases the worker had eventually been persuaded to join the union.

The collection of union dues and the checking of cards is probably an even more time-consuming and wearing business for the steward than recuitment, when, as is often still the case, it forms part of the steward's weekly duties. It is often argued that this regular and routine contact with members keeps a steward in touch with their feelings and opinions, but the role of debt collector is hardly an ideal one for the purpose of making friends and influencing people, and when the steward's pre-occupation with other matters (such as prolonged and difficult negotiations) or the member's own absence from work leads to an accumulation of arrears of contributions, the weekly dues collection round has a tendency to become a complaints session against the union. Since the check-off, administratively the most effective solution to this problem, was found to operate in only 19 out of 432 plants, it is clear that many engineering stewards must have heavy demands made on their time by dues collection, card checking, and the complicated, tension-producing business of dealing with members who fall into arrears.

Turning to the other major aspect of steward activity, their involvement in workshop regulation and negotiation, it is a common source of popular complaint about shop stewards that they are instrumental in the maintenance of work practices that are restrictive of managers' freedom to organize work efficiently. In the language of academic industrial relations this is an example of the imposition of unilateral rules from the workers' side. Managers in 318 establishments in our survey group (73·6 per cent) felt that they were not free to arrange their labour force as they wished and that this was a factor in preventing them from improving the organization of work in their plants. Over 96 per cent of the managers who felt restricted thought that the unions were a factor imposing restrictions on them. But they were far from blaming the unions entirely, in fact only 28 per cent thought that the unions were a large factor, which suggests that the degree of union unilateral control of work practices is not as great as has often been suggested.

We questioned managers in some detail about restrictions in an endeavour to be sure that we got replies based on their own experience and not just repetitions of the orthodoxy of managerial complaints. It turned out that managers were quite specific in reporting ways in which they felt unable to act freely. The kinds of restriction they reported are reproduced in Table 1 and this gives a good indication of the area of union control in the engineering workshop. It is interesting to note that union

Table 1 AREAS WHERE STEWARDS HAVE A DEGREE OF UNILATERAL CONTROL

Type of restriction	Number of establishments	Percentage of those reporting a particular restriction	Percentage of 432 establishments
Labour mobility	184	60·3	42·6
Changing Manning of machines	174	57·0	40·3
Job demarcation	162	53·1	37·5
Hampering work study	128	42·0	29·6
Resistance to dilutees	124	40·7	28·7
Union demarcation	98	32·1	22·7
Restriction on trainees from Government Training Centre	89	29·2	20·6
Restrictions on level of output	79	25·9	18·3
Restrictions on levels of earnings	65	21·3	15·0
Restrictions on apprentices	57	18·7	13·2
Seniority in redundancy	55	18·0	12·7
Seniority for promotion to better jobs	19	6·2	4·4
Overtime restrictions	9	3·0	2·1

demarcation comes much lower down the list than the traditional disputed areas of control–mobility of labour, the manning of machines, demarcation between jobs, and resistance to work study. It also shows the relatively small number of complaints about restrictions on the levels of earnings and output. One might have expected that overtime would have been an area where managers felt unions exerted a degree of control which was irksome, but the fact that only 2 per cent of managers mentioned it may merely reflect the way in which systematic

G

overtime has become an almost unquestioned way of life in the typical workshop. It is also revealing that when asked whether they thought that restrictions originated with shop stewards or with informal groups of union members, 50 per cent of the managers attributed them to the latter source and a further 10 per cent of cases thought that stewards and members were about equally responsible.

The area of control exercised unilaterally by management is obviously less easy to define since it comprises the whole area of decision making which union members and shop stewards have not insisted be subject to negotiation and consultation.* It is however possible from our survey to identify one aspect of workplace life where these engineering managements tend to *claim* a good deal of unilateral control – the area of works rules and discipline. Works rule books,[10] which appear to have been very rarely the subject of discussion with stewards, let alone agreement, were given to employees or available for inspection in 267 (62 per cent) of the 432 establishments, and they commonly contained a variety of fairly stringent rules of behaviour. Examination of nearly 200 of these books revealed that in many of them managements claimed very wide-ranging rights to suspend, dismiss, or otherwise discipline employees for breaches of the rules. In 84 per cent of the books this right was held to apply in a general way to the breach of any contractual element in the book.

Some evidence of the challenge offered by stewards when managements try to exercise the 'rights' in practice comes from the finding that 63 establishments, one in every seven, had been involved in formal works conferences in procedure on the subject of discipline over the two years prior to the survey, and in 16 of these cases a stoppage had occurred. For an issue to proceed as far as a formal works conference it must be regarded as particularly serious, so that these comparatively high figures suggest that a much larger number of cases have occurred where stewards have challenged management disciplinary activity. A further indication of the degree to which this area of managerial control may have been eroded is given by the number of managers (153) reporting that they had in

* Apart that is from the area of norm-governed behaviour that is thought of by both sides as appropriately regulated by fixed custom and practice, and therefore not within the area of decision making in any real sense.

operation a special procedure for dealing with individual dismissals. That dismissals are widely treated with caution is suggested by the fact that in the 432 establishments we found only 73 where supervisors have the power to dismiss workers without referring the matter to some higher authority in the management.

Another area of control that managements evidently regard as important for them to retain, and one where in these engineering plants they seem on the whole to have been successful, is related to redundancy. We asked a number of questions about this and carefully examined a collection of written redundancy procedures which they sent to us in the course of the survey. We found that almost without exception managers were adamant about reserving their prerogative to decide *when* the labour force must be reduced and *by how many*. It appears that managements will fight hard to restrict the influence of stewards to the selection of candidates for redundancy, the compensation to be offered, if any, to those who lose jobs, and sometimes to the degree of assistance to be given by managements towards the process by which workers get another job.

Our survey reveals something of the way in which engineering stewards are seeking, at least in the absence of managerial initiatives that would make it worthwhile for them to behave otherwise, to retain such unilateral worker control as has been traditional in the industry, and to extend their influence into areas of decision making which, equally traditionally, managements assumed to be within the area of their prerogative. Nevertheless the bulk of stewards' activity still falls into the (in engineering) wide sector where consultation and negotiation is regarded by both sides, with whatever degree of distaste in particular instances, as legitimate.* This is a large area including, at its most formal, work on such consultative bodies as Joint Production Consultative and Advisory Committees, and negotiation with management as a member of joint stewards committees or other plant negotiating agencies. More informally and in a day-to-day fashion the steward will be involved in bargaining over piecework or bonus prices and times or in the

* The terms of the 1922 engineering procedure agreement were widely enough drawn to make possible negotiation on most kinds of objections that workers would wish to make to management actions. In December 1971 the unions terminated this Procedure Agreement. An event which occurred after this text was drafted.

negotiation of special allowances, or lieu bonuses for workers not covered by schemes of payments by results, and more generally in a wide range of issues which it is legitimate to pursue through the procedural machinery, including the rules which regulate the degree of freedom needed by the steward himself in order to carry out his job effectively, or indeed, at all.

The practice in engineering of engaging in informal consultation with stewards before making changes affecting union members[11] is, if managers are to be believed, almost universal in these establishments; though managers were a good deal more cautious when we asked whether such consultation continued during the period when the changes were actually implemented. It seems that managers feel the need to have some means of sounding out shop floor opinion before they take decisions which may lead to resistance. Shop stewards are evidently a very convenient source of information about how workers feel on matters which management has it in mind to alter. That more formal and regular committees for consultation are also needed by management is indicated by our finding that despite the decline in number of formal JPCs,* a variety of other committees performing, in managers' eyes, similar functions seem to have arisen to take their place and our fairly detailed inquiries on this point established that stewards are active on many of them.

Discussions with managers suggest that when moves are made in the direction of more detailed and formal plant agreements, consultative committees provide a useful forum where matters of terminology and intention can be clarified prior to the main negotiations, often saving the latter from becoming bogged down in disputes and misunderstandings in areas where the parties are not fundamentally in conflict. Another expression of the felt need to provide means for an informal exploratory stage in negotiation, during which the issues in dispute can be sorted out and the position of the parties defined, is shown by the popularity of holding informal discussion with full-time union officials in the works before an issue in procedure goes

---

* A decline already well documented and confirmed by our study. One-half of our group have never had a JPC. 17 per cent have discontinued them, leaving 30 per cent with current JPCs of whom some six out of ten are dominated by stewards.

beyond the purely domestic stages to a formal Works Conference. Over half of these establishments had had this type of discussion at some time in the past two years, and as these firms are not confined to any particular region the practice would seem to be widespread.

Consultation, formal or informal, is one thing but negotiation is quite another, and the effectiveness with which stewards are able to act as lubricating agents in the system of industrial relations at the plant, by representing their members' views to levels of management with the power to make decisions, depends to a considerable extent on the existence of an effective disputes procedure. In mapping the workplace practices of a group of establishments covered by an industry-wide procedure agreement it was natural for us to make fairly detailed inquiries about the extent to which firms had attempted to design tailor-made arrangements for the domestic stage of procedural machinery. An industry procedure can obviously be more specific about stages outside the workplace than it can be about domestic arrangements, and in relation to the latter it can do little more than provide a bare frame which it is the responsibility of the firms themselves to clothe.

We assumed that the best indicator we could look for that firms had given systematic attention to this matter would be the existence of written domestic agreements deliberately designed to supplement the sketch outline in the 1922 *Procedure Agreement – Manual Workers*. We asked our managers whether they had such an agreement but only 51 (11·8 per cent) were able to reply that they had. This question was answered very fully and it transpired that 88 per cent of these plants were without any formal written procedure at the time of the survey. This is a significant finding in view of the fact (referred to in detail later) that these managers claim that most of the 'unconstitutional' stoppages that they experienced occurred within the domestic stages of procedure. In the absence of clearly defined and agreed domestic arrangements how, one is surely entitled to ask, can it be unequivocally established that trade union members have acted in breach of them?

We asked managers if they favoured the idea that procedural agreements should have the force of law and 70 per cent of them said that they did. There is little doubt that the answering of this question must have been heavily influenced by public advocacy of this idea by the Federation; however one wonders whether managers had really considered what courts of law would make of a situation where procedures were so informal. When procedural detail can only be established with reference to custom and practice and verbal understandings it is certain that in any dispute the parties will take widely differing views of what the procedure actually is. Unions in the workplace are likely to regard procedures from their point of view as restraints on management and to perceive the situation as one where many such restraints have been agreed verbally and over time, while managements on their part are likely in many cases to find such constraints irksome, imposed upon them and agreed to tactically for particular instances only, and may often subsequently act as if they did not exist.

Size of establishment seems to affect procedure, and written procedures were more common among the establishments with over 1,000 employees. They existed in 21 per cent of the firms in this size group. We were able to examine about half of the written grievance procedures (28 documents) and in the majority of cases (21) the text had been taken from that of the national procedure. What had been done in these cases was to restate the domestic part of the national procedure and to write in the particular titles of those responsible for negotiation on the management side at each stage. In addition, where conveners or senior stewards were recognized in the plant, the point at which these officers were entitled to enter the procedural negotiations tended to be stated. It appears that most general written procedures go a little way towards clarifying roles but apart from publicizing within the plant the existence of a constitutional means of dealing with disputed questions, they do little else.

Our discussions with managers indicated that few of the general domestic procedures had come into being out of any feeling that the skeletal and unspecific nature of the 1922 procedure was inadequate. Mostly they seemed to have originated somewhat casually as a result of the writing of a productivity agreement or from a felt need at some time to educate managers and stewards in the text of the national procedure. What does seem to be happening is that *ad hoc* procedures for dealing with particular types of issue are proliferating. 47 per cent of establishments claimed to have such a procedure for dealing with redundancy. 35 per cent claimed to have one for individual dismissals and a similar percentage for work study or PBR issues. 18 per cent claimed to have one for productivity bargaining but no other kinds of issue were covered by more than a few firms, even the contentious issue of discipline. What stands out from a study of such of these agreements as we were able to examine is how few of them (29 per cent) give clear evidence of having been worked out and agreed with the stewards as distinct from being laid down by management, though procedures for dealing with money matters such as prices and times of jobs are an exception to this, and their quality as rule systems tends also to be higher. Altogether our survey indicates how little impression has been made on the thinking of most individual managements by the volume of criticism of the procedural inadequacy characteristic of much British industry at the level of the plant, and also perhaps the relative ignorance among managers of the growing body of knowledge about the proper design of plant procedures. In a situation where managements seem so content with vague and informal 'constitutions' for their domestic relations, shop stewards can hardly be blamed if, from their point of view, it looks like a game with few established rules and to be played accordingly.

Table 2 NUMBER OF FORMAL WORKS CONFERENCES IN 432 ESTABLISHMENTS, 1967–1968

Subject	Number of Conferences
Miscellaneous pay issues	477
Time or basic rates	390
Piecework prices or times	372
Lieu bonus	126
Working conditions	111
Miscellaneous issues	97
Discipline	93
Union matters	52
Labour mobility	51
Measured daywork or job evaluation	45
Redundancy	41
Waiting time	36
Holidays	32

Only lengthy and detailed case studies of individual plants could hope to establish the pattern of day-to-day bargaining in which stewards are engaged. But we were able to get from managers the main subject of formal works conferences in their plants over the previous two years, and this information, printed as Table 2, gives some idea of the most contentious issues. As one would expect, in an industry where so much of pay is linked to results, matters involving or related to pay loom very large.

In federated engineering establishments with systems of payments by results, workshop negotiation on prices and times is governed by the so-called 'mutuality principle', whereby prices or times shall not be made or changed except by mutual arrangement between the worker or workers concerned and the employer. Notionally the price or time is negotiated between the employer's representative and the worker or workers directly concerned 'and there are cases in which "mutuality" exists in its purest sense, but there are many more in which work groups or unofficial shop committees keep a careful eye on the movement of rates and earnings. Strict "mutuality" is probably an illusion, for the workers' long term interest so obviously lies in union control of earnings if this is at all possible.'[12] Shop stewards are therefore heavily involved in bargaining over prices and times where PBR schemes operate.

We estimate that 270 establishments (62·5 per cent) in the survey group operate some kind of payment system which involves bargaining covered by the 'mutuality' principle. A typical bargaining tactic in such situations is for the workers and their representatives to argue that, when due to a change in the product or in the method by which it is made, prices or times need to be made or altered, the worker should not have lower earnings than he had before. Managers reported that this kind of argument was used in 85 per cent of establishments. However, the variable degree of success that workers and their stewards have in the bargaining is indicated from the finding that in 13 per cent of the establishments managers claim *always* to be able to reduce piecework prices and times when there is a change in means, method, or materials. Most of the other establishments say that they are able to do so sometimes and in only 8 per cent of cases are stewards able to insist on the maintenance of previous times or prices.

Stewards representing time workers in plants where most workers are on payment by results are of course engaged in bargaining processes by which they attempt to maintain some link between the earnings of their own members and those of production workers on PBR. A common device by which this is achieved is for them to persuade management to pay a lieu rate, a kind of compensating payment made to workers whose jobs are not suitable for inclusion in an incentive scheme. The extent of stewards' involvement in this kind of negotiation is indicated for these establishments by the fact that a system of lieu rates operated in 45 per cent of them. The practice may be even more widespread since, for reasons which are not known, one-quarter of the managements did not reply to questions on this topic, and only 28 per cent said definitely that they did not operate lieu rates.

In more general terms only 58 per cent of managers attributed the level of earnings in their plants mainly to piecework negotiations, and an even smaller percentage (50 per cent) ascribed the level specifically to negotiating pressure put on them by shop stewards. The rest of the managers attributed their level of payment to a mixture of more impersonal labour market forces and deliberate management policy. An idea of the degree to which managers, conscious possibly of the danger of unrest developing among workers or simply implementing some notion of appropriateness, try to maintain the existing or traditional structure of earnings, comes from our finding that over 73 per cent of these managers sometimes adjust the earnings of some workers upwards in order to preserve differentials *without* negotiation.

In recent years a principal target for critics of the system of workplace relations in Britain has been the preference of the parties for informality in their relations. The conviction has been growing among informed observers that excessive reliance on unwritten understandings, on 'custom and practice' and on *ad hoc* settlements with particular work groups has been at least partly to blame for a failure of adaption in the institutions of industrial relations. The centre of gravity of negotiation in the system having moved to the workplace, the preference for informality there has impeded the development of workplace institutions which would regulate conflict and coordinate shop floor bargaining. The result, so it has been supposed, is that workplace industrial relations processes are often chaotic and that, as the Donovan Commission reported: 'In circumstances of this kind they [shop stewards] may be striving to bring some order into a chaotic situation, and management may rely heavily on their efforts to do so.'[13]

One of the implicit themes in the Donovan recommendations for reform of the British system of collective bargaining was the desirability of a movement towards more formal and, by inference, written collective agreements at Company and plant level which could be the means to establish 'comprehensive and authoritative collective bargaining machinery to deal . . . with the terms and conditions of employment which are settled at these levels';[14] and to deal with the whole range of important issues which cannot be regulated in the system of national or industry-wide negotiations.

The Donovan commissioners were satisfied that, of the parties involved, only managements were effectively in a position to initiate such institutional changes. Since the Commission reported, a great deal has been written and said which has been aimed at encouraging managements to begin the process of introducing a greater degree of orderliness into industrial relations in the workplace. Such initiatives by managements will both make it possible for stewards to move away from what must often be the tiresome round of fragmented bargaining and will also make it necessary for them to adopt a rather different style of negotiation and to sharpen up their skills. Under the pressure created by this weight of opinion what has happened in federated engineering establishments? Has the idea of negotiating more formal and comprehensive agreements caught on? And if so, has the process been easy or hard, and what implications arise for the role of steward?

Something has been said above about the comparatively limited degree to which, in our survey group of establishments, domestic procedures have been clarified and formalized. We also made fairly extensive inquiries about substantive agreements. 228 establishments (53 per cent) claimed to have written agreements on wages and conditions at establishment or works level. 279 (64·4 per cent) said that they had negotiated a productivity agreement of some kind within the last five years and 183 (42·4 per cent) had introduced a new payment system based on measured daywork, job evaluation, or some similar recognized technique of scientific management. A much larger number, 311 (77 per cent), said that in the same period they had reviewed their pay system in order to improve its operation, and just under 50 per cent of the managers said that they proposed to engage in productivity bargaining in the foreseeable future.

It is a matter of some considerable difficulty to make a reliable interpretation of these figures, and we were aware that we were dealing in terms that were not uniformly understood. The term 'agreement' can clearly be taken to cover formal documents signed by the parties, and its use can be extended to cover documents agreed but not ratified in this way; but it can also be used, less properly, to refer to those written statements issued by management and not actively objected to by shop stewards or union officials. 'Productivity' agreements proliferated during the period of statutory incomes restraint and some of them were notoriously void of meaningful content and were merely instruments by which plant wage claims were slid past the machinery of incomes policy. A 'written agreement on wages or conditions' may be merely a record of some detail of shop floor bargaining or it can be a plant productivity package, comprehensive in scope and covering a new payment system, detailed and itemized changes in working practice, and the constitution for plant-level collective bargaining institutions.

From among those firms with something in writing on wages and conditions we were able to collect over 100 documents and from a study of these samples, and assuming that they are not untypical, it is possible to say something of what written substantive agreements at plant level in engineering are like.

The documents fall into three categories. First, sectional agreements covering either a particular department, a small group of workers, or even, as in a few cases, an individual worker. These agreements appear to put on paper, probably for the first time, pre-existing verbal agreements or understandings, or they modify them, or they represent an attempt to clarify a confused situation which has led to dispute. This category may be said to represent the written tip of the iceberg of verbal understandings by which supervisors and managers have, over a period of many years, succeeded in reconciling conflicting interests on the shop floor in order to keep the wheels turning.

The second category, and the kind of document most frequently found among the collection studied, record modifications to wage systems or the replacement of one wage system by another. They vary greatly in quality as written regulatory documents. Some are hardly intelligible to any but the parties involved while others make perfectly good sense to an outsider. Reading between the lines and in the light of subsequent discussions with some of the managers, it seems that many firms took advantage of the need to negotiate some document containing 'productivity' provisions (which could be submitted to the Department of Employment and Productivity in justification of a pay increase) to introduce reforms in their pay system, either by getting the stewards' agreement to new sets of rules by which better control of the PBR scheme might be achieved or by replacing the wage system with a different one.

The third category, and we found less than a dozen documents which could really be so classified, contains agreements which were comprehensive enough and contained a sufficient variety of topics to be called plant or Company agreements in the Donovan sense. These documents though evidencing a move in the direction of more fundamental workshop regulations were disappointing in their coverage of the range of topics that one might expect to see dealt with in agreements of this kind.

Though most of them dealt with payment systems and their control, with methods of timing jobs and the relation of pay to performance, and all had something significant to say about work practices, few of them set up authoritative union-management negotiating machinery for the plant, few said anything about the rights and duties of shop stewards or the facilities that they could expect to be afforded, and few included provision for the joint legislation of disciplinary rules or agreement on methods of enforcement.

Taking an overall view it appears that written agreements are on the increase but that comprehensive agreements are rare. The preoccupation of managers with a felt need to introduce greater rationality and control into their wage structure seems to have been a major factor in generating more formal agreements but ones which tend to be partial in their coverage.

Management initiatives towards greater formality are bound to affect the role of the steward as a major actor in the workplace system, but equally the *quality* of the management initiative may to a large extent determine the degree of resistance or cooperation offered by stewards to changes in a bargaining system which, whatever its defects from their point of view, has enabled many of them to defend successfully their own and their members' interests.

Some clue to quality is given by the documents studied, and it is hard to escape the conclusion that engineering managers have, on the whole, a long way to go before they can be called sophisticated in matters of workplace industrial relations reform. This is evidenced from three different aspects of the documents which record initiatives towards change in the system.

First, the poor coverage of topics which has been mentioned above. Secondly, the relative lack in the agreements of statements of intention, and the vague generality of many statements which are included. Many agreements say nothing about the reasons for change and the objective of the changed system. It does not necessarily follow of course that because an agreement says nothing about objectives, managers must be unclear in their own minds on this matter, but it is arguable that if the case really is that managers are not sure about the direction in which they want to develop their workplace relations and have not patiently and fully discussed and agreed changes with stewards then it will not be surprising if paper changes do not convert to changes in behaviour, and our field studies have revealed cases where in fact just this has happened. As the Donovan report wisely said, 'a factory agreement can assist competent managers', but 'a factory agreement does not accomplish things automatically. . . . All that is claimed for a factory agreement is that it is a means for the effective regulation of industrial relations within the factory where managers and workers choose to use it for that purpose.'[15]

These considerations lead into the third aspect of these documents which raises doubts about their adequacy and this is an aspect which turns on the meaning of 'agreement'. It is by no means clear that all of them have been agreed in any meaningful sense with stewards as representatives of the shop floor workers to whom they are to apply and by whose ultimate judgment, expressed in behaviour, they will stand or fall as a means to order in workplace relations. Only 75 per cent of the documents are signed and many of them, even among the signed ones, read more like statements of managerial policy than records of agreement on joint regulation. Our discussion with many of the managers who cooperated in the inquiry revealed that the notion of 'agreement' with stewards is a very fluid concept. Managers seem very prone to assume that a lack of immediate and forceful objection by stewards to acts of management implies agreement to them, and that agreement, even signed agreement, under the duress of (for instance) a statutory incomes policy means that stewards have accepted an obligation to honour the agreement as a moral commitment.

In case this should be considered a matter of mere semantics, it has to be remembered that many managers are equally prone to complain of the difficulty of getting stewards and more especially their members to abide by details of agreements when the practical implications become apparent and are found not to be entirely palatable. The evident perplexity of managers as to why people should behave, as they see it, in so 'unprincipled' a fashion is one factor leading many of them to believe that sanctions external to the workplace need to be applied for the breach of agreements. But as Alan Fox has recently written:

'industrial societies in which there is considered to be a problem of organizational order, but in which the dominant opinion seeks to minimize the use of coercion, may well find it necessary to ask a difficult question. In what circumstances can it be properly be assumed that employees have committed themselves to normative agreement, thus rendering them justly liable to punitive sanctions should they engage in rule-breaking. . . . It might, for example be established that no normative agreement can be said to exist in conditions where either party has failed to understand the issues; is not aware of the possible alternatives of action; does not appreciate the consequences of his choice, or for some other reason cannot be regarded as morally bound.'[16]*

THE MANAGERS' VIEW

How do managers regard the existence in their plants of organizations, trade unions, pursuing different objectives to the management and often opposed to it? Do these engineering managers accept a degree of conflict in the plant as natural

* Quoted by kind permission of the author and publisher.

and acceptable and to what extent do they view the workplace representatives of trade unions as of value in revealing sources of discontent among their workers and as a means by which they can secure the consent of the workers to change? It is hard to establish how far managers in Britain operate with a unitary or pluralistic view of the enterprise,[17] but our survey contains some clues as to how this particular group of managers see the matter, and it is both convenient and appropriate to consider the question in conjunction with a review of the degree to which stewards and union members were reported as using industrial sanctions to achieve their ends.

Three questions that we asked bore directly on managers' evaluation of unions and their representatives in the plant. We asked whether they thought that their relations with manual unions were good, bad, or indifferent; whether they thought that shop stewards were, on the whole, helpful or obstructive; and whether, given a choice, they would sooner deal with shop stewards or union full-time officers. Table 3 summarizes the replies and shows that the great majority of managers evaluated the unions and their stewards favourably in these three ways.

Table 3

	Number of establishments	Percentage of 432
Relations with manual unions are good	385	89·1
Shop stewards are helpful	346	80·0
Prefer to deal with shop stewards	321	74·2

Some people might argue that replies given by managers to questions such as these should not be taken too literally, and may reflect no more than a politely tolerant estimate of union activities which if they gave their real opinion they would more likely describe as disruptive and unfortunate brakes on much needed management initiative. However, that managers' replies can be taken seriously is suggested by comparing them with what managers said about the incidence of unconstitutional stoppages at their plants. We asked firms about their experience of stoppages of over half-an-hour's duration in the period of two years prior to the survey. The average number of stoppages each year per establishment was just under four, but 164 establishments (38 per cent) had not had any stoppages during this period. Table 4 breaks down the replies into groups with varying severity of experience and it correlates reports of the number of stoppages with the replies managers gave to our question asking whether they regarded the stoppage situation as a serious problem.

Table 4

Average number of stoppages per year, 1967–1968	Number of establishments	Number that regarded them as serious
4 or less	208	16
between 4 and 8	23	10
between 8 and 16	19	12
more than 16	13	11

When taken together, managers' qualitative evaluations of stewards and their tolerant attitude to a modest level of stoppages do suggest that they take a realistic view of the workshop situation and are prepared to accept as natural and inevitable a moderate degree of conflict between themselves and their employees and are not unduly disturbed when this conflict is expressed in strike activity. When stoppages are running at only about four per year most managers seem to regard the situation with equanimity. It is only when they are experiencing an incidence of about one stoppage a month that the great majority of managers feel the situation to be serious.

In order to get some information as to whether union members in these establishments generally had a tendency to resort to industrial action without first attempting to get a negotiated settlement we asked managers about their difficulties in operating domestic procedure, and where, in a scale of importance to them, threats of stoppages or other industrial action fell. It seems that managers regard such threats as a quite significant pressure during procedural negotiations, but that they are as much and perhaps even more concerned about procedural improprieties such as stewards intervening before a worker has seen the foreman, stewards taking information to workers before the foreman has been able to do so, and stewards shortcutting procedure by taking matters to higher levels of management without going through intervening levels in the management hierarchy.

We investigated the stage in procedure at which, in these managers' experience, stoppages most frequently occurred. The pattern of our findings is that an unconstitutional stoppage is most likely to take place at works management level, that is, when the issue has run through the domestic stage of the grievance machinery and just prior to invocation of the first formal stage of the national procedure for avoiding disputes – Works Conference. We found that it is much less likely for industrial action to be taken before this level is reached and that there is no significant difference in the chance of it occurring, when it does occur, before the procedure is started, at foreman level, or at the level of middle management. Once an issue has been lodged in the national system of employer conciliation – Works, Local, and Central Conferences, the likelihood of industrial action being taken is slight, though it is twice as likely to happen, on the figures we were given, after Works Conference than after Local or Central Conference.

It seems not unreasonable to interpret these replies as demonstrating the consciousness of managers in a situation of grievance handling that if some mutually acceptable settlement is not arrived at, there is always the chance of industrial action being taken when workers feel strongly about something. Managers may accept this as an inevitable part of the continuing power struggle and not always to be avoided as undesirable if it means successful resistance to unacceptable worker demands. For these managers it seems to be often more important to ensure that the element of industrial democracy injected into the system of workshop government by the need to negotiate, and the existence within their workshop of a system of democratically elected representatives, should not unduly interfere with the hierarchy of authority within the management itself nor restrict too much their ability to make settlements with their employees as individuals if they so wish.

Some people are worried that there is a process of growing anarchy in motion in our workshops. Our study hardly supports such an extreme view. Of course there is always the danger that resort to strike action may become a habit once it begins to be practised, but on the figures emerging from our study it seems that attention to a few outstandingly strike-prone establishments would quite transform the stoppage statistics. In our group of 432 establishments three plants alone accounted for no less than 41 per cent of all the strikes in the two years for which figures were given to us.

H   113

CONCLUSION

If the group of establishments that we studied are reasonably similar to the population from which they were selected, and we have no reason to suppose that they are in many respects other than fairly ordinary, then the survey reveals an engineering industry *less unionized* than is commonly thought and where shop stewards, despite considerable growth in their overall numbers, have rather less influence than is popularly supposed.

Despite the retention by workers and stewards of an area of unilateral control over work practices and some advance by them into the territory of 'managerial functions', on the evidence of this survey shop stewards in engineering can hardly be described as having gained a stranglehold on the factories and managers are far from having lost control.

It seems that by and large managers in engineering regard the shop steward system as both a convenient means by which they can get to know workers' opinions and discontents and a genuinely representative agency through which contentious workshop issues can be explored and negotiated. For those managers who care to take the initiatives it is available as a base on which to build institutions for more orderly and comprehensive joint regulation of the workplace.

The ready availability of this structure of relatively skilled workplace representatives should not lightly be taken for granted. The turnover among stewards suggests that the staffing of this structure is not altogether an easy matter and the cost to management of its upkeep, in terms of facilities afforded to stewards, is very modest. In view of the indispensable and largely constructive role which they play in the workplace industrial relations system, it seems reasonable to conclude that shop stewards in engineering might be cheap at twice the price.

NOTES

1 *Report of the Royal Commission on Trade Unions and Employers Associations*, HMSO, 1968, para. 110.
2 W. E. J. McCarthy, *The role of shop stewards in British industrial relations*, HMSO, 1966.

3 W. E. J. McCarthy and S. R. Parker, *Shop stewards and workplace relations*, HMSO, 1968.

4 A. I. Marsh, E. O. Evans, and P. Garcia, *Workplace industrial relations in engineering*, Kogan Page, in the Engineering Employers Federation Research Series. 1971. A copy of the questionnaire is included as an appendix.

5 The term 'establishment' in the federated sector of engineering denotes for formal industrial relations purposes 'the whole establishment, or section thereof, according to whether management in unified or subdivided' (*Procedure Agreement–Manual Workers*, clauses 11(2), 12). It is roughly synonymous with plants when these are negotiating units in procedure.

6 A. I. Marsh and E. E. Coker, 'Shop steward organisation in the engineering industry', *British Journal of Industrial Relations*, 1963 vol. 1, pp. 174 and 188.

7 Marsh and Coker, 'Shop steward organisation in the engineering industry', p. 188.

8 The Federation has not objected, in principle, to the recognition of conveners for many years now: A. I. Marsh, *Industrial relations in engineering*, Pergamon Press, 1965, p. 82.

9 Marsh, *Industrial relations in engineering*, pp. 81ff.

10 For a detailed account of the content of these rule books see E. O. Evans, 'Work rule books in the engineering industry', *Industrial Relations Journal*, vol. 2, no. 1, Spring 1971.

11 A practice advised in clause 1(c) of the *Procedure Agreement – Manual Workers*.

12 Marsh, *Industrial relations in engineering*, p. 171.

13 Donovan report, para. 110.

14 *Ibid.* para. 182.

15 *Ibid.* para. 167.

16 Alan Fox, *A sociology of work in industry*, Collier-Macmillan, 1971, pp. 53, 54.

17 For a discussion of this matter see Alan Fox, 'Managerial ideology and labour relations', *British Journal of Industrial Relations*, vol. IV, October 1966.

4 Perceptions, the 'Principle of Cumulation', and the Supply of Labour

DAN GOWLER AND KAREN LEGGE

INTRODUCTION

Recent research at the Manchester Business School* has revealed the existence of a phenomenon which throws some light on a number of problems besetting contemporary work organizations. This phenomenon, which we have termed the 'regressive spiral',[1] is a member of that class of social processes commonly referred to as 'vicious circles'.

The characteristics of the vicious circle have been summarized by Bredemeier and Stephenson, who comment:

> 'The "vicious circle" is a condition of interaction of two or more variables such that a change in any one will tend to alter the others in the same direction; and this change in the others, in turn, will feed back to further move the first changing condition in the same direction, and so on, as the variables interact. Gunnar Myrdal calls this the "principle of cumulation", pointing out that the direction of change may be either desirable (and therefore not necessarily "vicious") or undesirable.'[2]

In this paper we first show how the phenomenon was observed to operate in relation to problems of labour turnover, absenteeism, and the supply of hours to work organizations. Yet this

---

* This research was carried out under the direction of Professor T. Lupton whose ideas and general theoretical approach have contributed so much to this paper. We also owe a great deal to our colleagues and students who have given their time and energies to the development of these ideas.

poses a problem. If vicious circles operate to push employees out of an organization, and if the process is unchecked, the organization should in time be completely denuded of labour. Clearly this does not happen. Employees may be observed to stay, even in organizations where the principle of cumulation appears to be exacerbating the loss of man hours and effort. An attempt to answer this question provides the second part of our analysis, where we suggest that the principle of cumulation also applies to the processes which 'lock' employees into an organization and make them unwilling to move. Thus the final stage of our analysis is to seek some explanation of the relationship between these two forms of vicious circles – those that 'push' labour out and those that 'pull' labour into the organization. To do this we shift our analysis from the level of the organization to that of the individual, employing social-psychological as well as sociological concepts.

VICIOUS CIRCLES AND THE SUPPLY OF LABOUR

We first observed the 'principle of cumulation', as Myrdal terms the phenomenon, in a manufacturing organization, when attempting to analyse the affects of changes in employees' perceptions of the effort-reward relationship on absenteeism and labour turnover.

This initial study first[3] sought to ascertain the attitudes manual workers held towards the wage payment system. Briefly, it was found that workers, especially the men, not only had clearly distinguishable attitudes to each of the six elements comprising the wage packet,* but that they tended to balance and evaluate each of these elements in relation to one another. Furthermore, it was discovered that the structure of the wage packet failed to meet the expectations of many of the workers. First, there was a perceived imbalance in the effort-reward relationship, in that workers claimed that they were having to work 'too long for too little'. Secondly, there was a sense of uncertainty brought about by the relatively large size of unstable elements in the wage packet, for example, at least one-third of many men's earnings derived from overtime working, which was subject to a great deal of fluctuation. This sense of un-

---

* Viz. (1) basic rate, (2) job rate, (3) long service allowance, (4) overtime, (5) shift allowance, (6) bonus, paid as lump sum, twice a year [4].

certainty was increase by the workers' firm conviction that all elements in the wage packet except the basic rate were unstable and/or insecure, in that they 'could be taken away any time'. The workers' careful assessment of the characteristics of the elements in the pay packet is of crucial importance to later stages of our analysis, where we relate changes in employees' perceptions to changes in organizational structure.

Having ascertained that many workers' effort-reward expectations were not being met by the payment system, and having examined its inadequacies, we then sought to describe and analyse the organizational factors that exacerbated these failings. The following model emerged, and represents not only the pressures confronting the smooth operation of the wage payment system but some of the causes and effects of overtime, absenteeism, and labour turnover in the situation.

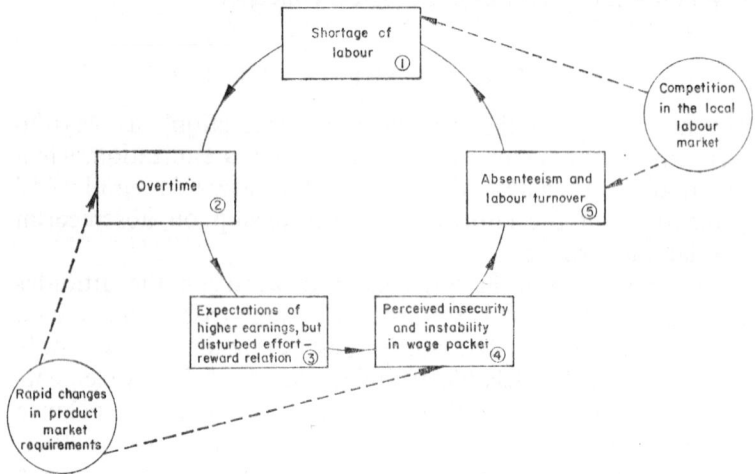

Figure 1

In Figure 1,[5] the shortage of labour (box 1) was one consequence of a marked increase in competition for workers in this area. This, coupled with the fluctuating production requirements stemming from highly market-oriented policies and seasonal variations in demand for the company's products, led at times to a considerable amount of overtime working (box 2). The consequences of this were two-fold (see box 3). First, it tended to promote expectations of higher earnings, as for long periods men's wages were inflated by overtime payments. It was during these periods that employees were likely to expand their financial commitments thus initiating a sustained demand for overtime.[6] Secondly, workers found that their effort-reward relation was out of balance, claiming that because of a low basic rate they were having to work 'too long for too little'. Further, the women employees' claim was not that they had to work too long for too little, but simply that they were just not paid enough for their forty-hour week. This situation has been described by Baldamus as a condition of 'wage disparity', which he defines as, 'Taking a hypothetical equilibrium between effort and pay on a given level of expectations as an arbitrary starting point, to be called a situation of wage parity, non-parallel movements of the components of effort value may be described as various forms of wage disparity.'[7]

Thus, in Figure 1 where expanding wage expectations were being met at the expense of increasing wage disparity (box 3), workers' attentions were focussed on the contribution each element made to the security and stability of their take-home pay (box 4).

Several problems arose at this point. First, men felt that they were being 'compelled' to work overtime on a fairly regular basis in order to make up their pay to an acceptable level. But there were also occasions where men were compelled to work more overtime than they 'needed', which tended to happen when production requirements resulted in long periods of twelve-hour shift working. Secondly, the young single men often complained that this compulsion to work overtime, for whatever reasons, seriously interfered with their external social life. The result was a predictable rise in absenteeism. This relationship between control over hours and absenteeism has been noted elsewhere, as Buck and Shimmin comment: 'The individual worker who is never given the opportunity to work overtime can only vary his working week by going absent, and the same applies where overtime is on a compulsory all-or-none basis, as is likely in continuous or line processing.'[8] Thus the cumulative consequences of boxes 1, 2, 3, 4 were that the organization was caught in a 'double bind'. When overtime working *diminished*, male workers tended to leave because they found they were unable to accept their now reduced incomes. When overtime working *increased* there was a loss of male labour as a result of absenteeism through men taking time off after long, tiring periods of overtime working, or deliberately substituting overtime hours for 'normal' hours.[9]

Further, levels of absenteeism were aggravated by the perceptions of wage disparity held by both male and female workers. Baldamus, when discussing wage disparity, contends that it leads to such manifestations of 'unrest and strife'[10] as strikes, excessive labour turnover, absenteeism, gold bricking, and slowdowns. For the general workers* in this factory, the possibility of collective action in the form of strikes and slowdowns was most unlikely, owing to such factors as the numerical weakness of the trade union concerned, the high proportion of women employed, and the absence of a tradition of organized militancy. Thus attempts to resolve wage disparity were dealt with on an *individual* basis, by absenteeism, labour turnover and by low levels of personal effort.

In other words, the labour turnover and absenteeism (box 5) served to aggravate the labour shortage (box 1) already brought about by the other factors discussed above. Thus the 'vicious circle' was completed, and a self-reinforcing system was generated. Further, within this system, there were other equally vicious circles. For example, there existed a 'feedback' loop from box 3 to box 2, with overtime working resulting in heightened wage expectations which led to pressure for even more overtime, and so on. Again, there was a feedback loop to box 5, for as it has often been observed, the disruptive effects of high labour turnover leads to even more labour turnover, and so on.[11]

This mode of analysis not only demonstrated the self-perpetuating nature of the problems discussed above, but provided an explanation as to why the organization had suffered from an increasing loss of both men and man hours.

On the basis of this fieldwork we began to construct a general model of these processes. Consequently, we began to look elsewhere for similar circumstances. Examples of this phenomenon were then found in a range of organizations in such diverse areas of the economy as the garment and leisure industries, and the health service. The next three sections of the paper describe some of these examples.

* The term 'general workers' covers both male and female unskilled and semi-skilled workers, who provided the largest proportion of the labour employed in this plant.

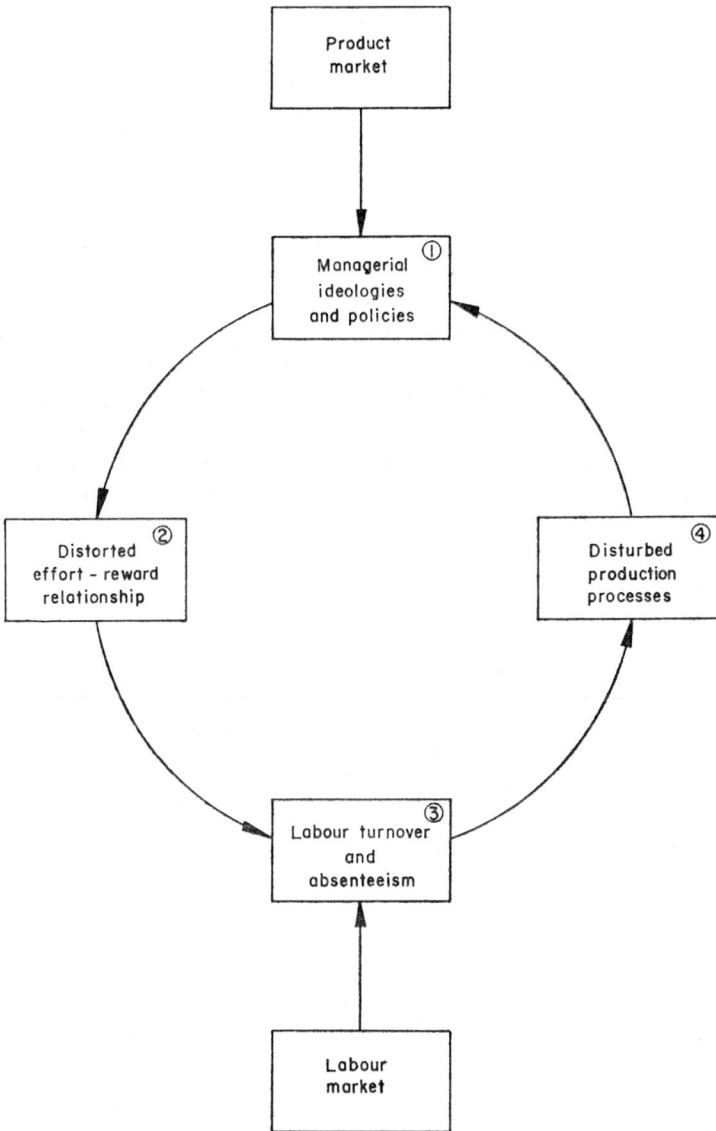

Figure 2

A GARMENT-MANUFACTURING ORGANIZATION

In the largest department of a vertically integrated garment-manufacturing organization, self-perpetuating labour turnover was observed to be operating among female machinists[12] and these processes are represented in diagrammatic form in Figure 2. In brief, the situation was as follows. Managerial ideas about the competitive nature of their product market and the labour intensive nature of their production process resulted in a marked reluctance to increase wage rates. For labour costs were considered to be a decisive influence upon the organization's position in its product market. Furthermore, believing themselves unable to compete effectively in the product market for low price, standardized garments, the management found it necessary to meet their competition through greater product variety. This involved both a rapid increase in the range of garments manufactured, and, at the same time, a decrease in the life span of styles (box 1). One effect of this change in market strategy was to increase greatly the number of 'job changes'* machinists experienced, initially through a greater variety of shorter production runs. As in the previous example, the difficulties in workflow administration influenced and were influenced by the wage payment system.

In short, the machinists were paid chiefly on a linear piece-work scheme. The amount they earned was in a one-to-one relationship with the number of garments they produced, calculated at one of three hourly job rates, dependent upon the skill involved. During initial training or when learning to work a new machine, perform a new operation, or a known operation on a new garment, the machinist 'fell back' on to a low time work rate.

The result of the increase in job changes meant that machinists were faced with learning to handle new materials, to operate unfamiliar machines, or perform unaccustomed operations upon a newly introduced garment. This resulted in low piecework earnings as well as a large proportion of time being paid at the fall-back time work rate, which was perceived by both manage-

* Job change was considered to involve three factors, and consequently was compared against them. They were: (a) machine change, (b) operation change, (c) garment change. 'Job change' for a machinist could contain any or all three of these factors.

ment and machinists as being too low.* Thus, not only were levels of earnings perceived to have deteriorated but levels of effort were perceived to have increased. The hours spent learning unfamilar machines and operations, in ironing out the snags on incoming garments, etc., were considered by the machinists to involve more 'effort' than working at full speed on accustomed operations, machines, and garments. Yet the monetary return on the fall-back time rate (especially for the younger girls) was lower than on piecework over standard performance. As far as the machinists were concerned the effort-reward relationship had shifted unfavourably (box 2).

Shorter production runs involved even more difficulties in workflow administration and in the operation of the wage payment system. For example, the problem of satisfactorily balancing a work team became more difficult. Machinists were often redeployed from one class of work to another, possibly on fall-back time work rates. The sectionalized flow method of production which made machinists partially dependent on workmates' speed of operations for their own levels of production and earnings also accentuated these difficulties. This in turn led to increased resentment at low earnings, to labour turnover and absenteeism (box 3), and further redeployment of labour (box 4).

The recruitment difficulties experienced in a tight labour market and problems of training such labour that could be obtained (i.e. older part-timers, foreigners with inadequate English) meant that as labour turnover (box 3) increased, replacements on the teams took longer to arrive. This meant that, as labour turnover increased, the remaining machinists' rate of job change increased. For, apart from the greater number of production runs, they were compelled to cover the work of a learner or absentee in order to maintain the flow of production.

This process was further exacerbated by the influence of short production runs upon training. It was quite possible that by the time a replacement had been trained to do a job and

* This was consistent with a managerial ideology which held the financial incentive in very high regard. Consequently, they believed if 'fall-back' rates were low, workers would be 'motivated' to work harder and so move on to the piecework rate. To be on the full piecework rate was believed by the management to be both beneficial to the machinists, i.e. through higher earnings, and to the firm through higher production and hence lower unit costs.

123

assigned to a team the class of work would have changed. The replacement would then have to undertake a further period of training, which would aggravate her effort-reward relationship* (box 2), possibly resulting in labour turnover (box 3), etc.

Finally, on the shorter production runs there was a higher percentage of badly cut components than on longer runs. If experience of the material and print was relatively limited, there could occur substantial stretching, needle cutting, distortion of stripes, and machine trouble (box 4). All these factors resulted in more work and responsibility for the chargehands, and in more irritation and loss of potential earnings for the machinists. Added to this, the role of the chargehand, initiating machinists' job changes while they themselves were under pressure, often led to strained relations with the machinists, which aggravated growing labour turnover problems.

Management recognized that the wage payment system could not cope with changed production patterns, but were reluctant to adjust either the time work rates or the job rates, or deliberately to set 'loose' times and steadfastly maintained their 'piecework' ideology (box 1).† Moreover the product market was considered to be too competitive to allow large increases in labour costs to be absorbed by price increases, while the high overhead costs from the other departments of this organization made savings in labour costs all the more necessary. Furthermore, management was aware that the machinists' lower performance was itself distorting unfavourably the balance between labour costs and overheads. *Hence, for a period of two years, management refused to make any major adjustment to either job rates, time work rates, or the structure of the wage payment system to relieve the machinists' perceptions of a distortion in the effort-reward relationship.*

In conclusion, the vicious circle described above deprived the organization of labour. However, there were other forces at work which served to alleviate some of the worst effects of the 'regressive spiral'. We will return to this point later, after considering two further case studies.

* Workers were on fall-back rates during training.
† In fact, they appeared to be reinforced in their beliefs [13] and held that any retreat from the principle of the financial incentive would result in lower levels of employee effort, thereby making the situation worse.

A LEISURE INDUSTRY CASE*

The sector of the leisure industry in which this organization operated had, in the last decade, experienced a rapid growth rate, but which during the two years prior to the study had started to level off. The industry's general response to this rapid development has been and continues to be a move towards a greater range of services offered to the customer (box A, figure 3). However, the effect of this product diversification upon the organization concerned was to help generate and perpetuate a vicious circle similar to those described above. This process is represented in diagrammatic form in Figure 3. It shows how an initial shortage of labour was increased by self-perpetuating labour turnover which resulted in the further reduction of the quantity and quality of manpower available to the organization.

This diagram shows that a shortage of labour (box 1), initially generated by the demand for labour outstripping its supply, was not adequately dealt with because of the management's reluctance to offer levels of pay sufficient to attract the required quantity and quality of manpower. This reluctance was a result of fierce price competition in this industry, which demanded a very close control of costs. Since wages and salaries provide a large proportion of costs in this business, the management were very hesitant about agreeing to any substantial increases in pay (box A).

However, and whatever the cause, the shortage of labour had several deleterious effects upon the work of those employed in the organization. First, it resulted in an increase in the workload of the undermanned labour force. Secondly, this pressure of work resulted in not enough time and care being taken over the training of recruits, who were often left 'to pick up the job' as quickly and as best they could. This lack of training was especially unfortunate for those employees, e.g. reservation clerks, whose job involved a high degree of role visibility, i.e. work activities at the interface between the organization and its customers. Briefly, the training did not equip this class of employees with sufficient knowledge and expertise to cope with the increasing variety of services being offered by the organiza-

* An unpublished case study conducted by staff and students at the Manchester Business School.

tion to its potential customers. In fact, this often resulted in strained relations between reservation clerks and customers. Frustrated and disappointed customers tended to vent their anger upon the reservation clerks, who at certain times of the year have a great deal of work and stress to contend with.* This, coupled with the shortage of labour and relatively low levels of pay, resulted in the reservation clerks perceiving that

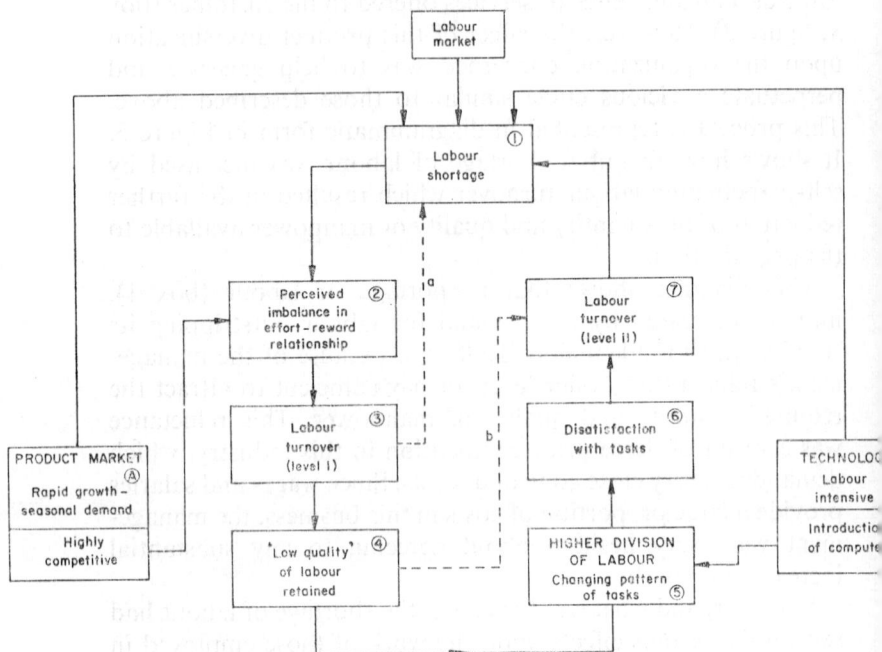

Figure 3

there was a marked imbalance in their effort-reward relationship, which contributed to more labour turnover,† thus increasing labour shortage, and so on. The self-perpetuating relationships between boxes 1, 2, and 3 therefore result in a vicious circle within the wider 'regressive spiral', influencing

* Feelings of relative deprivation were introduced by the practice of transferring employees at certain times of year from satisfying external roles, e.g. company representatives, to dissatisfying internal roles, e.g. reservation clerks [14].
† See dotted arrow a.

126

and being influenced by the other difficulties being faced by this organization.

At this point we now link the problems discussed above with a wider set of difficulties and show the nature of their inter-action.

One consequence of the organization's problems with the recruitment and retention of labour resulted, at least in the management's perceptions, in the increased proportion of 'low quality' labour (box 4). This type of assertion is usually very difficult to verify. However, the social composition of the workforce had changed in favour of female, secondary wage earners, whose commitment to employment has often been observed to be weak, this type of labour being prone to high levels of labour turnover and absenteeism.* Thus management's perceptions of their employees were probably correct in so far as the latter were not greatly interested in their work and patently not likely to adopt the behaviour and attitudes approved in the managerial value-system.

These difficulties were very much reflected in the general clerical operations of the organization. One consequence of all this was that the errors and failings of this 'low quality' clerical labour compounded the difficulties of the reservation clerks. The reservation clerks felt they were in a very exposed position, being confronted by a temperamental public on the one side and an unreliable organization on the other.†

Management's solution to their problems on the general clerical side appeared, at least in the short term, to make the situation worse. The solution to these and other problems was the introduction of a computer and more sophisticated means of information processing (box B).

The immediate effects of this 'substitution of capital for labour' was disturbance to the whole social fabric of the organization, a not uncommon occurrence on the introduction of computers[15]. Furthermore, this introduction radically altered the nature of many general clerical tasks (box 5). First, it increased the division of labour and bureaucratization of many clerical jobs, thus further depriving them of what little

---

* See dotted arrow b.
† This appears to be quite common for those occupying boundary or interface roles in service organizations and would appear to repay further analysis and research.

intrinsic satisfaction they had (box 6). Also, and somewhat paradoxically, other clerical workers found themselves confronted with an enlarged and more complicated set of tasks, which were beyond either their competence or their interests. Again these difficulties being experienced by the general clerical employees influenced and aggravated those being suffered by the reservation clerks. Finally, the consequence of the restructuring of clerical tasks was more labour turnover (box 7) which compounded the existing labour shortage (box 1), and so on.

Thus the management was faced with hiring more skilled staff at higher cost, yet was unwilling to increase labour costs in the light of intense price competition in the industry. Further, the organization suffered from a lack of high-calibre managers, itself a product of growth and competition in the industry, which hindered the discovery and implementation of the ideas and policies necessary to break or slow down the vicious circle described above.

A PUBLIC SERVICE CASE

The vicious circle considered here was discovered in a number of hospitals during a recent study into the training needs of ward sisters[16].

In the situation outlined in Figure 4, we show that an increased and variable demand for beds, provided a 'product market' that was completely outside the control of the nursing staff (box A). The ward sister had no official voice in either the number or type of patient admitted to the wards. Such decisions were made by the medical consultants who had beds in the wards concerned. In fact, the lack of coordination between consultants at times appeared to lead to the admittance of 'too many' patients, at least too many in the light of nursing staff and other facilities. However, pressure on the part of the consultants for beds was difficult to resist, since the nursing staff had been socialized in a 'care-of-the-sick-at-all-costs' culture overlaid with a very heavy emphasis on the hierarchical nature of authority.

Moreover, although the workload on a ward varied, the staffing levels were not equally flexible. First, wards on which there was temporarily less pressure were unwilling to relinquish trained staff, even temporarily, for fear of being caught shorthanded in the event of a rush of emergency cases. Secondly, there was a general shortage of trained staff in these hospitals owing to the increasing number of more attractive alternative white collar jobs for women in industrial, commercial, private, and public service sectors (box B). Hence wards were often caught with a shortage of trained staff (box 1) in relation to the amount of work on hand, and, unlike in some production units in industry, level of 'production' could not be substantially adjusted downwards. Once the patients were in the ward the value system in which the nursing staff had been socialized demanded that they were treated.

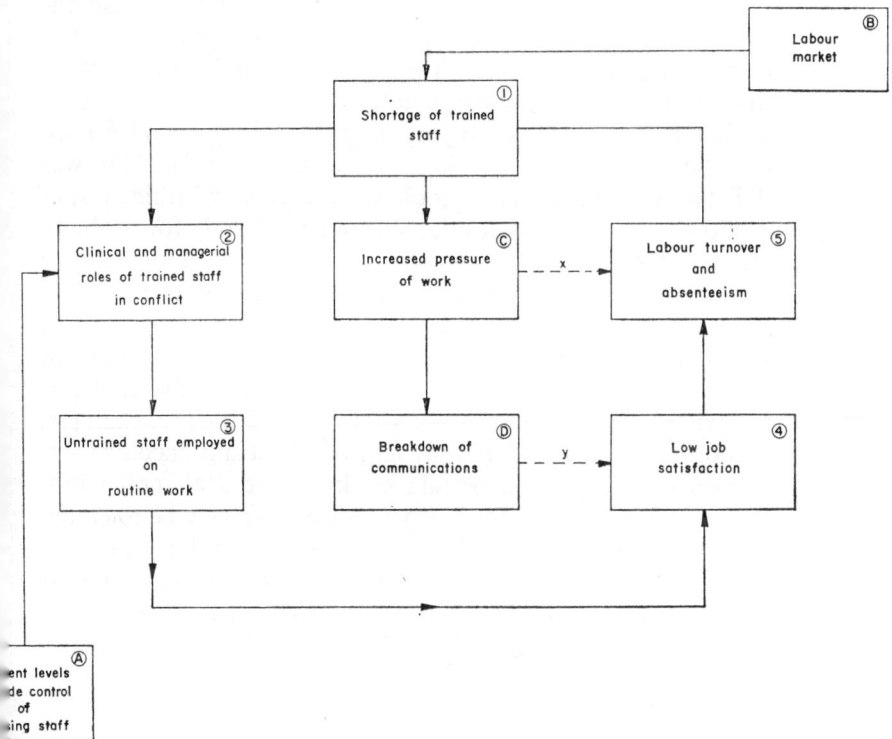

Figure 4

Moreover, the training of nursing staff placed an emphasis on clinical rather than administrative aspects of their work. Thus, when staff took charge of a ward they had difficulty in perceiving their role as one of supervision, coordination, and instruction

I

(box 2). The shortage of staff and pressure of work in any case demanded their participation in the clinical work.

This also led to problems with the training of student nurses. First, the wards to which students were allocated depended not only on the pressure of work but upon which aspect of nursing the students had arrived at in the progression of their training. Secondly, they might be allocated to wards inundated with emergency cases and under a great deal of pressure.* When this occurred the teaching function of first-line supervision† broke down altogether, for numerous emergency cases prevented students from being able to stand and watch at prescribed times. In emergencies not only were they in the way, but the trained staff did not have the time to explain what they were doing and why. Moreover, shortage of staff on the wards meant that students were pressured into jobs that they could do – basic nursing such as emptying bedpans, taking round drinks, etc. (box 3). More interesting 'important' work for them was difficult to organize as it took up the time of trained staff needed on urgent work. Hence students frequently found them- selves spending a large proportion of their time on a new ward engaged in low-status tasks, from which they learnt nothing new, and certainly were unable to apply the theory they had learnt in the classroom. Low job satisfaction was a frequent result (box 4) which was further exacerbated by the students' awareness that related aspects of their job – for example, authoritarian supervision, long and often socially inconvenient working hours, did not pertain in alternative white collar jobs they might undertake. Such aspects of the job may be tolerated if the intrinsic nature of the work is rewarding, but otherwise contribute to labour turnover and absenteeism (box 5). Levels of student labour turnover and absenteeism further contributed to the shortage of trained staff available (box 1) and hence perpetuated the vicious circle described here.

This vicious circle was reinforced by further self-perpetuating pressures (see boxes c and d).‡ Because of the shortage of staff and pressure of work, communications on the ward had a tendency to breakdown. First, there was little time to talk, and thus, unless information was transmitted immediately, it tended

* This is especially the case in such wards as outpatients and casualty.
† The ward sisters.
‡ See dotted arrow x.

to get lost, often resulting in further pressures upon the nursing staff. Secondly, if the sister was busy on an emergency case and was interrupted by a student, who was not in a position to differentiate between important and trivial questions, with what the former perceived to be time-wasting information or requests, the reply was often somewhat brusque. This often seemed to discourage students from attempting to communicate with senior staff, which apart from potentially deleterious effects on the running of a ward, also contributed to the student's lack of job satisfaction, and so on.*

STRUCTURE AND PERCEPTION

Certain common themes emerge from these case studies, and examination and analysis of them has led us to the following conclusions. These are that the 'principle of cumulation', or the 'regressive spiral', is likely to occur when

i. the quantity of products† demanded is subject to seasonal increase and/or fluctuation;
ii. the variety of products manufactured or processed is subject to increase and/or fluctuation;
iii. the situation involves a relatively tight control of labour costs, and
iv. when alternative job opportunities exist, i.e. when there is effective competition for the type of labour required by the organizations concerned.

The interaction between the circumstances outlined in (i) to (iv) result in the generation and self-perpetuation of forces which adversely influence the organization's ability to recruit and retain *certain types* of labour.

Generally speaking, these studies‡ suggest that the structural pressures developed in the organization's product and labour markets adversely influenced employees' perceptions of the relationship between effort and reward. This had unfortunate

* See dotted arrow y.
† 'Products' includes both goods and services.
‡ Other studies conducted by researchers at the Manchester Business School have supported the propositions presented here [17]. Further, we have examined and analysed other published studies and are of the opinion that they also lend a certain amount of support to these views [18].

consequences for the organizations concerned, since the response to the perceived distortion of the effort-reward relationship was to reinforce the pressures generated in the organization's product and labour markets.

The 'mechanisms' which transformed these market pressures into perceptions of an imbalance in the effort-reward relationship were the changes brought about in the organization's control systems, e.g. workflow administration and wage payment systems, which in turn influenced the role and relationships of those concerned. It is through the examination of these 'mechanisms' that we have developed a number of hypotheses which relate directly to the concerns expressed in the introduction to this paper. These were the description and analysis of the self-perpetuating forces which serve to 'pull' employees into the work organization as well as those which 'push' them out.

Our attention to the forces which lead to the retention of labour had been stimulated by the simple fact that even the organizations in the grip of the 'regressive spiral' still seemed to retain some employees. Moreover, these employees could have obtained jobs elsewhere. In other words, it appeared that they had chosen not to avail themselves of alternative employment.

Legge's study[19] of the behaviours of workers in a garment factory appears very relevant here, and it was this piece of research that led us to look more closely at the problem of labour retention. Very briefly, Legge noticed that over a relatively short period of time, two to three years, the social composition of the workforce under investigation changed in favour of married, part-time, immigrant workers, who lived fairly near the factory concerned. The basic finding was that this change in social composition was a result of the fact that the workers retained in this factory occupied *external* roles which gave rise to different perceptions of the effort-reward bargain offered by this form of employment[20].

Initially we were well satisfied by this explanation of labour retention. However, when re-analysing data from our other studies we came to the conclusion that this was only part of the story, and as a consequence began to look closely at the *internal* occupational role, as well as the external roles. Furthermore, we began to take an interest in the relationship between these internal and external roles and perceptions of the balance between effort and reward. This led us to an analysis of the occupational role, particularly with reference to intra- and inter-organizational labour mobility[21]. The following section of the paper presents an outline of this analysis.

OCCUPATIONAL ROLE DIFFERENTIATION AND INTEGRATION

In our analysis of the occupational role we distinguished four components; they are

    i. job requirements;
    ii. job expectations;
    iii. job performance, and
    iv. job experience.

Job requirements are *those rules and procedures which define the non-discretionary element in the occupational role,* for example job descriptions, authority relationships, official control systems, and so on. They are, therefore, those activities which are either prescribed by management, or formally agreed between management and employees and/or their representatives. Furthermore, all these mechanisms of managerial control are designed to direct employees towards the attainment of organizational goals, however vague or ill-defined these might be.

We define *job expectations* as *the set of ideas, feelings, values, and beliefs which the employee brings to his occupational role.* This definition suggests three important distinctions. First, job expectations involve an employee's role *cognitions,* that is, his intellectual understanding of what the job requires of him. Secondly, it involves his *normative prejudgments* about what the work entails, for example, whether he believes his job to be worthwhile, etc. Finally, these cognitions and prejudgments have an *affective* element, namely that the employee has feelings about the nature of his occupational role. These three elements may collectively be referred to as *attitudes.*

Our third element, *job performance,* is defined as *all the activities engaged in by the employee in the space and time defined by his occupational role.* In the occupational role, the larger the proportion of and the more effective the control upon its non-discretionary component, the more *routinized* will be these activities. Many commentators have pointed out that a large number of manual workers have little or no discretion over the number and pattern of hours he works, and frequently the content, method, and pace of his work is so standardized and controlled that he becomes a mere adjunct to the machine he operates, etc. Other commentators, notably Jaques[22], point out, on the other hand, that there is likely to be as many difficulties where the occupational role has a very high discretionary content. For it engenders a sense of uncertainty and anxiety in the role-incumbent, due to decision making on the allocation of scarce resources in high risk situations.

We may in fact argue that, as discretion is closely related to the nature and severity of sanctions, the difference between high and low discretion jobs is more apparent than real. It might be contended that the real difference between jobs with high and low discretion is that, where job discretion is high, sanctions for substandard work are likely to be deferred and unspecific, and where job discretion is low, sanctions are likely to be immediate and specific. What we can say, though, is that those jobs which enjoy high levels of discretion as to *how* they are to be performed, do allow the incumbent's job performance to be as much or more influenced by his job expectations than his job requirements, i.e. what the job incumbent does is just as much influenced by what he is predisposed to do, as what he is compelled to do.

Finally, job performance is also influenced by the 'informal' activities which develop around the occupational role, including such activities as the formulation of managerial cliques[23], coalitions, and work groups[24], each with their own sets of values, beliefs, and behaviours. However, these have not been designed to attain organizational goals, and, therefore, may not necessarily direct employees towards such ends.

The fourth component of the occupational role is *job experience*. We define this as *the employees' retrospective thoughts, feelings, and evaluations about his job performance*. Thus, whereas job performance may be seen as external to the individual, job experience is the 'internal' and wholly subjective response to these 'external' behaviours.

It is clear from these definitions that the structure of the occupational role is greatly influenced by others with whom the incumbent interacts, in other words his *role-set*[25].

134

Although in the analysis that follows we describe the relationships between the components of occupational role as a closed system, each of these components is influenced by a number of *external* factors, for example, the behaviour of the various members of the individual's occupational role-set. Indeed, each component of the occupational role results from the incumbent's interaction with relevant members of his role-set, as for example, his superiors in the case of job requirements, his immediate supervision and work group in the case of job performance, and, in the case of job experience and job expectations, his colleagues and members of role-sets associated with activities outside the work situation. In the case of job expectations, the configuration of role-sets become especially complex over time and space, as those participating in the incumbent's primary socialization and the whole array of non-work activities could be involved.

The relationship between this analysis of occupational role and the above discussion of vicious circles is through the processes of occupational role *integration* and occupational role *differentiation*. Briefly, we hypothesize that the process by which an employee becomes *locked into an organization* is through the components of his occupational role becoming integrated. In other words the process occurs through the components fusing together, and in practice becoming, *to the incumbent*, indistinguishable. This may be explained by reference to Figure 5[26], which illustrates the relationships between the four components comprising the occupational role.

This 'model' of the occupational role is made up of six propositions[27], where each component is treated as either an independent, dependent, or intervening variable. For example, the influence exercised by job requirements (box 1) on job performance (box 3) is subject to the intervention of job expectations (box 2). Thus, in this example, job requirements are treated as the independent variable, job performance as the dependent variable, and job expectations as the intervening variable. Another proposition is that the influence exercised by job performance (box 3) on job expectations (box 2) is subject to the intervention of job experience (box 4). In this example, job performance is treated as the independent variable, job expectations as the dependent variable, and job experience as the intervening variable, and so on.

135

Clearly this makes any analysis of the occupational role a relatively complex affair, which restrictions of space do not permit us to deal with here. Consequently, for the purposes of the problems under consideration only some of the relationships will be discussed.

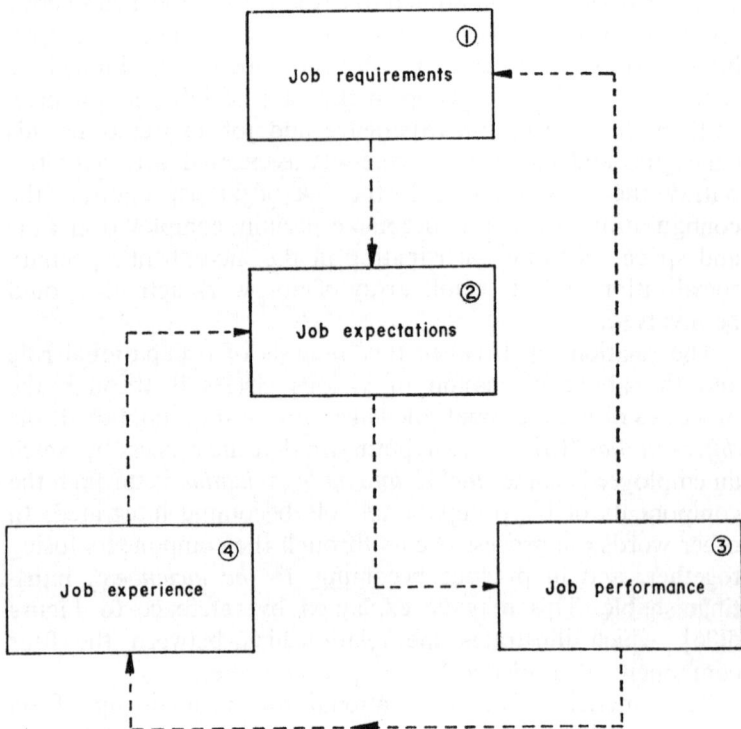

Figure 5

We begin by considering how the relationship between job performance (box 3) and job expectations (box 2), mediated by job experience (box 4), may lead to occupational role integration.

First, the process of occupational role integration is brought about by the 'fusion' of job experience with job expectations. This fusion may be said to occur when the occupational role incumbent treats the decisions he has to make in the light of preconceived ideas, and his job experience and job expectations fuse into a rigid set of job attitudes.

This integration of experience and expectations, where the present and future are mainly interpreted in terms of the past, is usually a relatively long-term process, and the result of physical and attitudinal ageing[28].* However, this process may be accelerated by *routinization of job performance*. That is, if what the employee does is highly repetitive and subject to little change, he will have very few new work experiences to compare against previously acquired ideas and feelings, and this may actually assist the fusion of job experience with job expectations. Further, if an employee's job performance is highly routinized it is probable that his related job requirements are also highly routinized[29]. And so if, as we have just argued, there is a tendency through ageing for expectations to become so also, *the interaction between these components and the whole process of integration becomes self-reinforcing. Thus here again the principle of cumulation can be seen to be operating.*

Secondly, we consider that what the employee actually does (job performance) exerts an influence upon what he is pre-disposed to do (job expectations) by his evaluation (job experience) of his performance. This is, of course, the *conditioning* argument[30], i.e. given certain circumstances are maintained over a relatively long period of time, the employee becomes predisposed to do that which he consistently does do[31]. Again, we suggest that the circumstances which are likely to promote this conditioning are those where the work is repetitive and where the employee has a low degree of job discretion.

Thirdly, we argue that apart from the influence of employee job expectations upon job requirements, the degree of difference between what employees actually do and what they are required to do depends upon the 'tightness' of a number of constraints, e.g. the technology and managerial control system[32]. It is this 'tightness' which mainly determines and maintains the amount of discretion in the occupational role. Thus, where job discretion is low and/or the constraints are tight, *job performance is in no significant respect different from job requirements*. So, for the incumbent of the role, these two components are perceived to fuse into one.

* There are a number of influences at work here, e.g. personality and cultural factors. Furthermore, it may be that certain institutional arrangements and policies, e.g. pension schemes, annual appraisals, and so on, actually encourage the employee to 'fuse' the present and future with the past.

137

Finally, we suggest that an employee's job experience exercises influence upon his future behaviours (job performance), depending upon the strength of his existing attitudes (job expectations). However, at high levels of occupational role integration, as previously discussed, where job experience fuses with job expectations, this mechanism of behaviour change becomes seriously impaired, and, as a result, the incumbent's behaviour may become rigid and further routinized. Again, we see the principle of cumulation at work.

This analysis would suggest that *lack of change in and routinization of the job requirements is a major factor in the integration of occupational role components.* Further, in all our case studies, job requirements were subject to frequent change, and in all but one, these changes tended to involve *decreased* routinization of work whether through greater variety of hours to be worked, or of job content itself. *Hence role integration for the majority of employees studied in these situations did not occur.* Their occupational roles were *differentiated*[33], in *that they perceived differences between the four components which comprise its structure.*

ROLE INTEGRATION AND LABOUR MOBILITY

We hypothesized earlier that the level of role integration was related to labour mobility and a key factor in the development of the vicious circles discussed. Our theoretical basis for this hypothesis rests on a concept from social psychology, namely *cognitive dissonance.* Dissonance theory centres around the proposition that, if an individual perceives various ideas, objects, or events to be inconsistent with one another, he experiences tension and internal conflict, which motivates him to eliminate its cause and/or mitigate its effects by changing his perceptions and/or his behaviour[34].

We suggest that, as the level of occupational role integration increases, the ability to tolerate dissonance decreases. The process is as follows. First, as the degree of occupational role integration increases, the perceived inconsistencies between the components concerned diminishes. As 'cognitive consonance' increases, there is a concomitant increase in the difficulties in coping with any dissonant change in the components of occupational role. The difficulties are made particularly severe when one of the main mechanisms of dissonance reduction, i.e. attitudinal change, is damaged by rigidity of cognitive and affective structures, i.e. thoughts and feelings, brought about by the fusion of job experiences and job expectations. Finally, given these difficulties with the reduction of dissonance, the incumbent of the highly integrated occupational role learns to avoid those situations where he believes he will be faced with such problems. This increases the level of occupational role integration, and so on. The process is illustrated in Figure 6[35].

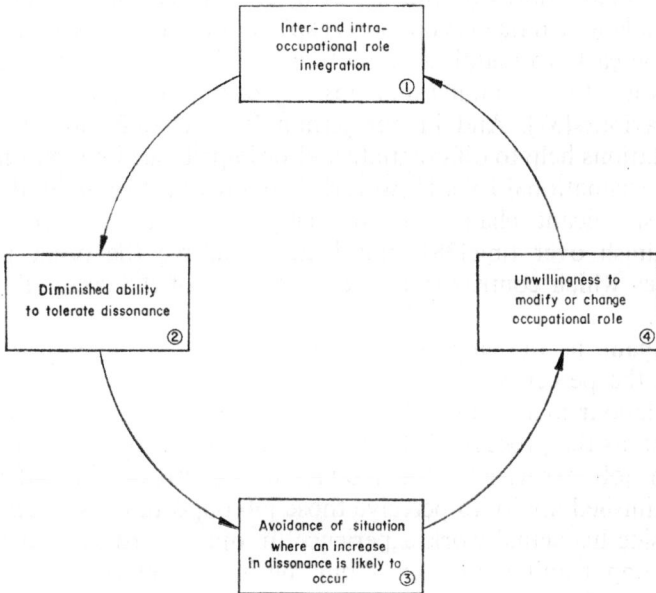

Figure 6

If, however, he is *forced* into a dissonant situation or choice, the incumbent of a highly integrated occupational role is quite likely to resort to some form of *covert* aggression, e.g. absenteeism, reduction of effort, and psychosomatic illness. In those situations where the individual has some support from others, or where groups are involved in some dissonant situation or choice, the result may be *overt* aggression, e.g. strikes, go-slows, and so on. We would argue, though, that the incumbent of a highly integrated occupational role is unlikely to cope with a dissonant situation by labour turnover. This would be perceived as moving to an even more highly dissonant situation, with the threat of changes of an unfamiliar and possibly unwelcome nature in all the components of occupational role. Again, by definition, labour turnover and the move to another job, involves a process of forcible differentiation of the occupational role, and with it an increase in cognitive dissonance[36].

Other factors combine with the process of occupational role integration to promote this immobilization of labour. For example, the employee's domestic roles are likely to be similarly integrated. Marriage and the birth of children may exercise a considerable influence upon job expectations, and thus maintain in the early to middle stages of an individual's working life, a pressure to re-examine and possibly change job attitudes and behaviours[37]. And in our terminology, changes in job expectations help to differentiate and/or impede the integration of the occupational role. However, these pressures brought about by significant changes in the employee's domestic role-set diminish over time[38], and hence reinforce the other processes which contribute to the integration of the occupational role.

Again, as the employee's role becomes more integrated so will the perceived number of alternative job opportunities in the labour market diminish. There are several reasons for this. First, as the process of attitudinal ageing fuses job expectations with job experience, the individual concerned will suffer a diminished ability to perceive those job opportunities which lie outside his actual work experience. In other words, alternative job opportunities may exist but the incumbent of the highly integrated role will become less and less aware of them. Further, if the members of his occupational role-set are similarly placed, the amount of information he receives from them about alternative job opportunities will also diminish. Indeed, given a high degree of occupational role integration in an individual's role-set, and given the validity of the avoidance of dissonance argument, one might expect to find a 'conspiracy of silence' on such dissonance-arousing topics as alternative employment in such groups.

Secondly, when real* or perceived job opportunities diminish, the employee will naturally be unwilling to change his employ-

* Obviously, as the employee ages 'real' job opportunities do diminish, and so contribute to the locking-in process.

ment, thus reinforcing the factors 'binding' him to the organization which then contributes to the further integration of his occupational role, and so on. See Figure 6.

ROLE DIFFERENTIATION AND VICIOUS CIRCLES

In the case studies we have outlined, the components of the occupational roles of many employees were highly differentiated, in that job requirements and job expectations were perceived to be different and contrasting. Furthermore, the imbalance between these two components of occupational role were shown to result in a style of job performance markedly different from the official job requirements, and in turn feelings and evaluations about job performance out of line with initial job expectations.

In this situation of high occupational role differentiation, two processes may occur. First, the employee can modify his job expectations in the light of working experience. In doing so he initiates the process of role integration through rationalizing the differences between job expectations and job experience, and thus encouraging the process of fusion. Alternatively, the employee may consider his job expectations and requirements so incompatible, that the process of evaluation may only serve to highlight the differences. In such circumstances, the dissonance may be most easily reduced by seeking a new occupational role. Clearly which alternative the employee choses will depend on a range of factors, such as the degree of difference perceived between job requirements and job expectations (itself partially dependent upon socialization, stage in the life cycle, etc.) and, crucially, the nature of job experience.

In the case studies we have discussed, then, the high levels of occupational role differentiation, fostered by the rapid change and unpredictability in job requirements, naturally encouraged labour turnover as a means of coping with the dissonance generated by conflict between job requirements and job expectations. In these circumstances, it is interesting to consider how an organization brings about greater occupational role integration, and with it lower labour turnover.

In the organizations we studied several possibilities were visible. In two organizations attempts were made to retain staff by restructuring job requirements, in the hope that these would match more closely the job expectations of present and/or future employees. Thus, for example, the whole training system for student nurses was being reconsidered, while the leisure industry organization was forced into examining the feasibility of changing job requirements in the light of the job expectations of existing staff, and the necessary adjustments, both in terms of job design and recruitment policies, required.

Secondly, all the organizations were dependent *upon a haphazard process of employee self-selection.* In other words, they really relied upon employees accomodating their own job expectations to the organization's changing job requirements and finally integrating these two components. This took several forms. In some cases, as in the hospitals, the process of accommodation depended largely upon the employees' primary socialization in *deferred gratification*[39]. Thus, although the student nurse might find the routine activities upon which she was largely engaged out of line with her job expectations, she was often able to reduce the dissonance generated through anticipation that after qualifying this present 'conflict' would be removed as she herself would work on more professionally demanding (and rewarding) tasks.

In the garment-manufacturing factory self-selection took place, *and temporarily arrested the vicious circle,* through the recruitment and retention of a category of employees whose evaluation of one aspect of job requirements, namely the effort-reward relationship, differed markedly from the majority of the employees. While they *perceived* the formal effort-reward relationship in a similar light to the rest of the employees, i.e. 'too much work for too little money', they did not *evaluate* this as dissonant with their job expectations. This group of employees, married women, generally with dependent children, placed a high priority upon flexibility of hours and part-time working, e.g. evening shift work, time off in school holidays, and so on. Moreover, drawn mainly from the immediate locality in which the factory was situated, they also valued highly the short journey to work[40]. Thus these employees' job expectations were less concerned about the nature of the job requirements, as related to an occupational role, than as related to their domestic roles. *In other words job expectations were mainly concerned with the relationship between job requirements and domestic roles, rather than the occupational role itself.* As such

142

the organization was able to satisfy these expectations without difficulty[41].

Finally, in the same organization, self-selection operated in another manner. Because of the problems of labour turnover experienced, the organization felt compelled to recruit increasing numbers of foreign and immigrant employees. These employees, many recently arrived in the country with a minimal understanding of English, had little job experience of comparable working situations, and thus only a generalized set of job expectations and little detailed knowledge of job requirements. In practice *these two role components were largely integrated in their perceptions.* Moreover, certain structural pressures helped maintain this integration. For some of the foreign workers, freedom of movement between firms (and hence experience of a variety of job requirements to develop and enlarge their job expectations) was limited by government regulations.* Again, inadequate understanding of English placed this group of employees at a disadvantage, both in acquiring knowledge of feasible job opportunities in the local labour market, and of actually acquiring jobs where understanding and use of English were absolutely essential.

CONCLUSIONS

We consider that the processes we have described and analysed in this paper suggest that organizations (or units within an organization) oscillate between two modes of adaption to organization change, both essentially 'vicious circles'. These are illustrated in Figure 7. We contend that the structural pressures arising out of response to environmental change encourage the process of occupational role differentiation and the arousal of dissonance. In these circumstances, for the reasons discussed above, it is likely that the dissonance aroused will be coped with by labour turnover. This process, illustrated in the case studies, is shown by model B. However, these structural pressures ultimately result, through the self-selection of those with job expectations compatible with the existing job requirements, in changes in the social composition of the workforce. This process

---

* We are referring to the Aliens Employment Act 1955, section 2 (*a*) and (*b*), which was in operation at the time of the study.

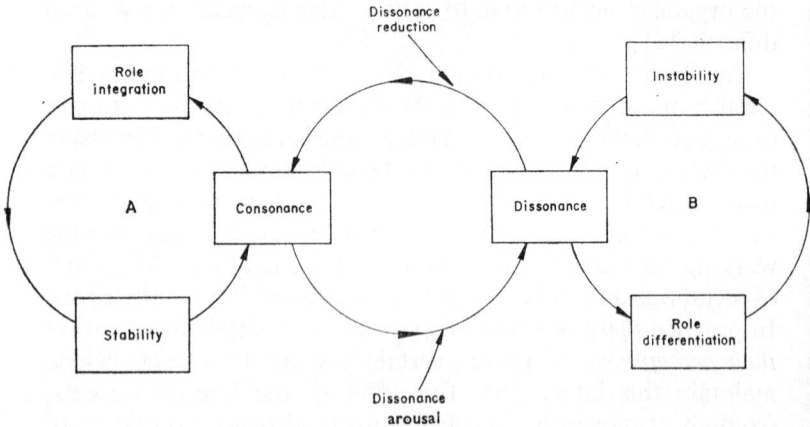

Figure 7

generates occupational role integration, which acts as a self-reinforcing 'vicious circle' (see model A).

In this paper we have illustrated in detail several 'model B' situations and considered the processes whereby an organization (or units within it) can shift to a 'model A' stance. Examples of 'model A' situations have frequently been illustrated in the literature, most notably perhaps in Merton's discussions concerning the dysfunctions of bureaucracy[42] and Crozier's analysis of the 'vicious circles' of bureaucracy[43]. The problems inherent in situations producing occupational role component integration are indicated most clearly in Crozier's work. First, a succession problem is likely to arise over time. Not only does the highly stable labour force age and eventually retire, but the process of role-integration itself, with its concomitant routinization of performance, narrowing of environmental awareness, and general resistance to change, impedes the introduction and implementation of the long-term planning that would alleviate this problem. Secondly, if such an organization is to remain viable in the face of environmental change, and if employees with high levels of occupational role integration are either unable to perceive environmental change, or to cope with its implications, then new occupational roles must be created. Thus organizations that have developed a high level of structural rigidity (and bureaucracies afford numerous examples) contain the seeds of eventual 'dis-integration'. Succession problems, in

144

a context of environmental change, inevitably involve the recruitment of new employees into the organization and/or the creation of new roles, which in turn results in a process of role component differentiation for the employee thus involved. The organization, we would argue, then reverts back to the model B stance, until the processes of self-selection discussed above, and ensuing role component integration, act to redirect it towards the situation shown by model A, and so on.

Clearly the time period over which these processes operate and the severity of their oscillation, will depend in part upon the speed and extent of environmental change* and organizations' existing mechanisms to cope with it. However, if our arguments are valid, mechanisms to cope with environmental change must include those consciously designed to prevent not only the dysfunctional consequences of occupational role differentiation, *but of occupational role integration as well.* We are of the opinion that the investigation of occupational role integration will also throw some light on the problem of the 'institutionalization' of those in prisons, hospitals, and asylums, and indeed vice versa.†

NOTES

1 K. Legge, 'The operation of the "regressive spiral" in the labour market', *Journal of Management Studies*, vol. 7, no. 1, February 1970.
2 Harry C. Bredemeier, and Richard M. Stephenson, *The analysis of social systems*, New York: Holt, Rinehart and Winston, 1970 edition, p. 174, footnote 34.
3 D. Gowler, 'Determinants of the supply of labour to the firm', *Journal of Management Studies*, vol. 6, no. 1, February 1969.
4 *Ibid.* pp. 77–8.
5 *Ibid.* Figure 2, p. 79.
6 E. G. Whybrew, 'Overtime working in Britain', Research Paper no. 9, Royal Commission on Trade Unions and Employers' Associations, London: HMSO, 1968, p. 52.
7 W. Baldamus, *Efficiency and effort*, London: Tavistock, 1961, p. 104.

* Particularly conditions in the external labour market. For example, we would expect a rising level of unemployment to contribute to a move towards or intensification of the process outlined in model A.

† We are at present commencing investigations into the problem of 'institutionalization' with the intention of comparing findings with our studies of occupational role integration.

8 L. Buck and S. Shimmin, 'Overtime and financial responsibility', *Occupational Psychology*, vol. 33, 1959.
9 See also Whybrew, 'Overtime working in Britain'.
10 Baldamus, *Efficiency and effort*, pp. 105–6.
11 The self-perpetuating nature of much labour turnover has been discussed by other commentators, notably: Food Manufacturing EDC, *A study of labour turnover*, London: HMSO, 1968; P. J. Samuel, *Labour turnover? towards a solution*, London: IPM, 1969.
12 Legge, 'The operation of the "regressive spiral" in the labour market.'
13 H. Behrend, 'Financial incentives as the expression of a system of beliefs', *British Journal of Sociology*, vol. 10, no. 2, 1959.
14 For discussions of the concept of relative deprivation, see, for example, W. G. Runciman, *Relative deprivation and social justice: a study of attitudes to social inequality in twentieth century England*, London: Routledge and Kegan Paul, 1966; also, J. A. Davis, 'A formal integration of the theory of relative deprivation', *Sociometry*, vol. 22, 1959.
15 E. Mumford and Olive Banks, *The computer and the clerk*, London: Routledge and Kegan Paul, 1967; E. Mumford, and T. B. Ward, *Computers: planning for people*, London: Batsford, 1968; E. Mumford, *Computers, planning and personnel management*, London: IPM, 1969.
16 We are greatly indebted to Mrs Julia Davis for this case study, drawn from her researches, and for permission to adapt a diagram that appears in her book; *A Study of Hospital Management Training in its Organizational Context*, Manchester, Centre for Business Research, 1972.
17 D. Gowler, 'Socio-cultural influences on the operation of a wage payment system: an explanatory case-study', in D. Robinson, *Local Labour markets and wage structures*, London: Gower Press, 1970.
18 See note 11.
19 Legge, 'The operation of the "regressive spiral" in the labour market',
20 *Ibid.* pp. 15–17.
21 D. Gowler and K. Legge, 'Occupational role development: part I', *Personnel Review*, vol. 1, no. 2, January 1972.
22 E. Jaques, *Equitable payment*, Pelican revised edition, Harmondsworth: Penguin Books, 1967.
23 R. M. Cyert and J. G. March, *A behavioural theory of the firm*, Englewood Cliffs, N. J.: Prentice-Hall, 1963.
24 F. J. Roethlisberger and W. J. Dickson, *Management and the workers*, Cambridge, Mass.: Harvard University Press, 1939; T. Lupton, *On the shop floor*, Oxford: Pergamon, 1963.
25 R. K. Merton, *Social theory and social structure*, 3rd enlarged edtiion, New York: Free Press of Glencoe, 1968; R. K. Merton, *On theoretical sociology: five essays, old and new*, New York: Free Press of Glencoe, 1967.
26 Gowler and Legge, 'Occupational role development: part I', Figure 1.
27 For a presentation of the six propositions and discussion, see Gowler and Legge, *ibid.*
28 *Ibid.* For supporting arguments on the relationship between ageing and attitudes, see D. B. Bromley, *The psychology of human ageing*, Harmondsworth: Penguin Books, 1966.

146

29 See, for example, R. Blauner, *Alienation and freedom*, Chicago: University of Chicago Press, 1964; also, C. Walker and R. H. Guest, *The man on the assembly line*, Cambridge, Mass.: Harvard University Press, 1952. It should be mentioned, however, that there are satisfactions in repetitive work which may also contribute to occupational role integration. See A. N. Turner and A. L. Miclette, 'Sources of satisfaction in repetitive work', *Occupational Psychology*, vol. 36, 1962; also, Baldamus, *Efficiency and effort*, chs. 6 and 7.

30 For an analysis and description of the processes inducing conformity in employees, see H. Kaufman, *The forest ranger*, Baltimore: John Hopkins Press, 1967, ch. 6 (paperback edition).

31 For a discussion of the use of this concept in relation to workplace behaviour, see W. R. Nord, 'Beyond the teaching machine: the neglected area of operant conditioning in the theory and practice of management', in G. W. Dalton and P. R. Lawrence, *Motivation and control in organizations*, Homewood, Ill.: Irwin, 1971.

32 For the influences of technology and managerial control systems upon the behaviours of individuals and groups, see L. Sayles, *Behaviour of industrial work groups*, New York: Wiley, 1958; also, J. Woodward, *Industrial organization: theory and practice*, London: Oxford University Press, 1965; J. Woodward, *Industrial organization: behaviour and control*, London: Oxford University Press, 1970. For the crucial influence of first-line supervision in maintaining congruence between job requirements and job performance in work groups, see Gowler, 'Socio-cultural influences on the operation of a wage payment system: an explanatory case-study'; also, N. Millward, 'Piecework earnings and workers' controls', *Human Relations*, Vol. 25, no. 4, Sept., 1972.

33 Gowler and Legge, 'Occupational role development: part I'.

34 L. Festinger, *A theory of cognitive dissonance*, London: Tavistock, 1962 (first published by Row, Peterson and Co., 1957); J. W. Brehm and A. R. Cohen, *Explorations in cognitive dissonance*, New York: Wiley, 1962.

35 See Gowler and Legge, 'Occupational role development: part I', Figure 8.

36 *Ibid.*

37 J. Klein, *Samples from English cultures*, vol. I and II, London: Routledge and Kegan Paul, 1965; also, M. Fogarty, R. Rapoport, and R. N. Rapoport, *Sex, career and family*, London: Allen and Unwin, 1971.

38 We regard this as an important point, and are publishing a paper on the relationship between external role integration and internal occupational role integration in the near future.

39 For a discussion of this concept see S. M. Lipset and R. Bendix, *Social mobility in industrial society*, Berkeley: University of California Press, 1967, pp. 247-9 and 255-6 (1st edition 1959); also, D. Lawton, *Social class, language and education*, London: Routledge and Kegan Paul, 1968.

40 M. Jefferys, *Mobility in the Labour market*, London: Routledge and Kegan Paul, 1954.

41 See Fogerty, Rapoport, and Rapoport, *Sex, career and family*; also,

A. Myrdal and V. Klein, *Woman's two roles: home and work*, 2nd, revised edition, London: Routledge and Kegan Paul, 1968; A. Hunt, *A survey of women's employment*, Government Social Survey, ss 379, London: HMSO, 1968.

42 R. K. Merton *et al.*, *Reader in Bureaucracy*, New York; Free Press of Glencoe, 1952; R. K. Merton, 'Bureaucratic structure and personality', in A. Etzioni, *et al.*, *Complex organizations*, New York: Holt, 1961.

43 M. Crozier, *The bureaucratic phenomenon*, London: Tavistock, 1965. See also, A. W. Gouldner, *Patterns of industrial bureaucracy*, New York: Free Press of Glencoe, 1965; P. Selznick, *TVA and Grass Roots*, Berkeley: University of California Press, 1953.

5 Technology and Other Variables: Some Current Approaches in Organization Theory[*]

CELIA DAVIES, SANDRA DAWSON, AND
ARTHUR FRANCIS

INTRODUCTION

For many purposes industrial sociologists view organizations merely as convenient contexts for the examination of work-related behaviour. This is, of course, a valuable exercise and one which yields solutions to certain kinds of problems. For some purposes, however, it is more helpful to make the organization itself the focus of study, and this paper concerns work which is squarely within this second focus. It deals with the study of organizations as such and it is concerned with the problem of explaining why typical configurations of inter-actions are found in specifiable organizational types. In other words our central interest here relates to the explanation and prediction of organizational structure.

The paper is primarily concerned with the work of Joan Woodward and the ways in which this has been developed in recent years.[†] It is divided into two main parts. The first is a brief clarification of concepts, paying particular attention to the use made of the concepts of control systems and uncertainty.

[*] This is an amended version of a paper read to the Industrial Sociology Section of the British Sociological Association Annual Conference, London, April 1971.

[†] Joan Woodward's illness and tragic death in May 1971 meant that we were unable to benefit from her views and comments on this paper. We acknowledge a debt to our colleagues in the Industrial Sociology Unit at Imperial College in the writing of it, but must stress that the responsibility for the views expressed here is our own.

In the second part we have explored some of the assumptions which inhere in this particular approach and tried to meet some of the criticisms which have been raised. In particular, we have examined the place of a 'non-social factor' such as technology in sociological explanation and asked whether this inevitably leads to what is commonly called a 'deterministic' position.

The paper should not be construed as a definitive critique of the 'technology' or 'task analysis'[1] school, nor as a full evaluation of the work of Woodward. It is intended rather as a contribution to a sociological debate about the nature of this type of explanation and an attempt to clarify some issues in relation to it.

DEVELOPING A CONCEPTUAL FRAMEWORK

The work of Woodward published in 1958 and 1965 is familiar to many people. It is perhaps salutary to note at the outset, however, that one of the reasons this earlier work[2] had a substantial impact among academics was the almost complete lack of a programme for organization theory at that time and the dearth of good descriptive data concerning organizational functioning. Her work was an attempt 'to discover whether the principles of organization laid down by an expanding body of management theory correlate with business success when put into practice'.[3]

There is no need to report here the findings of the South East Essex Study, except to say that technology, then defined in terms of type of production process on a scale from unit to process production, was found to be consistently related to specified structural characteristics.* The widely accepted assumption that there are principles of management valid for all types of production systems was at once called into question. Given these findings Woodward and her colleagues were faced with problems both of explanation and of deciding on future research strategies.

* The particular structural characteristics measured related to the 'shape' of organizations, i.e. to the observed characteristics or roles and relationships. They included: numbers of levels of authority in the management hierarchy, span of control of first-line supervision, and ratio of managers and supervisory staff to other personnel. However, technology was also found to be related to the extent to which top executives possessed models of the organization and the extent to which these models differed.

150

Their first step was to create a typology of technology. This did appear to be associated with different types of organization structure and was particularly successful at each end of the technology scale. It could not, however, be comprehensively developed, and a sustained attempt to measure technical variables was eventually abandoned. This gave rise to two developments: a broadening of the concept of technology, and a consideration of the concept of control.

It was seen to be necessary, for any useful definition of technology, to include a reference not only to the physical hardware of production but also to the knowledge required to operate it, and the meanings attached.[4] However, because of the overtones of manufacturing and machine tools that technology as a concept has, we now find it more useful to talk in terms of 'task'. For a working definition of task we have adapted Perrow's definition of technology,[5] making it more flexible so as to include both 'doing' and 'thinking' tasks. Tasks then are the actions that an individual performs upon an object, or the thoughts applied to problems, with or without the aid of tools or machines, in order to make some change in the object or solve the problems. It should be noted that the 'in order to' contained in this definition implies a goal, and further that this goal may or may not be one with which the actor agrees.

Consideration of the existence of goals set for some actors by others brings us to the concept of control or rather control systems. This is a concept developed initially by operational researchers, notably Eilon,[6] but though we have been influenced in our terminology by them, the use we make of this notion is a different one.

Two elements of the control system are salient for our attempts to explicate the link between task and structure. One is the making of decisions about the design and programming of the varying tasks involved in production. The other is ensuring that people actually do the work necessary to perform the programmed tasks. Taking first that part of the control system concerned with ensuring that the work actually gets done, it is clear that the type of supervisory roles, and the nature of the relationships between supervisors and workers, depends on the way in which both supervisors and workers perceive and interpret their situation. It has been hypothesized that one

151

factor among many that would affect their interpretations of the situation is the nature of the physical hardware in the workplace.[7] Thus it is contended that there is a link between the production task and the organizational structure by way of this part of the control system.

Turning to that part of the control system which is related to the design and programming of the tasks, the link with technology is complex. There are at least two aspects to it. One is the extent to which the nature of the production task demands or allows these sorts of decisions to be made before production starts. In process production, for example, it was found that nearly all design and programme decisions were made while the process plant was being designed and virtually no decisions of this nature needed to be made once the plant was in operation. Everyone knew what had to be done and who should do it. In unit production the opposite was found to be true, all programming of tasks being carried out concurrently with production. It is clear that the structure of an organization in which all production tasks are fully known and are fixed for a length of time does not need to be so complex and therefore differs in a number of other ways from that structure obtaining when many different decisions have to be made as production is carried out.

The second aspect of this link is the effect of the production task on the way in which programming decisions can be made. Initial research suggested two effects, one the extent to which such decisions required an administrative structure (for example, a formal information system and rigid role definitions for managers), and the other the extent to which such decisions were based on the pursuance of one objective. In some cases of batch production, for example, the control system appeared extremely fragmented with different managers making their own programming decisions in order to meet their own objectives.

Thus an attempt was made to create a typology of control systems according to the degree to which control was personal or mechanical and the extent to which objectives were unitary or fragmented.[8] It was argued that technology constrains managerial choice as to the control system that can be adopted,*

* The implicit assumption here concerning managerial goals and 'rationality' is examined on p. 158 below.

there being more constraints at the two ends of the technology scale than in the middle. However, once a choice has been made about the control system, this in itself constrains the shape of the organizational structure. The researchers, therefore, attempted to create a typology linking control systems with structure.

From work on control systems it became increasingly clear that an additional and key variable to be taken into account was that of uncertainty. It was suggested that one of the most significant aspects of task was its associated degree of uncertainty. It is this which affects the ability both to programme before production and to routinize decision making. For the purposes of our research both that uncertainty which is experienced by those in the situation and that which might 'objectively' be measured are relevant. Sources of uncertainty include lack of knowledge about the outcome of production processes and lack of knowledge about the production system as a whole, due perhaps to the complex nature of the interdependent parts of the system.[9]

The relationship between technical variables, control, and uncertainty is a complex one. The nature of the product, the product range, the market served, raw materials and the techniques and hardware available to process them – all these are sources of uncertainty, and therefore major determinants of the way in which the production task can be controlled. Whilst the control system is, in this sense, a function of the task, studies have shown that it can also influence the impact and distribution of uncertainty throughout the organization. A control system, then, can either increase or reduce the amount of uncertainty.[10]

This brief discussion of major concepts is not, of course, exhaustive. In the current programme of research in the Industrial Sociology Unit projects are being undertaken which pay particular attention, for example, to the impact of environment on the task and structure, to cultural differences in organizational ideologies, to characteristics of formal information systems, and to interdepartmental differentiation. Empirical work is now being undertaken in a variety of settings, manufacturing and non-manufacturing organizations, including public services, hospitals, trade unions, prisons, and among others, the construction, coal, and steel industries.

153

Hence the programme of research which the late Joan Woodward inaugurated and directed at Imperial College may largely be seen as an expansion and elaboration of the ideas discussed above. It also reflects the various interests of a diverse group of some twenty research and teaching staff.

There are a number of organization theorists in the USA who have adopted similar but not identical perspectives to our own in explaining the relationships between task or technology and structure, among them Perrow, Thompson, and Lawrence and Lorsch. For example, Perrow[11] in a recent publication makes clear that his particular interest lies in exploring the relationship between types of structure and unpredictability in the task. He identifies two aspects of unpredictability: number of exceptional cases encountered by the individual, and the degree to which search procedures are analysable. Where we diverge from him, however, is our emphasis on control systems as an intervening explanatory variable.

J. D. Thompson[12] has developed typologies of technology, interdependence, and coordination. From a purely theoretical point of view he has suggested interrelationships between these typologies. This contrasts markedly with the more empirical approach of Lawrence and Lorsch.[13] In operationalizing their concepts of differentiation and integration they rely heavily on members' perceptions of the organization. Their suggestion is that the successful performance of different tasks in various departments in organizations results in different habits of thought and patterns of behaviour amongst members. This differentiation creates difficulties in integrating the work of the several departments and so various 'integrating devices' have to be used. What these are depends largely on the level of uncertainty encountered in each department about its own performance and that of others.

It is interesting that such similar approaches as these three and our own have been developed more or less independently. However, one of the problems in the field of organization theory at the present time is the degree of overlap in the use and articulation of concepts. What remains to be done, of course, is to evaluate and synthesize these various approaches, though this is a task which we cannot attempt here.

USING TASK ANALYSIS – SOME IMPLICATIONS

We now turn our attention to an examination of some of the common misconceptions which have grown up about the sort of theoretical approach we have outlined above. We link this with a discussion of some of the assumptions which are built into our approach and which may be seen as a legitimate cause for debate. One of the most popular misconceptions concerns the nature of technology itself and its place in sociological explanation.

For some sociologists, technology has been regarded as intrinsically uninteresting and 'non-social'. A sociology of sociology might well inquire into the treatment accorded to these 'non-social' factors when writers have tried to introduce them. It would seem, at least to a superficial observer, that there are striking parallels in the reactions of sociologists to, say, ecological theories of crime and technological theories of organization. Advocates of 'non-social' factors in both cases are accused of being 'determinists' in an orthodox sociology which regards technology, ecology, and perhaps biology,[14] as environmental factors. Such factors are said to be important, possibly for background descriptive purposes but never to be part of the explanatory framework itself – never actually causal in their impact. Many of course would deny this simple position and accord 'non-social' factors some importance at the extremes; thus technology may impose limits or constraints, or ecology may provide a 'structure of available opportunities',[15] but nonetheless their main research effort is directed elsewhere. This 'orthodox' position is well summarized by Steward when he says of sociology that 'environment is relegated to a purely secondary and passive role. It is considered prohibitive or permissive but not creative. It allows man to carry on some kinds of activities and prevents others.'[16]

Thus it seems that anyone who would seek to examine aspects of the natural environment, to assess the importance of 'non-social' factors, is immediately faced on the one hand with the dilemma of whether he is a 'real' sociologist, and on the other with the label of determinism.

J. L. Roach has faced a similar dilemma with respect to the sociology of poverty and his development of a theory of lower class behaviour. He contends that sociological determinism has become socio-cultural determinism and that, for example, the emphasis in sociology on meaning and on the symbolic world has prevailed at the expense of an examination of the material conditions of economic deprivation and that this is unduly restrictive. Hence he suggests that 'the determinants ordinarily given causal emphasis in sociology – e.g. meaning, social relations, status needs – must be treated as variables which intervene between material conditions of poverty and the behaviour of the poor'.[17]

So it seems that even if one were to accept that technology is essentially a 'non-social factor' in organizations, there is a case for its inclusion in any explanatory model of behaviour. However, we would contend that technology cannot be so conveniently pigeon-holed.

Those who have regarded technology as a central variable in their studies of organizations have ordinarily adopted a broader and more complex definition. Technology is viewed as a part of culture in that it reflects man's knowledge, skills, objectives, and designs. Meissner makes this clear:

'We would say that the technology of a work-place consists of pieces of steel, stone and wood in certain shapes. But that is not what is meant. When we speak of technical conditions of work – of the technology of work-places – we refer to the fact that these material things (their presence, shapes and interconnections) are the product of designs, the manifestations of ideas of those who planned a process and the means of facilitating it.'[18]

However, this kind of formulation does not cover altogether the complexities of defining technology. The technical hardware not only reflects an existing body of knowledge; additional knowledge is required to utilize it. A more inclusive definition of technology would therefore cover not only the hardware of production and its designers' implied meanings but also operating knowledge.

This is the approach of Woodward who defined the specific technology of an organization as 'the collection of plant, machines, tools and recipes available at a given time for the execution of the production task and the rationale underlying their utilization'.[19] Parsons, in a different and wider context, adopts a similar position: 'Technology I should conceive as modes in which knowledge is put to instrumental uses in the interest of goals or purposes, the significance of which is not given in the body of knowledge itself.'[20]

We have discussed technology at length because we were aware that for some sociologists technology is still merely 'hardware' and thus it seemed necessary to point out that even in this limiting and material sense it is too important a factor in explanations of organizational behaviour to forget. However, as Woodward's definition suggests, the Unit has always acknowledged a relationship between technology and man which is both complex and reciprocal. This is reflected in our developing interest in control systems and uncertainty as intervening variables, acting in both directions, between technology and structure.

Whether the relationship between technology and structure is a qualitatively different one from that, more often studied, between technology and worker orientations is a further point for discussion. Empirically the two are related, analytically they may be kept distinct, and it is only the first of these issues which we have tackled in any detailed fashion in this paper.* It could be argued that the link between technology and management behaviour is more direct in that a 'management culture' may be in operation.† In the cross-cultural research of the Industrial Sociology Unit certain similarities in management orientations have already been noted. However, once one studies organizations in a wider context than that concerned explicitly with production management in manufacturing organizations, the existence of diverse goals and reference groups among different sorts of executives becomes more apparent.

'Determinism' has already entered our argument as it has often been assumed that explanations involving technology are deterministic ones. We now turn to a more detailed discussion of this assumption.

Determinism is often used by sociologists in a pejorative

* This is not to suggest that members of the Industrial Sociology Unit have not been concerned with worker behaviour. But in the present context we personally would be more interested, for example, in linking the structure of trade unions with their tasks rather than looking at member attitudes, or in linking the structure of the industrial relations set-up in a firm with its technology rather than directly associating technology and grievance behaviour.

† If this were so, it would fulfil the conditions of 'shared needs' which Silverman postulates is necessary for any explanation which suggests a direct link between technology and behaviour. See p. 158 below.

sense, yet it inheres in many of the activities of social scientists, for they all employ models of man in explaining behaviour. This form of determinism is rarely attacked, indeed rarely mentioned, except perhaps for the purposes of introducing the student to a new subject and emphasizing that different disciplines may look at the same behaviour, asking different questions and getting different answers. However, Bendix and Berger[21] point out that whenever use is made of concepts such as 'role', 'class', 'status-group', 'subculture', etc., we have chosen the way of sociological determinism as we are viewing individuals as acting at the dictate of group influences. We do it without qualms, in the belief that a limited view of causation will advance understanding.

Of course, determinism is used in several senses other than this one. Let us discard at once that type which is equated with a unicausal mode of explanation. There are no serious advocates of this position and no serious critics who have accused Woodward of it. A more pertinent contender for discussion is the proposition that behaviour is determined by a number of different external factors still acting directly upon an individual. Silverman,[22] however, has usefully pointed out that this kind of argument in fact postulates some intervening assumption; he suggests universal needs. Two other possible assumptions that one might make here are that there are shared cultural norms, or that there is a direct and prohibitive link between 'causes' and behaviour. Whether either of these assumptions is long tenable seems to us an interesting but still open question.

The assumption, however, which we ourselves are making is that we can only understand the links that we have suggested between external factors and behaviour by reference to the perceptions of those instituting and operating the control system. In particular we assume that they perceive themselves to be rationally pursuing their stated goals. This should not be construed as a managerial view of organizations. We do not believe that unity of purpose, total consensus, and complete rationality are the hallmarks of organizations. But in so far as dominant power groups exist, state that they agree on particular objectives, attempt to pursue these through organizations, and lay claims to rationality in doing so, it seems to us a useful exercise to trace through what would happen if their claims were valid.

Given this assumption, though, two things prevent us from predicting structure directly from an analysis of the task. The first is that in some instances it is difficult for managers to perceive which is the 'rational' choice of control system for particular tasks. This, as we pointed out earlier, has been found to apply particularly to firms which fall in the middle range of Woodward's scale of technology – i.e. in batch production, where there appear to be a number of different choices of control systems which are equally good or bad in terms of pursuing the goal of efficient production. This is one of the reasons for the need to place such emphasis on the control system intervening between task and structure.

The second problem about predicting structure and behaviour is, of course, that top management's definition of the situation may be neither consensual nor totally controlling and both the degree of consensus and control are variables which may themselves be linked to task. For example, the control system in process production is much more likely to be geared to the objectives of top management than the control system in construction, because in process production the control system is designed and built into the operating system by a small group of engineers who are called upon to justify the rationality of their designs by the demonstration of mathematical models. By contrast, the control system in construction is very largely designed and operated personally on site, by craftsmen at fairly low levels in the organization. Their objectives for the production system may be affected by their own personal goals and the rightness of their decisions cannot be demonstrated by reference to an agreed body of knowledge.

Thus different tasks allow different amounts of freedom to various people to seek their own goals. We see then that making the initial assumption about top management's rational pursuit of objectives puts us in a position where we can begin to predict where it is likely that these objectives may not be pursued, and where conflict over objectives is more likely to occur.

A further criticism of research articulated about the concepts we have already discussed has been that after the manner of Taylor and Fayol we are concerned merely with the 'mechanics' of organization.[23] It should be clear from this paper that our interests are by no means so limited. We feel, however, that implicit in this sort of criticism is a question which has a more general relevance in industrial sociology. This is a problem still largely unsettled for organization theorists and concerns the nature of their legitimate objects of study.

For us at least, these legitimate objects of study can usefully be defined, as we suggested in the introduction, as *typical configurations of interactions found in specifiable organizational types*. Such a definition of structure allows us to explore 'why' questions rather than mere 'how' questions,[24] for we are concerned not simply with *how* organizations differ in terms of their structure and technology, but with why behaviour is patterned in distinct and different ways in various organizations. In particular, we are concerned with why and when task, control, and uncertainty become salient explanatory variables.

For some, our concern with the structures of organizations *per se* will involve us automatically in 'reification'. As this is a sensitive area in organizational theory we must emphasize that for us organizations as such do not behave or have goals and we do not think that such assumptions are inherent in our research. To the extent that our interest is in the behaviour of management – or more properly in that of the dominant groups or coalition who determine policy in organizations – we take their perceptions of the situation as important factors in our research and these may well be expressed in reified terms.

Woodward's approach then leads one to make certain assumptions about the distribution and meaning of power in organizations. These may or may not be valid in all organizational contexts. They were initially built into explanations of structure and behaviour when all the research activity of the Industrial Sociology Unit was directed towards commercial manufacturing organizations. Such assumptions, then, demand further attention in our research, particularly as the research programme has been diversified to include examination of non-manufacturing, non-profit-making organizations.*

CONCLUSION

We would argue that the kind of approach we have outlined in this paper with its concentration on variables intervening

---

* We are each concerned to investigate the validity of these particular assumptions in our own current research work, Celia Davies and Arthur Francis in hospitals and Sandra Dawson in the post office and prisons.

between technology and structure cannot easily be categorized as 'technological determinism' and contrasted with an 'action frame of reference'. This is something which has happened in the past and has encouraged people to weigh and value the respective contribution of each. But such issues become irrelevant once one seeks to examine not the importance of, but the mutual interactions between, identifiable variables and behaviour. Our position is that in the real world it will neither be true that adopting a technological deterministic approach allows prediction of all behaviour nor that taking an 'action perspective' means that knowledge of technology is no predictor at all. Indeed, there is a wealth of empirical evidence to the contrary and what seems to happen is that technology is very often a partial predictor.[25]

In adopting this approach to technology, a major problem concerns methodology both in terms of how to collect the data and how to draw up relevant models. The general research strategy of the Industrial Sociology Unit has been to concentrate on those areas where the characteristics of an organization's technology or task are found to predict structure and behaviour least well, and to try to elucidate the character of the intervening variables. The development of the concept of a control system incorporated not only the idea that control systems are constrained by technologies but also that they are man-made attempts to perceive and cope with a technology. They thus intervene between technology and behaviour. Our current concern with uncertainty is also a step in the same direction, as is our interest in identifying other salient intervening variables.

There have been three major aims in this paper: to elucidate important theoretical strands in Joan Woodward's work and in the 'Task Analysis' approach more generally, to identify some of the misconceptions which have been developed around this particular approach, and to discuss some of the assumptions which have become part of this perspective. We have argued that technology, or task, cannot be dismissed on the grounds that it is the basis of simplistic exercises in determinism. Rather, the problem for organization theory is one of building complex models in which technology must play a significant part in conjunction with a variety of other variables.

NOTES

1 See in particular: P. Lawrence and J. Lorsch, *Organization and envirionment: managing differentiation and integration*, Boston, Mass.: Harvard University Press, 1967; J. Lorsch and P. Lawrence (eds.), *Studies in organizational design*, Honewood, Illinois: Irwin-Dorsey Press, 1970; C. Perrow, 'A framework for the comparative analysis of organizations', *American Sociological Review*, vol. 32, 1967; C. Perrow, 'Technology and structural change in business firms', in B. C. Roberts (ed.), *Industrial relations: contemporary issues*, New York: Macmillan, 1968; C. Perrow, *Organizational analysis: a sociological view*, London: Tavistock, 1970; J. D. Thompson ,*Organizations in action*, New York: McGraw-Hill, 1967; S. H. Udy Jr., *Organization of work: a comparative analysis of production among non-industrial peoples*, New Haven: Human Relations Area Files Press, 1959; S. H. Udy Jr., 'The comparative study of organizations', in J. G. March (ed.) *Handbook of organizations*, Chicago: Rand McNally, 1965.
2 The findings of the South East Essex Study were first pubilshed in 1958: J. Woodward, *Management and technology*, HMSO, 1958. A fuller version of this study was given in J. Woodward, *Industrial organization: theory and practice*, London: Oxford University Press, 1965.
3 .Woodward, *Management and technology*, p. 4.
4 See p. 156.
5 Perrow, 'A framework for the comparative analysis of organizations', p. 195.
6 S. Eilon, 'Problems in studying management control', *International Journal of Production Research*, vol. 1, 1962.
7 Woodward, *Industrial organization: theory and practice*, pp. 175–7.
8 J. Woodward, *Industrial organization: behaviour and control*, London: Oxford University Press, 1970, p. 53.
9 T. Kynaston Reeves and B. A. Turner, 'A theory of organization and behaviour in batch production factories', *Administrative Science Quarterly*, March 1972.
10 There are added complications here in that individuals take advantage of certain organizational situations in order to increase the amount of uncertainty over which they have control with a view to increasing their power within the organization; see for example: M. Crozier, *The bureaucratic phenomenon*, London: Tavistock, 1964; D. J. Hickson and C. R. Hinings, 'A first interpretation of Canadian data on a strategic contingencies theory of intra-organizational power', paper presented to the Industrial Sociology Section of the British Sociological Association annual conference, London, April 1971.
11 Perrow, 'A framework for the comparative analysis of organizations', and *Organizational analysis: a sociological view*.
12 Thompson, *Organizations in action*.
13 Lawrence and Lorsch, *Organizations and environment*, and (eds.), *Studies in organizational design*.

14 Dennis Wrong, for example, reacts against this orthodoxy and replies to criticisms of 'biological determinism': 'I think we must start with the recognition that in the beginning there is a body. As soon as body is mentioned the spectre of "biological determinism" raises its head and sociologists draw back in fright.' D. Wrong, 'The oversocialised concept of man', *American Sociological Review*, vol. 26, 1961.

15 S. Greer and P. Orleans, 'Mass society and parapolitical structure', *American Sociological Review*, vol. 27, 1962.

16 J. Steward, *Theory of culture change*, University of Illinois Press, 1955. Similarly, Ralph Linton claims that 'between the natural environment and the individual, there is always imposed a human environment which is vastly more significant'. R. L. Linton, *The cultural background of personality*, New York: Appleton Century, 1945.

17 J. L. Roach, 'A theory of lower-class behaviour', in L. Gross, *Sociological theory: inquiries and paradigms*, New York: Harper and Row, 1967.

18 M. Meissner, *Technology and the worker*, San Francisco: Chandler, 1969.

19 Woodward (ed.), *Industrial organization: behaviour and control*, p. 4.

20 T. Parsons, 'The impact of technology on culture and emerging new modes of behaviour', *International Social Science Journal*, vol. 22, 1970.

21 R. Bendix and R. Berger, 'Images of society and problems of concept formation in sociology', in L. Gross (ed.), *Symposium on sociological theory*, New York: Harper and Row, 1959.

22 D. Silverman, *The theory of organizations*, London: Heinemann, 1970.

23 This term has been used by John Child; see *Sociology*, vol. 5, 1971, Book Reviews.

24 Dahrendorf has made this distinction in an essay which laments the loss of problem consciousness in sociology. R. Dahrendorf, 'Out of Utopia', *American Journal of Sociology*, vol. 64, 1958.

25 This is apparent in the work of a number of writers. See for example: R. Blauner, *Alienation and freedom: the factory worker and his industry*, Chicago: University of Chicago Press, 1964; R. Dubin, 'Supervision and productivity: empirical findings and theoretical considerations', in R. Dubin *et al.*, *Leadership and productivity*, San Francisco: Chandler, 1965; A. W. Gouldner, *Patterns of industrial bureaucracy*, Glencoe, Ill.: Free Press of Glencoe, 1954; L. R. Sayles, *The behaviour of industrial work groups: prediction and control*, New York: John Wiley, 1958; E. Trist *et al.*, *Organizational choice*, London: Tavistock, 1963; A. N. Turner and P. Lawrence, *Industrial jobs and the worker: an investigation of response to task attributes*, Boston Mass.: Harvard University Press, 1965; C. R. Walker and R. H. Guest, *The man on the assembly line*, London: Harvard University Press, 1965; D. Wedderburn and R. Crompton, *Workers' attitudes and technology*, London: Cambridge University Press, 1972; J. Goldthorpe, D. Lockwood, F. Bechhofer, and J. Platt, *The affluent worker: industrial attitudes and behaviour*, London: Cambridge University Press, 1968.

6 The Task Analysis Framework in Organizational Analysis

PETER ABELL AND DAVID MATHEW

In recent years a number of authors, Woodward,[1] Perrow,[2] Thompson,[3] Lawrence and Lorsch,[4] – to name but a few – have become associated with a general orientation to organizational analysis which gives primacy to the concept of organizational task in 'explaining' many features of organizational structure. Although there are differences between the various authors, there is sufficient intellectual unison to enable one to speak of the 'task analysis framework'. In concise form we want to try to lay bare its basic logical structure, raise some queries, and interpret the ideas connecting task to organizational shape.

Since in a very loose sense an organizational task is what an organization 'does', it might seem surprising that anybody should feel inclined to deny the importance of this concept in organizational analysis. For surely what an organization is designed (consciously, or unconsciously) to do, must influence the 'way it is made' (i.e. its structure). After all, structural functionalism, that most influential of sociological meta-theories, suggests that there is always an intimate relation between structures and functions. Though the concept of task is not identical to that of function, they are closely related and thus task analysis is in some sense a variant of functional analysis.

The significance of task analysis, however, seems to reside in the catholicity of its explanatory claims. Our own view is that organizational tasks, or rather *task decomposition structures* (defined below), are a *sine qua non* in organizational analysis but they by no means exhaust the field of explanatory variables in this field of inquiry. And indeed conceptual imperialism of

164

any sort should be frowned upon at the present stage of development of organizational theories.

Clearly our first objective must be to establish as clear and precise a definition of the concept of task as possible.

TASK DEFINED ?

The concept of task and technology seem often to have been used interchangeably but it seems to us important to keep them analytically distinct, though we feel sufficiently insecure about the precision we want to try and force on these concepts to put our sub-title in interrogative form.

Task may be deployed at any level of abstraction within a given organization. Thus we may speak of the total organizational task – or even the task of a group of organizations; the task of a division; the task of a department or sub-department; or the task of an individual person occupying an organizational position.

We will define a task as:

a process whereby a distribution of inputs is converted (transformed) into a constrained distribution of outputs by the application of a technology(ies) *

As defined, the concept thus involves three subsidiary concepts: (*a*) inputs, (*b*) technologies, and (*c*) outputs. We can then view an organization or any part thereof as performing a task by applying an appropriate set of transformation procedures (technologies) to a set of inputs and thus converting them into a set of outputs. This will sound almost trite to the uninitiated reader. And indeed taken at face value it is – the claims of task analysis, however, derive from the complexities of this disarmingly simple statement and the consequences they have for organizational structure. Not least of these complexities is the measurement problem associated with the three subsidiary concepts.

TYPES OF TASK

Most organizations, though not all, have two types of task

* This definition, in effect, takes a very objective stance and in particular implies that the distributions of inputs, outputs, and technologies are given and well defined and organizationally understood. Later in the paper we will question these assumptions in the context of individual performance.

THE SOCIOLOGY OF THE WORKPLACE

system (therefore task decomposition structures – see below): (a) *material tasks* – the transformation of material inputs into material outputs; (b) *informational tasks* – the transformation of information inputs into information outputs (directives, communications, requests, etc.).*

Much of the complexity of organizations resides in the fact that these different systems interrelate in complex ways. For instance, material tasks cannot be accomplished without some information – every task, however routinized, involves some element of decision making (information handling). The maps of material and information tasks onto organizational parts are complex, requiring fairly well-developed formalisms to sort them out.

One of the major appeals of the concept task, as developed here, is that decision making becomes a species of the genus – thus facilitating a very general level of organizational analysis.

TASK DECOMPOSITION STRUCTURES

If a given organization performs a global† task then the task is well defined if we specify the distributions of the sets of inputs and outputs and the technology. In practice, global tasks must be decomposed into a set of local tasks. The structure of decomposition whereby a well-defined global task is progressively refined into more and more local tasks, we refer to as a task decomposition structure. It will characteristically have the structure of a single-rooted tree. There will, in a *well-defined organization*, be a decomposition structure for each global task. In practice, of course, the decomposition structures are not necessarily well defined and the concept must very much be treated as an *ideal type*.

Since a given global task may usually be decomposed into more and more local tasks in a variety of ways – constraints being imposed by the available technologies – the problem of optimal decomposition and refinement arises. However, little can be said about this until some derivative concepts, uncer-

* There are clearly additional complexities surrounding this distribution and both types of task could be further classified. Also in some situations the distinction between material and informational inputs and outputs is not clear-cut. For instance, a financial decision (an informational task) may involve the handling of materials, cheques, etc.
† Task defined at the organizational level.

tainty, interdependence, and inventory capacity, have been defined.

A WELL-DEFINED ORGANIZATION (W.D.O.)

Although the idea of a well-defined organization[5] has not traditionally been associated with the task analysis framework, it does seem to us to enrich the framework and so we will take the liberty of introducing it here. It should be emphasized that a w.d.o. is an *ideal type*.

A well-defined organization comprises:

i. a finite set of organizational *positions* $P = \{p_i\}$, $i = 1, 2, \ldots n$.

ii. a finite set of *individuals* (position incumbents) $I = \{i_j\}$, $j = 1, 2, \ldots m$.

iii. An *allocation mapping* $\gamma \colon I \to P$; γ will map I *onto* P as all the organizational positions must be filled. The mapping need not be 1–1 since an individual may occupy more than one position. Though we do not allow a single position to be mapped onto more than one individual.*

iv. The allocation will, in general, be in terms of certain properties of the individuals – 'appropriate skills'. In a w.d.o., we assume (*a*) the set of properties is well defined and (*b*) that there is a well-defined mapping of individuals into sub-sets of these properties.

Let the set of properties be $C = \{c_i\}$, $i = 1, 2, \ldots k$. We can then define the mapping $\theta \colon I \to C$; θ is, in general, one to many. Since θ allows for 'overlapping sets of skills', it generates rather interesting simplicial complexes $K(C; \theta)$ and $K(I, \theta^{-1})$.[6]

v. A task decomposition structure for each global task G into a set T of local tasks.

vi. A *task allocation map* $\alpha \colon P \to T$. This map must be *onto* and merely describes how individual positions are ascribed to local tasks. In the simplest case it may be 1–1, in more complex situations it will be one to many.

---

* It is important to emphasize in this respect that each individual position in an organization is kept distinct, even though two or more may perform 'the same type of task', e.g. they may be lathe operators.

If we allow the same local task to be performed by more than one position, α^{-1} will also be one to many.

vii. An *authoritative coordination relation* H mapping P into itself, traditionally referred to as the formal hierarchy. The H relations are the channels through which communications and directions are supposed to flow. At this stage, we leave its multiple nature unanalysed and specify that H will be symmetric.

These seven features do, in our opinion, establish a reasonably accurate language for describing a W.D.O. In practice, organizations do not exhibit the 'niceness' of this formal picture; there is invariably a degree of ambiguity especially about the allocation mappings. The central maps are depicted in Figure 1 along with some interesting compound maps.[7]

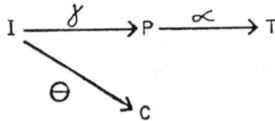

$$I \xrightarrow{\gamma} P \xrightarrow{\alpha} T$$

$$\theta \searrow C$$

$\theta^{-1} \; \gamma$ (mapping qualifications onto positions)

$\gamma \; \alpha$ (mapping individuals onto tasks)

$\theta^{-1} \gamma \alpha$ (mapping qualifications onto tasks)

Figure 1

The central maps of a well-defined organization

SOME CONCEPTS DERIVATIVE OF THE CONCEPT TASK

1. *Technology*

Woodward[8] defined organizational technology as follows: 'the collection of plant, machines, tools and recipes available at a given time for the execution of the production task and the rationale underlying their utilisation'. The fundamental idea behind this definition' seems to be in accord with our definition of technology as a set of techniques for effecting transformations on a set of inputs. There is perhaps much to be gained from a more detailed analytic breakdown of this concept, particularly since it seems to cut across the well-established analytic distinctions of material, belief, and value systems. We will not, however, pursue this further here, but

168

merely note that for a task to be performed effectively, there will be a problem of accommodating individuals to all three systems.

An important point is that just as the concept of task can be applied at different levels of abstraction in an organization, then of necessity so can technology. Furthermore, the often implicit assumption that there is a single organizational technology (relevant to explaining internal structures) is often unwarranted. At the very least, one can distinguish between the technologies appropriate for handling physical and informational inputs. The distribution of tasks and therefore technologies, across an organizational structure, may well make it illegitimate to generalize about the organization as a totality. For instance, since, as we shall see, certain aspects of tasks are important for understanding variations in span of control, the average of control in an organization is often less revealing than its variance.

2. *Task uncertainty*

The idea that individuals or groups of individuals (as task performers) in organizations often face uncertainties of one sort or another has long been documented. It has entered the theory of the firm in terms of uncertainties and risks in the factor and product markets and has even been elevated to play an integral role in parts of motivation theory where it is postulated that organizational behaviour can be seen as a constant endeavour to render one's environment more certain – in particular by getting others to do predictable things in all conceivable circumstances.[9] But the idea that the distribution of uncertainty in an organization can influence its shape is particularly associated with the task analysis framework. Unfortunately, the concept has been used in a wide variety of ways and often very imprecisely. Our definition of task does enable us to tie down the concept rather well, though at the empirical level the measurement problems are appalling. Since there are three components of a given task, we can associate uncertainties with each; it should be emphasized that at this stage we are concentrating upon the concept of W.D.O.; later in the paper we will relax this assumption.

a. The input uncertainty of a task. If we assume a known

169

probability distribution of each input, then the task input uncertainty is given by a suitable measure* of the variance in each of these distributions. Clearly information theory measures of uncertainty are appropriate here and provide additive measures facilitating an estimate of aggregate uncertainty. There are, however, a number of empirical problems with this conception.

There is a problem when measuring input uncertainty in connection with the time period over which the distributions are measured. In general by reducing the time unit, we may expect the uncertainty measure to reduce and there is, therefore, a rather acute problem of locating significant time units when using this concept. In a W.D.O., these problems do of course not exist since even though it allows for multiple task performance, each task and its input variations are well defined. But even in a W.D.O. an additional uncertainty is created by possible variations in the mix of tasks per unit time. We may refer to this as *task-switching uncertainty*, something particularly evident in batch production systems.[10]

There is also a particular problem in connection with decisions (informal tasks). Here the nature of the task often requires complex search procedures actually to establish the input distributions. This clearly relates to the *cognitive structures* individuals erect, in particular the ways they impose categories on their environment.

b. Technological uncertainty. It is relatively easy to get an intuitive idea of this concept but almost impossible to tie it down with exactitude because of the lack of definition of technology itself. Broadly speaking it is a measure of the variation in available techniques for effecting the required transformation on the set of inputs. Less precisely, the alternative ways of doing the job. Technological uncertainty is obviously related in a complex way to input uncertainty but the details of this relationship, it seems to us, can only be examined in the context of empirical investigation.

* The measure of variance appropriate will depend upon the measurement properties of the inputs. There is clearly a complexity problem here – each input may perhaps be further bioken down into a set of variables each with a probability distribution. The level of refinement that must be imposed in a given investigation is an empirical problem. There is also a series of issues surrounding the perceptions and cognitive structuring of the task performer, issues we will return to later.

c. The output uncertainty. This can be defined in a completely analogous way to input uncertainty; it is a measure of the variance in the probability distribution of outputs.

3. *Task interdependence*

Tasks become interdependent in so far as, either directly or through the agency of intervening tasks, the output of one task is the input of another; or if their outputs have to be coordinated either directly or indirectly. This conception is close to that of Thompson[11] though we believe the issues to be more complex than his three basic types indicate. However, we have no need of any further refinement of the concept here. In a w.d.o., task interdependence can be defined at any level of abstraction (e.g. interdependence of departments, divisions, individuals, and so on). Thus we can think of maps from various levels of refinement on the task decomposition structure onto appropriate sets of organizational positions which preserve the pattern of interdependence (*i.e.* connectivity).

4. *Input/output inventory*

If two tasks are directly interdependent in the sense that the output of the first is the input of the second, then a particularly important issue, which will have profound implications for an organizational structure, is the extent to which it is or is not possible to build up inventories between the task sites. If the output of t_1 is the input of t_2 and it must be handling 'without delay', then there is no inventory capacity in this link. In a system of interrelated tasks, the distribution of inventory capacity is an important determinant of control structures.

TASK PERCEPTION AND PERFORMANCE

These are two principal reasons why real organizational tasks differ from our ideal type: the first is that an individual's perception of his task is not necessarily in exact correspondence with the task allocated by the task decomposition structure, and the task allocation map to the position he occupies, and the second is that any task is only more or less well defined. Examination of the former complication is beyond the scope of this essay, but the latter introduces important new problems. There are two criteria by which to judge how well defined any real task is; these are, first, to what degree exceptions to the defined task categories occur at input, output, or transformational stages, and secondly, to what degree the task input, output, and transformation techniques are defined in purely objective terms calling for no 'intuition' or 'subjective judgment'. These criteria are similar to but more general than Perrow's[12] concepts of 'familiarity/unfamiliarity' of stimuli encountered and 'understandability' of raw materials. The similarities are plain; the generality of our concepts lies in the fact that they apply to all stages of task accomplishment at any level of abstraction of an organization.

The degree to which exceptional cases are encountered in the task we will call the *novelty of the task* and, like Perrow, we would distinguish between analytic and intuitive search procedures in response to both existing and anticipated exceptional occurrences.* Of course, the concept of uncertainty can always be defined over a sufficiently large unit of time to embrace all potential novelty. But, nevertheless, the distinction is, in practice, useful.

TASK AND ORGANIZATIONAL STRUCTURE (SHAPE)

Perhaps the most original claim deriving from the task analysis framework is that the nature of the task influences the appropriate (optimal?) control structure. So there is, for any particular task decomposition structure an optimalizing control system.

A fundamental aspect of control is the variation in span and depth in an organization, because these two major topographic features in many ways constrain other aspects of organizational structure like the concentration of decision making.

A typical finding is that of Woodward demonstrating that as an organization moves along the technological continuum from 'unit' to 'continuous', there is a tendency for the mean span of control to decrease and depth of the organization to increase. Why should this be so – can we explain this empirical regularity by some deeper lying theoretical scheme involving the above outlined concepts?

There must in any rationally constructed organization be an endeavour to find optimal spans of control. Control resources are costly but so is ineffective control. A rational organization

* We give here only a brief analysis of the problems. They will be pursued at greater length in a forthcoming paper.

will equate control benefits and costs at the margin. In general as span decreases, control costs increase (i.e. the ratio of controllers to controlled increases) but the potential effectiveness of the control increases.

Let us first of all concentrate upon one local task in an organization and its control.

(i) As task input or output uncertainty* increases, then one of two things may happen. First, the *discretionary power* of the task performer may be increased (i.e. there will be a change in the *distribution of decision making*). Secondly, the degree of *control surveillance* may be increased allowing the 'supervisor' to pay closer attention to the task performer's decision problems.

Similarly, for technological uncertainties – either or both discretionary power and control surveillance will increase as technological uncertainty increases.

Let us suppose increasing discretionary power involves increased costs (i.e. more proficient task performers must be employed with higher rates of renumeration) and so does control surveillance – then a rational organization will face a problem in minimizing control costs by balancing one sort of cost off against the other. In general, there will be an upper bound to discretionary power – this leads to the first major hypothesis:

(H.1) *For a given level of discretionary power the control surveillance will increase with increases in input, output, and technological uncertainty.*

The capacity for control surveillance is clearly variable ultimately depending on at least two factors: (*a*) the inherent control ability of the controlling unit (a supervisor or a department), and (*b*) the *control technology* – the ability to generate, process, and feed back the requisite sorts of information.

A corollary of hypothesis H.1 is then:

(Cor. 1) *For given levels of discretionary power and capacity for control surveillance, an increase in input, output, or technological uncertainty will decrease the span of control.*

* For the sake of clarity in presentation, no mention is made of novelty, and nature of search procedures, though parallel arguments will obviously apply to these concepts.

173

The implicit assumption being that the degree of control surveillance increases with decrease in span of control. Clearly with increasing uncertainties, the tendency for spans to reduce can be offset by increasing the capacity for control surveillance.

If we now turn to task interdependence, an additional complication arises, in connection with the coordination of the tasks: if the output of task t_1 is the input of task t_2 then it is a prerequisite for efficient performance of t_2 that the output of t_1 is produced in a manageable way. This becomes particularly acute if there is no inventory capacity in the link. Discretionary power is of more limited use in connection with interdependency – especially with indirect patterns, where some global coordination is called for. Thus in general with complex systems of task interdependency we can expect the coordination problems to increase and therefore control surveillance must likewise increase. If in addition there is little capacity for inventory in the system, we must expect an even greater impact on control surveillance.

> (H.2) *For given levels of discretionary power and capacity for control surveillance an increase in task interdependence will decrease span of control.*

and

> (H.3) *For given levels of discretionary power and capacity for control surveillance, a decrease in inventory capacity of a system of interdependent tasks will decrease the span of control.*

The aforegoing theoretical ideas are summarized in Figure 2. The structure of the diagram should not be taken too literally; in all probability the determinants will show a complex pattern of interaction and direct effects – this is an area where empirical research is needed.

We are now in a position to make a tentative interpretation of Woodward's results. If we assume that in her sample, which was drawn from one geographical locality, the discretionary power of task performers does not vary in a systematic way with the technological scale, then the variations in span or control she observed must be a function of variations in (*a*) capacity for control surveillance, (*b*) task uncertainties, and (*c*) task interdependence and inventory capacity.

Perhaps (*a*) increases along the scale 'unit' to 'continuous' as a consequence of the increased sophistication of 'the technical control systems'; (*b*), on the other hand, probably decreases. Both of these effects would predict an increase in average span along the scale 'unit' to continuous. However, empirically the situation is the reverse which suggests that increases in (*c*) more than offset the effects of (*a*) and (*b*). Implying perhaps that task interdependence and inventory capacity are much stronger determinants of control spans than the other variables.

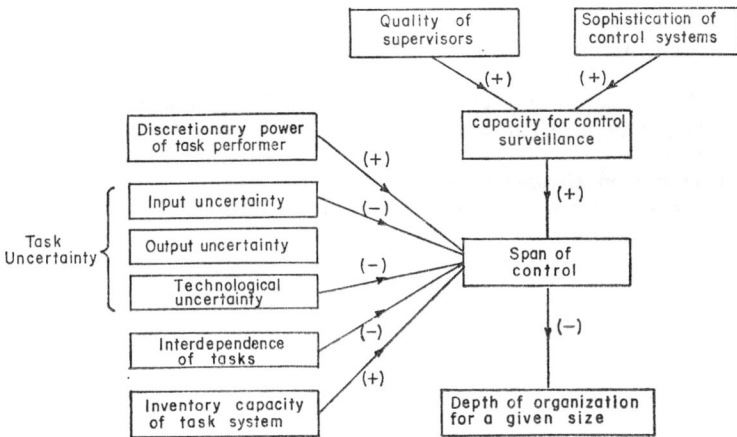

Figure 2

It remains to relate span to depth. The first point to make is that for an organization of a given size, if the average span decreases, the depth *of necessity* must increase if the normal hierarchical structure is preserved. Thus it is not surprising that Woodward found that at the 'continuous' end of her technological scale, organizations had on the average more levels. This result could only have been avoided if there had been a systematic reduction in size with increasing sophistication of technology.

NOTES

1 J. Woodward, *Industrial organization: theory and practice*, London: Oxford University Press, 1965.

2 C. Perrow, 'A framework for the comparative analysis of organizations', *American Sociological Review*, vol. 32, 1967.
3 J. D. Thompson, *Organizations in action*, New York: McGraw-Hill, 1967.
4 P. Lawrence and J. Lorsch, *Organizations and environment: managing differentiation and integration*, Cambridge, Mass.: Harvard University Press, 1967.
5 The concept will be explored in more detail in Peter Abell and Vera West, *Explorations in the analysis of organizations*, forthcoming.
6 See Abell and West, *Explorations in the analysis of organizations* (forthcoming).
7 See *ibid.* for a more detailed analysis.
8 Woodward, *Industrial organizations: theory and practice*.
9 M. Crozier, *The bureaucratic phenomenon*, Chicago: University of Chicago Press, 1964.
10 T. Kynaston Reeves and B. A. Turner, 'A theory of organizations and behaviour in batch production factories', mimeo, Imperial College, 1970.
11 Thompson, *Organizations in action*.
12 Perrow, 'A framework for the comparative analysis of organizations'.

7   Computers and Supervisors*

KEITH E. THURLEY

The debate about the implications and consequences of automation for industry, society, and the individual is now very
familiar to us all. We may quarrel about the terminology used
(automation or cybernation?) or about the need to trace
automatic developments back to the industrial revolution or
beyond, but the plethora of international conferences and
publications in the last ten years have at least established
automation and the use of computers as a problem or a set
of problems of major importance. Underneath the debate there
often seems to be a deep-rooted anxiety. Although scientific
and technological advance offers us power and mastery over
our environment – as Edmund Leach has recently said – 'Men
have become like gods, but instead of rejoicing we feel deeply
afraid.'[1] 'Cybernation creates changes in our social system so
vast and so utterly different from those in the past that it will
challenge to its roots our present understanding about the
viability of our way of life.'[2]

Main questions

1. the effect of the introduction of computers on supervisory
   functions;
2. the problems of adapting the existing supervisors to new
   techniques and problems;
3. the question of training and retraining for any changes in
   roles demanded by the new technology.

* This is an amended and extended version of a paper which has appeared
in German in G. Friedrichs (ed.), *Computer und Angestellte*, vol. II, international
edition, Frankfurt-am-Main: Europaische Verlangsantsalt, 1970. It also appeared
in an earlier version in India: in *Productivity*, 1969, National Productivity Council,
New Delhi, India. The original paper was given to the Industrial Sociology
Group of the BSA, when it was founded in the later 1960s.

As with other aspects of the automation debate, there is a visionary view of the problem which promises radical change and exciting developments. There is also the cautious and more cynical view which disbelieves in the likelihood of the predicted changes occurring at any speed. Those who take the former view may go on record querying the possible need for supervisors under conditions of sophisticated process automation.

'The foreman's position tends to become equivocal. If he possesses sufficient technical skill and knowledge, he may act as a roving technical adviser; and if he has also the necessary personal qualities, he may become the accepted leader of an integrated team. But, however good he is at managing men, unless he has extensive technical knowledge and experience, he is apt to find himself a fish out of water, merely keeping records and arranging rotas. Where there is a qualified engineer on each shift, it is doubtful whether there is a place for him at all.'[3]

Leavitt and Whisler argued further in their study of management in the 1980s, that middle management would be replaced by overall coordinators, systems analysts, and programmers.[4] Management controls would be centralized at more senior levels, the autonomy of departments would be broken down and *lower-level management decision making would then be subject to programming and rationalization.* The rump of independent areas for decision making left to foremen after the recent growth in specialist functional departments might finally then be eliminated by the creation of an integrated computer-based production control and planning system.

Against such predictions one can quote the evidence of the ILO report on Automation and Non-Manual Workers on the effect of the introduction of computers on administrative hierarchies:

'The same studies note, however, that in the early stages of computer operations *middle management is very busy with the practical and organisational problems involved.* Other studies have not confirmed the prediction that middle management jobs will substantially diminish. Rather they indicate that, although the functions required of middle managers change under office automation, the need for them remains.'[5]

As Professor Zalewski argued in the Geneva Conference of 1964 on Employment Problems of Automation and Advanced Technology, it is equally possible that supervision will not be made redundant but will become more crucial:

'Co-ordination of specialised tasks will become the prime function of the supervisor, while subordinates will be expected not only to supply information and report progress, but to identify problems and initiate proposals for their solution. Apart from giving orders, the supervisor will supply the general information that enables subordinates to direct their specialised activities towards the fulfilment of organizational objectives.'[6]

Zalewski sees the necessity for upholding the authority of supervisors 'for it is his function of co-ordinating diverse efforts towards a common goal that entitles him to make responsible decisions at a policy level'.[7] This argument finds some support from a case study of the introduction of a computer-controlled production control systems in an English factory:

'For example, the foreman has *now no responsibilities or worries concerning the planning of the work* in his section for weeks ahead; neither is he responsible for ensuring that the materials, tools, blueprints, etc. are physically available before he issues the work to a specific operative; nor to see that the sections responsible for prior operations are, in fact, keeping up to schedule, in order not to invalidate his own programme. All these facets are now part of the total scheme and no work authorities are issued to him unless all these prerequisites are satisfied. On the other hand his function as a manager of a team of men has been re-emphasised, his responsibility to see that they are adequately trained and competent for the tasks in hand, to ensure that machine tools are maintained and to assist in the continued effort to improve methods of manufacture. In all levels of management there exists, in differing degrees, *this tendency to anticipate difficulties, to be concentrating on tomorrow's needs* rather than the immediate problems of the day. Now the foreman gets a completely detailed work plan for two weeks ahead; the superintendent knows the plans for a month ahead; the production manager has the next four months under completely detailed analysis and review; the works manager has a whole twelve months' plan before him. Each in his turn has to make appropriate appraisals and decisions to ensure that plans laid down by top management are carried out.'[8]

The main issues at stake appear to be, therefore:

a. The degree to which centralization of decision making is demanded by the introduction of computers to assist managerial planning of production schedules, controls of scrap loss, maintenance programmes, etc.
b. The degree to which supervisors find their total functions restricted to organizational and leadership functions.
c. The degree to which the necessity for direct supervision of operative behaviour is eliminated by changes in the role of operators; i.e. by the development of complex man/machine *production systems in which 'operators' themselves are supervising and monitoring* the results of closed loop process control system.

With these problems, as with the other supposed effects of automation and computers, it is *desperately important to avoid yet another speculative debate*. We need further clarification of our hypotheses and we need detailed factual evidence. There is, unfortunately, very little systematic and objective data on supervisory roles and behaviour in the now extensive literature on automation. Fragmentary information can be gleaned from published case studies. Much more data is no doubt available within companies that have experienced the introduction of ADP and other types of computer-based systems. We can hardly hope to dispose of our problems with our current amount of data. It is however, important to consider the types of factors influencing supervisory behaviour under various technological systems, as this may provide some detailed clues, as to the *possible effects of the introduction of computers*.

RECENT STUDIES OF SUPERVISORY ROLES

It was argued in a previous paper,[9] that much of the research into supervision conducted by social psychologists was limited

180

ın its usefulness by its exclusive emphasis on leadership style. Researchers have been concerned to demonstrate the correlations or lack of correlations between varying aspects of individual supervisory behaviour and operative productivity and morale.[10] Recent studies of foremen roles in Sweden,[11] the Netherlands,[12] Finland,[13] in the United Kingdom,[14] and Japan[15] have tended to use observational and questionnaire methods in attempting to describe and analyse supervisory functions in a more comprehensive manner. A common objective of these studies appears to have been the attempts to obtain realistic information about training requirements, and many of the researchers have adapted their techniques from work study practice as well as psychological and survey research. One result has been the gradual compilation of case studies of supervisory behaviour in different types of technology. It is useful here to try to summarize the main characteristics of the supervisory role as described in such case studies.

1. *Supervisory systems.* Analysis of individual supervisory roles is greatly enriched by considering the interrelationships between roles as a 'supervisory system of control' over some or all aspects of a production system, i.e. plant, materials, men, and general process conditions. Membership of a supervisory system could be established by checking the degree to which the individuals concerned were directly and personally involved with shop floor problems and were recognized by operatives and managers as carrying authority and status in their role, above that of the ordinary operatives.

2. *Levels of supervision.* Supervisory systems thus vary from the single role to the multi-focal type. The levels show a gradation from roles which are semi-operative to those which are semi-managerial.

3. *Supervisory tasks.* The tasks performed show an enormous variation in content. *The supervisory role is an 'empty box' which is filled according to the situation.* There are no necessary common tasks for all supervisors. There may be, however,

    a. essential tasks necessary to meet minimum production requirements and which can only be performed by supervisors;

181

    b. tasks essential to the production system which could be performed by supervisors or by others;

    c. tasks which are not essential but valued by managers, supervisors, or operatives.[16]

4. *Types of supervisory system.* Systems can be classified according to functions performed or by the shape and complexity of the role system or by the degree of role specialization and interdependence between roles. Another important characteristic of each system is the degree to which the boundaries are defined and mutually agreed. Two crucial variables are the *degree of formalization of the role system* and the *level of skill and discretion shown by operatives being supervised.* These two factors can be combined as in Figure 1 to show four ideal types of supervisory system.

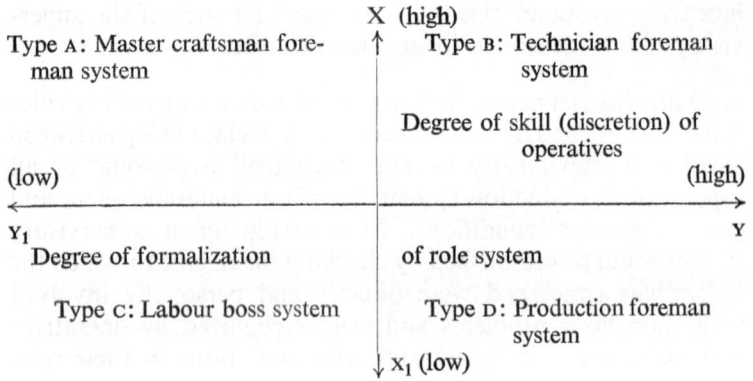

                                     X (high)

Type A: Master craftsman foreman system $\uparrow$ Type B: Technician foreman system

                             Degree of skill (discretion) of operatives

(low)   (high)

$\longleftarrow$ ——————————————————— $\longrightarrow$

Y_1 Y

  Degree of formalization   of role system

Type C: Labour boss system   Type D: Production foreman system

                            $\downarrow$ x_1 (low)

Figure 1
Types of supervisory system

5. *Supervisory functions.* These vary with the influence of many factors (see below) but they can be classified by the extent to which they involve predictable activities and tasks. Certain types of organization and environment provide numerous contingency problems which demand action by those within the supervisory system. Contingencies might include variations in the production process, shortages of raw materials or components unpredictable variations in performance by operatives, faults or breakdowns in plant, shortages of space, and so on. *The actions taken by supervisors to deal with contingencies appear to be the most critical parts of their role.* Although

adequate planning may make it possible to avoid certain types of problem, in reality it is beyond the influence and power of supervisors to affect the causes of many contingencies. Reactions to problems arising out of the production system are thus crucial.

6. *Typical organizational problem.* Difficulties experienced by supervisors with their roles reflect situations of 'role stress' as well as that of 'role ambiguity'.[17] *Supervisors operate in situations in which the correct performance standards are not decided; in which opinions differ as to priorities, and definitions of authority; and in which the main stimuli to action may come from requests and demands from a whole variety of persons – managers, supervisors, and operatives. A supervisor is found to respond to a number of 'messages' sent to him by persons in his role set. These messages may be contradictory and in this case the supervisor is* involved in the problem of conflicting expectations as to what he will do or should do. Gaps certainly exist between the perception of the supervisor's tasks by senior management and the tasks perceived by supervisors themselves or observed to be typical. 'They don't want to acknowledge any non-standard conditions, which we have all the time' (Superintendent quoted by Kahn *et al.*)[18] Such a gap reflects a blockage of upward communication from supervisors to management which appears to be widespread in large industrial organizations. Recent studies of supervision confirm that despite this, the most crucial role relationships for supervisors are with each other and with various managers. Relationships with their subordinates appear to be less significant or vital to them.

DETERMINANTS OF SUPERVISORY BEHAVIOUR

If these characteristics give us a broad picture of the supervisory role, can we go further and explain variations in role system behaviour patterns and attitudes?

In the paper quoted above[19] we discussed the relationship between the type of technology and the type of supervisory system. The conclusion was reached that there was no direct correlation but that many of the factors that were directly affecting supervisory behaviour, for instance the incidence of

plant breakdowns or changes in planning schedules, were themselves partly created by the type of technology. We are dealing
here with types of 'socio-technical systems', in which technical,
social, cultural, and economic factors are interdependent.[20]
One way of establishing the extent to which non-technological
factors are contributing to supervisory behaviour is to examine
similar technologies in differing cultures. A recent study[21] of
supervisory systems in Japan contained one observational
study of a steel-tube-making shop which was compared with a
study in a British factory making tubes. Superficially the
supervisory systems were not too dissimilar (Figure 2).

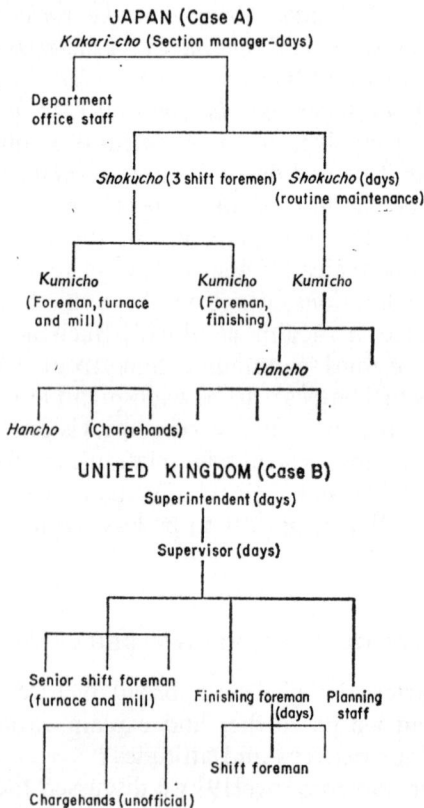

Figure 2

Supervisory systems in Japan and the United Kingdom
(steel tube manufacture)

184

Table 1   LOCATION OF WORK ACTIVITIES FOR
SUPERVISORS IN TWO TUBE MILLS
(*Average percentage of time at work*)
(*Tour method*)

	Own work area (Shop floor		Office	
	Japan	UK	Japan	UK
Shift foreman (mill)	31	66	53	18
Chargehand (mill)	60	74	18	2

If the location of work activities are examined (Table 1) the importance of office work in the Japanese case is underlined. Much of the observational data, however, showed considerable similarities in the proportions of time spent, for instance, on routine tasks or on meeting contingencies of various types (Table 2). The figures for observed contacts, which are shown in Figure 3, also have many similarities, although contacts with workers appear to be more numerous in the Japanese case.

Table 2   AVERAGE PERCENTAGE OF TIME AT WORK
SPENT IN ROUTINE TASKS OR IN MEETING
CONTINGENCIES

(*for supervisors in two tube mills*)
(*Tour method*)

Percentage of time spent in	UK (Mill foreman)	Japan (Kumicho)	UK (Charge-hand	Japan (Hancho)
Routine task contingencies:	43	47	49	59
(a) Problems given to supervisor		6	1	4
(b) Minor variations in plant, components, or human behaviour	9	13	7	6
(c) Major variations and breakdowns	11	3	6	1
(d) Problems due to introduction of new methods	4	8		1
(e) Problem due to shortages of materials or men	1	3		1
(f) Problems of communication failure	1	3		1

185

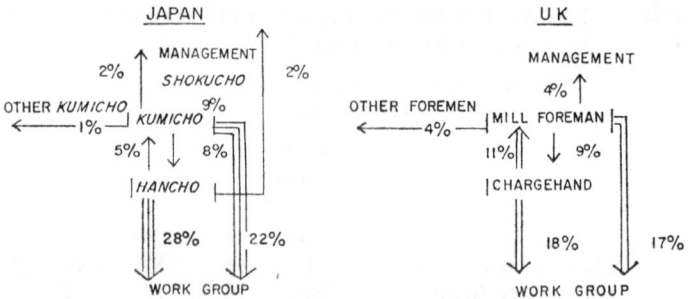

Figure 3

Observed communication network for four selected supervisory levels in
two tube works in Japan and the UK.
Average percentage of time spent (tour method) (face-to-face contacts)

Can we conclude (on the basis of these similarities) that
technology determines the shape of supervisory role behaviour?
They may well be used as *prima facie* evidence that 'essential
tasks' – demanded by the technology, exercise a strong influence
on the nature of supervisory work. The interview, questionnaire,
and discussion group data, however, showed that perceptions
of role and attitudes varied considerably between the two
systems. Broadly speaking, the Japanese supervisors showed a
certain contrast between the *Kumicho*, who were largely over
40 years old and who perceived their role as monitoring events
for senior management, and the *Hancho*, who were younger,
better educated, far more self-confident, and much more
identified with the shop floor workers. The confidence of the
mill foremen in their own authority stands out by contrast,
as well as the extremely limited formal responsibility of the
chargehands. In terms of Figure 1, one could say that the UK
supervisory system tended towards type A whilst the Japanese
case was nearer that of type D. A general conclusion from their
study and from the other nine companies studied in Japan was
that the Japanese supervisory systems showed a great deal of
deliberate organizational design by management, in contrast
with the reliance in Britain on traditional social patterns of
foremanship. In Japan, the status levels of lower and middle
management and management development systems show more
signs of a common traditional inheritance than the foreman

186

systems, which were often confused after much organizational reform.

This digression, therefore, teaches us that supervisory role behaviour is determined by a balance of influences arising from:

a. the production system and its demands;

b. the beliefs and plans of management for its supervisory control system;

c. the relative importance of traditional supervisory role systems in a particular industry's occupational system;

d. the social composition and characteristics of the work-force itself (education, aspirations, political beliefs, etc.).

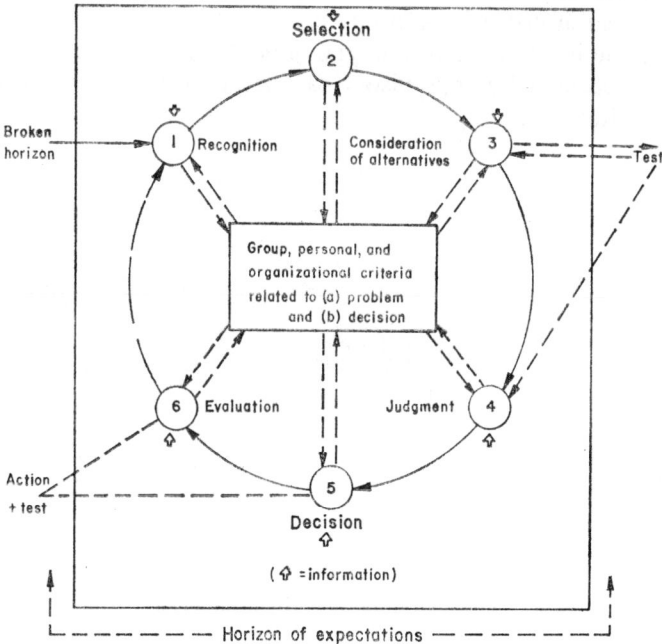

Figure 4

Problem solving for supervisors [22]

187

DECISION MAKING AND PROBLEM SOLVING FOR SUPERVISORS

If dealing with contingencies is important for supervisors, it is necessary to look at how they are dealt with. We can use a simple problem-solving model to clarify the activities involved (Figure 4).

This has been used to examine a number of cases of problem solving by construction site agents, foremen, and contracts managers on six building sites in the UK. Three conclusions stand out from this study –

   i. the importance of previous experience in shaping the type of problems recognized, in perceiving alternatives open and in learning appropriate strategies;

   ii. the importance of the attitudes of supervisors towards search procedures of any type;

   iii. the importance of the type of goals or objectives actually accepted by supervisors as relevant for their particular situation.

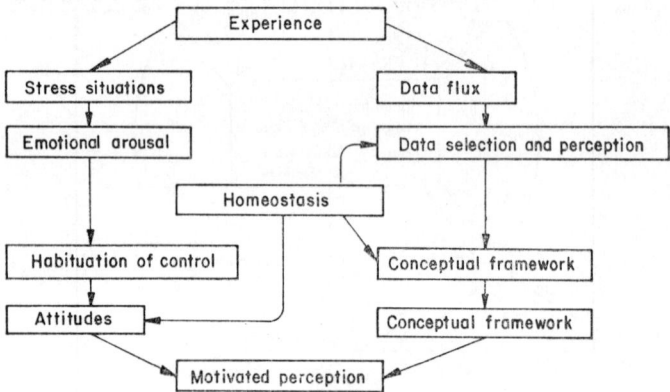

Figure 5
Perception modified by experience

These points are elaborated by Will Howells's model of perception as modified by experience[23] (Figure 5).

We can say here that there are tendencies for attitudes, ways of thinking, and facts perceived to be connected. If supervisors have learnt how to choose strategies entirely or largely from

188

observing other supervisors, if they feel that judgment from 'experience' is superior to 'academic' techniques of data collection, and if they are not expected by senior management to produce results from their problem solving (because managers do not expect or believe supervisors to be capable of decision making) – then we can readily understand why such problem solving is often ineffectual. The construction study showed many examples of supervisors 'patching' problems and trying to find temporary solutions which got them out of the immediate problem. In any fundamental difficulty, however, the problem remained unsolved.

Recent work by psychologists analysing the various types of methods of thinking have underlined three separate approaches.[24]

    a. use of memory to perceive relationships between variables;
    b. use of patterns (extrapolating from one set of relationships to another set);
    c. use of an operational strategy to test relationships between variables.

What we are saying is that supervisors in the UK construction study showed much evidence of stereotyped thinking or the use of deductions by patterned thinking, rather than operational thinking. The results of these strategies were satisfactory if the problem conformed to type and was a familiar one, e.g. allocation of work. In any new situation, or where the problem had to involve others across the boundary of the supervisory system, the response was usually quite inadequate. We can summarize our supervisory theory at this point by saying that supervisory effectiveness would seem to depend on how far the 'essential' supervisory tasks and problems arising from a given production system can be performed and solved by the supervisors with their *particular set of skills and attitudes, methods of thinking, and objectives. Where the rate of change is fast or where there is much variation in such production demands it requires the acceptance of operational strategies by supervisors and the support of management in their problem-solving role.*

INTRODUCTION AND APPLICATION OF COMPUTERS

Generalizations about the implications of automation or about the effects of using computers are frequently sterile because of the lack of precise definition of terms and the fast increasing variety of possible applications. Probably the best starting point is to take Professor Crossman's definition of automation as '*the replacement of human information processes by mechanical ones*'.[25] This enables him to build up a taxonomy of automation[26] based on nine characteristics of information processing (see Figure 6), as under:

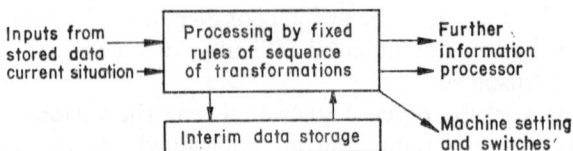

Figure 6

Information processing

1. Type of input data (digital, analog, or patterned)
2. Use of feedback (open or closed loop) for input data
3. Source of programme (fixed, preloaded, adaptive, or learning)
4. Type of programme (open chain, branching, looping, or heuristic)
5. Determining of programme (determinate or probablistic)
6. Size and type of memory (storage of current data)
7. Size and type of memory (storage of permanent data)
8. Type of output data (digital, analog, or patterned)
9. Timing of output data (either in step with input (real time) or indepent (off line)[27]

Another useful classification of types of computer control system is given by J. Rose.[28] He distinguishes between systems designed as stabilizing, control, optimizing a steady state system or optimizing a transient state system. The latter (as found in batch production of chemicals) is the most difficult to design and operate. These classifications are useful in allowing us to distinguish types of computer application and to identify precisely what aspects of information processing are being handled on the computer. They prevent generalization from particular cases and the illusion that total automation of management information systems is just round the corner

(Dearden).[29] In this article, Dearden argues that computers are best used when the data deals with interacting variables, and comprised accurate values. Where there is need for speed and were operations are repetitive, it is probably also true that computer investment will be most worthwhile as an economic investment. Otherwise, there are many barriers to the use and development of computer systems. As Emery remarks, 'Decision making and judgment cannot be reduced to the narrow band of formal logical structure to which computers are restricted.'[30]

SUPERVISION AND THE COMPUTER

Coming back to our first and central issue, can we say that supervisors are handling information processing, are operating faulty control systems; carrying out heuristic problem solving procedures in a limited and unsystematic way? Certainly. There could be many case studies showing such limitations. Are supervisory tasks capable of being handled automatically? The answer here seems to depend on the nature of the problem and task. Allocation of work and planning almost certainly could be handled in this way, inspection may be eliminated by the feedback controls in the process itself, and even disciplinary action could perhaps be expressed in a computer programme. It is more difficult to see how action to increase work motivation or the improvement of job methods could be dealt with by the computer. Nevertheless, there are few aspects of supervisory work that *theoretically* could not be assisted and perhaps transformed by the automation of information processing.

We do not really get to the heart of our problem until we consider the value to an *organization* of possessing a discrete set of roles and norms which we call a supervisory system. Collectively, within the sub-culture built up among the foremen there exists a complex memory of previous situations, actions, successes, and failures, earlier referred to as experience. The virtue of possessing such a memory store immediately at hand to production developments is the possibility of quick response based on local information (real knowledge of shop floor conditions). As argued previously, the shape of supervisory systems has up to now depended largely on historical accident, social conditions, and the type of technology. In Britain at least there is some evidence that the traditional systems are becoming disfunctional. Yet in complex technologies, where plant becomes increasingly interdependent, the need for accurate and operational thinking close to the area of operations becomes even more important. 'The time span of the supervisor's job is considerably extended in correspondence with the sorts of variability with which he is normally coping.'[31] Work on the application of computer-controlled planning systems to building contracts in Britain at the moment is clearly recognizing this point. The systems are usually planned to increase the amount of data available for site agents to take their decisions on weekly programmes. In many cases of developing automation, the emphasis has been placed on the importance of the know-how of the design and systems engineers.[32] The problem of communication between the analysts and supervisors and local management is commonly noted. It should be clear that we face grave difficulties in trying to develop designs for integrated control systems in ignorance of the 'memory' of operational strategies built up inside the traditional supervisory system. The actual strategies themselves, of course, may be inappropriate to a new production system. The point is that in the processes of developing the design and of gradually pushing forward with the objective of optimizing the methods of running the system, the earlier supervisory system can serve as a model and an indication of problems likely to be encountered. The arguments all point to the necessity of developing integrated teams of systems engineers and supervisors utilizing the experiences of the past for the current and future design activity.

THE APPLICATION OF A COMPUTER TO THE
PRODUCTION CONTROL SYSTEM FOR A SECTION OF A
STEEL TUBE WORKS IN THE LATE 1960s – A CASE
STUDY

The situation

A UK manufacturer decided to experiment with the use of a computer for assisting the planners dealing with a batch production shop of a steel tube works employing about 700 men. At the time of this decision, the sales were handled centrally by the company on a computer-based system. The orders came to the works and were then programmed manually by a central planning office. The programmes were then sent through to the production department. A simplified model of the system is shown in Figure 7.

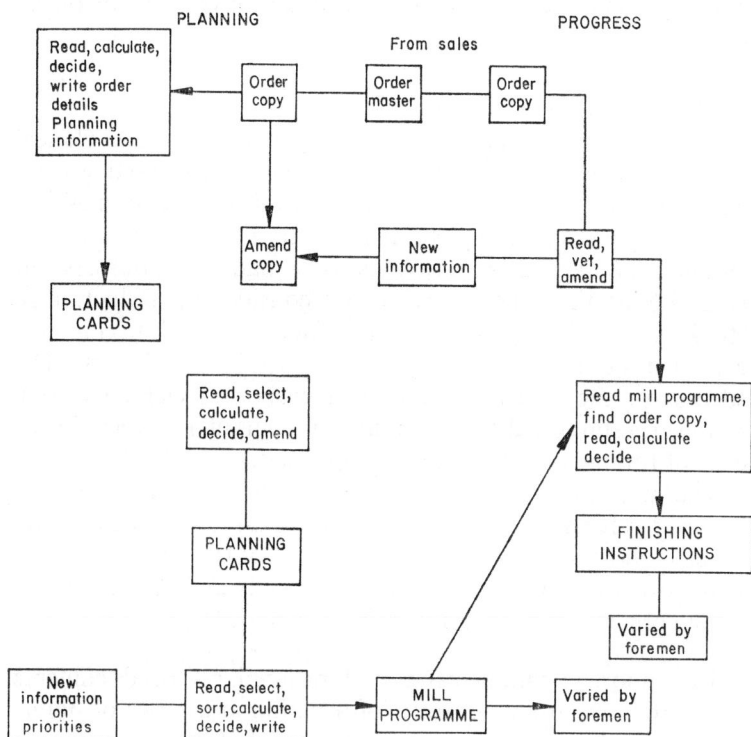

Figure 7

Planning and progress system pre-computer

This system did not prevent a large number of delivery dates being unfulfilled. Fifty-four were employed in the planning office. The programmes were sent out and then varied by the foremen according to production contingencies. The decisions taken by the foremen were critical because only they were in possession of up-to-date information about such contingencies.

Such decisions showed much awareness of the importance of factors immediate to the production process, but the result was not satisfactory because of gaps in the communication system between foremen and also because of their unawareness sometimes of critical factors external to the production situation (for example, the urgency of certain orders for particular customers). In particular, materials were wasted due to such communication gaps. By the time the finishing stage had been reached, planning often had to be done all over again on an ad hoc basis.

Introduction of the computer

The computer project was started by converting the clerical stock-taking system to a more efficient computer-based system. This took a programmer and an organization and methods man six months to complete. It involved a new documentation system and allowed large savings to be made in labour costs at stock-taking time. There was also a considerable reduction in stock levels. There was some resistance as stock-taking was regarded as a financial 'perk' or extra by employees. The success of the scheme in reducing costs and clerical errors, however, established the credibility of computer systems in the eyes of foremen, and middle management.

The main problem was then tackled by a series of training groups for foremen and clerks. They discussed the stock-taking scheme and then the overall planning problem. The proposed new system could be shown diagramatically as in Figure 8.

The crucial changes in this system included:

1. A more comprehensive and rational set of documents providing more accurate information at a series of points throughout the process, produced from a common source – the planning card master.
2. The splitting of the planning office into (*a*) a basic programming office and (*b*) an operations centre in the works itself, next to the foreman's office where replanning took place in collaboration with the foremen.

The system was introduced over an eighteen-month period. Some 60 foremen were involved as well as the 54 planning clerks. Anxieties grew in the latter; some three months after the start there was a crisis in the planning office over possible future redundancies. In the event, numbers were reduced to 40 clerks by natural wastage and redeployment. The operations centre was controlled by an ex-foreman and some of the younger, brighter clerks were transferred to this centre,

Effects

The effect on the production control system has been successful, in spite of difficulties raised by staff anxieties, the capacity of the computer used, and the accommodation available for the operations centre. The decisions on the actual order of the programme could be worked out in a realistic way, combining knowledge of urgency of orders with such factors as the reduction of changeover time, steel availability, and the loading of particular operations. The finishing foreman, in particular, now had more accurate and realistic instructions on the programme to be followed. The finishing flow-lines are now operating at a profit against standard cost of production, whereas before January 1968 there was usually a loss.

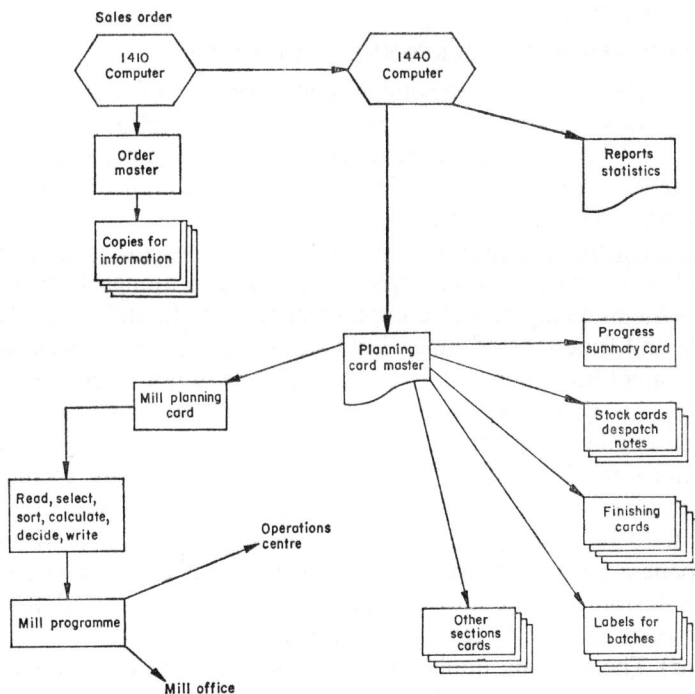

Figure 8

Proposed new system

195

The whole system allows little tolerance from instructions once the final programme has been decided. This reduces the old autonomy of foremen to decide the programme on their own initiative. It requires more awareness of the importance of planning and of the interconnection between decisions at one part of the process with those at another section. Organizationally, the old distinction between clerks and foremen in the operative centre is less in evidence. It is clear that the operations centre needs to be run on a team basis pooling ideas and knowledge from many parts of the system. The implication is the development of this centre with a new role and status for planners, closely allied to the role of the foremen. At the moment, there is some evidence that the older role system is preventing the full development of a computer planning system.

CONCLUSION

IMPLICATION FOR PERSONNEL POLICIES

(a) There are no inevitable consequences of the use of computers on supervision, because of the variations in such uses and in the types of supervisory system and behaviour in existence. We can only underline the type of choice open for personnel policy makers.

(b) On the question of organization, it is possible to keep a traditional system of supervision in existence alongside teams of systems analysts and computer engineers. In this case, the role and functions of supervisors will certainly be restricted to personnel functions and even these may be minor in character.

(c) An alternative is to try to develop teams of supervisors and engineers partly concerned with design, partly with optimizing the system. Such teams may eventually include operators as well, at least for part of their time. There would seem to be more possibility of developing such teams within Japanese industry than in the English case, if only because of the flexibility built into Japanese supervisory roles and their personal attitude to technical change.

(d) The training implications are fundamental if the course of action under (c) is favoured. Supervisors have helped to develop an operational method of thinking and the appropriate attitudes towards search procedures, change, and measurement.

This would require on-the-job training and probably the use of group problem-solving exercises off the job. In Britain and probably throughout Western Europe, some type of sensitivity, and group training will be necessary as well. In Japan, the training may require the reverse emphasis on individual work: the development of individual skills and thinking.

(e) Organizationally, managers would have to plan for a system of collective supervisory objectives, e.g. types of improvement, if the supervisors are to be supported in any new problem-solving role. It is clear that this would be disturbing in both the Japanese case and the British, for different reasons.

(f) Training of the systems analysts inevitably follows many personnel policy decisions. Probably they need experience in case study work and in management exercises and projects in order to develop their self-understanding and communication skills.

(g) A final and crucial point for personnel policy lies with the future selection and development of supervisors. It is unlikely to be true that traditional selection and promotion systems can be tolerated, if the other policies are carried out. As the size and nature of the supervisory problem expands, however (as with an integrated production system), the status of the supervisor as a 'shop floor' job could change radically. In this case, one can conceive of supervisory jobs being merely types of managerial work which most managers would experience at various stages in their career. A project system of organization would certainly make such a change more feasible.

NOTES

1 E. Leach, 'A runaway world, men and nature', *The Listener*, 16 November 1967, vol. 78, no. 2016, p. 621.

2 D. Michael, *Automation, the silent conquest*, New York: Vintage Books, 1962 (quoted by J. Rose, *Automation, its uses and consequences*, London: Oliver and Boyd, 1967, p. 117).

3 E. R. F. W. Crossman, *Automation and skill*, Problems of Progress in Industry, no. 9, DSIR, London: HMSO, 1960, p. 51.

4 H. Leavitt and T. Whistler, 'Management in the 1980s', *Harvard Business Review*, November/December, 1958.

5 *Automation and non-manual workers*, Labour and Automation Bulletin no. 5, Geneva: ILO, 1967, p. 21.

6 Andrzej Zalewski, 'The influence of automation on management', in J. Stieber (ed.), *Employment problems of automation and advanced technology – an international perspective*, London and New York: MacMillan, St Martins Press, 1966, p. 358.

7 *Ibid.* p. 358.

8 J. W. Grant, 'Production control system for Letchworth factory', *The electronic data processing symposium 1961*, London: Pitman, 1963, p. 43.

9 K. E. Thurley, 'Changing technology and the supervisor', in J. Stieber (ed.), *Employment problems of Automation and advanced technology – an international perspective*, London and New York: MacMillan, St Martins Press, 1966, pp. 334–53.

10 R. L. Kahn and D. Katz, 'Leadership practices in relation to productivity and morale', in D. Cartright and A. Zander (eds.), *Group dynamics, research and theory*, Harper and Row, 1961, pp. 554–70.

11 H. Wirdenius, *Supervisors at work*, Stockholm: P.A. 1958.

12 P. Hesseling, *Strategy of evaluation. Research in the field of supervisory and management training*, Van Gonum, 1966.

13 M. Lehesmoa (see H. Wirdenius, 'Formani arbete', 1961).

14 K. E. Thurley and A. C. Hamblin, *The supervisor and his job*, Problems of Progress in Industry, no. 13, London: HMSO, 1963; J. Kelly, 'The study of executive behaviour (by activity sampling)', *Human Relations*, vol. 17, no. 3, 1964, p. 277; Maria Pinschof, 'Notes on the role of production foreman in one case study', *Journal of Production Engineering*, vol. 3, no. 3.

15 K. E. Thurley, 'The foreman problem in Japanese industry', *Industrial Training International*, vol. 2, October 1967.

16 A. C. Hamblin, 'The nature of supervisory tasks', *Sociologie du Travail*, vol. 5, July/September 1963, p. 225.

17 R. L. Kahn, D. M. Wolfe, R. P. Quinn, and J. D. Snock, *Organizational stress*, New York: John Wiley, 1964.

18 *Ibid.* p. 342.

19 Thurley, 'Changing technology and the supervisor', p. 349.

20 F. E. Emery and E. L. Trist, 'Socio-technical systems', in *Proceedings of the 6th Annual International Meeting of the Institute of Management Sciences*, London and New York: Pergamon Press, 1960; *Management sciences, models and techniques*, vol. II.

21 The research is being reported in a series of articles in *Sangyo Kunren Zashi* (Industrial training), Japan Industrial and Vocational Training Association, Tokyo, May 1967 onwards.

22 J. Decks, S. A. Majid, M. Pinschof, and K. E. Thurley 'Problem-solving behaviour in construction project management', unpublished paper given to Anglo-Swedish conference on human factors in the construction process, Sept. 1967.

23 W. Howells, 'Managers and systems', *Journal of Management Studies*, vol. 3, no. 2, May 1966, pp. 150–62.

24 Z. P. Dienes, *Thinking in structures*, London: Hutchinson, 1965.

25 E. R. F. W. Crossman, 'European experience with the changing nature of jobs due to automation', in *The requirements of automated*

jobs. N. American Conference Final Report, OECD 1965, p. 161 (italics author's).

26 E. R. F. W. Crossman, 'Taxonomy of automation – state of the arts and prospects', in *Manpower aspects of automation and technical change. European Conference Supplement to Final Report,* OECD 1966, p. 75.

27 Figure 6 is from *Ibid,* p. 81; points 1–9 from p. 83.

28 Rose, *Automation, its uses and consequences,* pp. 8–9.

29 J. Dearden, 'Can management information be automated?', *Harvard Business Review,* March/April 1964, p. 128.

30 F. E. Emery 'The Next Thirty Years: Concepts, Methods and Anticipations'. *Human Relations,* vol. 20, no. 3, 1967, p. 232.

31 F. E. Emery and J. Marek, 'Some socio-technical aspects of automation', *Human Relations,* vol. 15, no. 1, 1962.

32 H. N. Laden and T. R. Gildersleeve, *System design for computer applications,* New York: John Wiley, 1966.

8 Hotel Pilferage: A Case Study in Occupational Theft

GERALD MARS

INTRODUCTION

The data to be discussed principally concerns institutionalized pilferage as this was observed in a hotel – one of a number of industrial situations in which I have collected material as a participant observer and one of several where pilferage was widespread.* The intention was not, however, specifically to examine pilferage. Observation of and participation in pilferage were by-products of an anthropologist's modified field approach or through working in a number of jobs before receiving formal anthropological training – what can be termed 'retrospective participant observation'.† Material on the hotel was in part obtained as a worker and suffers, of course, from the

---

* These include fairgrounds, stores, bars and docks. In addition, material has been collected but not supplemented by my own participation from informants working within medical departments of the National Health Service, in public parks and in a public corporation.

† There has been a considerable amount of journalism on this topic but little sociological study. Indeed, academic authors appear largely to have ignored the phenomenon even when knowledge of it could hardly have been avoided. Thus, in representative textbooks of industrial sociology [1], no mention is made of pilferage or theft at work despite it obvious implications for other aspects of work relationships. Even in monographs covering specific 'pilferage prone' industries such as docks [2] and restaurants [3], the topic remains unexplored.

One of the notable exceptions to the general silence is well reported by [4]. Another is provided by a recent book of readings on various aspects of deviance in bureaucracies, including pilferage (Smigel and Ross [5]).

It appears likely that researchers, especially if they have been participant observers, have not missed details of pilferage nor failed to realise its significance, but that they have not wished to intrude on three sets of vested interests. These are, firstly, the interests of workers who benefit by the practice. Secondly, the interests of management who collude with workers as part of an indulgency pattern which, as they perceive it, may permit calm industrial relations and, I

dangers of possible selective recall. As is usual in participant observation, there are dangers too in generalizing from a single case. Inquiry would suggest, however, that the techniques of pilferage found in the hotel have a considerably wider application.

Discussion of the case will compare certain aspects of hotel pilferage with pilferage as this was observed in dock work-gangs and which are more fully recorded elsewhere[7].

In dock work-gangs a regularly hired body of twenty-six men were found organized together to unload cargo. Some work tasks facilitated access to cargo but access alone was insufficient for safe pilferage and had to be buttressed by the support of other workers in the gang. Support was offered from within the gang by checkers, who would falsify paperwork; by fork drivers who would stack cargo into barriers so supervisors could not see illegitimate activity; and by signallers who acted as look-out men whilst carrying on their normal work. The gang foreman, though formally responsible for hiring, firing and the discipline of his men, had no role in pilferage. Even his formal powers of hiring and firing were considerably modified by the collective action of the gang who could threaten collective restrictions on output if a foreman acted in ways perceived as being against gang interests. If a gang found unacceptable new inductees introduced by the foreman, for instance, they would threaten a slow up. A similar result would follow the dropping of a man regarded as integral to the gang. One important criterion for gang membership was a man's participation in and the security of his behaviour in respect of pilferage. This meant not only that he be seen to participate but that he act within the limits on quantity and type of cargo which normally apply. Labour turnover in the gangs was extremely low and the gangs emerge in many respects as typical solidary work groups[8].

The turnover of waiting staff in hotels, on the other hand, tends to be extremely high – in the case study hotel it approached

suspect, the payment of below market wages; and, thirdly, the interest of the researcher himself who may, on ethical grounds, be reluctant to disclose information much of which he may have received in confidence. When to these interests are added the claims of scientific truth it is evident that the question of ethics involves irreducible conflicts, a position taken by Becker in discussion of associated fieldwork problems. (In McCall and Simmons [6], pp. 260–275.)

30 per cent per year – whilst wages paid by any comparable standards are low. Corporation bus conductors in the same city, for instance, doing a job requiring less skill, averaged approximately 25 per cent more direct take-home pay for about 30 per cent less hours. Both of these factors, high labour turnover and low wages, were used by waiters to justify the industry's institutionalization of pilferage – the overall term for which, in hotels as in many other places, is 'the fiddle'. 'Knock off', a common expression among hotel staffs, refers to a sub-type of fiddle, the illicit obtaining of concrete benefits – usually food or artifacts such as cutlery and linen. Present attention, however, is devoted to money fiddles in the hotel's dining-room and lounges, and how this was organized by waiting staff. It should be mentioned that this type of fiddle is not usually obtained at the expense of customers, but at the expense of the hotel – unlike bar fiddles, for instance, which are frequently at the expense of customers. It is distinct too from the theft of guests' personal possessions which is regarded by waiters as deviant and, when it occurs, which is rare, is simply called 'theft'. It is important too to realize that fiddles are regarded as a legitimate entitlement – as part of wages. A typical comment from a very skilful and highly trained waiter on this issue was, 'Who'd work for £12. 10s. a week for the hours I put in? No one but a bloody nutcase, I can tell you. Fiddles are a part of wages. The whole issue runs on fiddles, it couldn't work otherwise.'

Data was obtained unsystematically from the staff of a 200-bedroomed hotel in Blackpool, a seaside resort in the north of England. Its dining-room, like those of most hotels, is open to non-residents and it employs twenty waiting staff. I had previously worked in smaller establishments, and these provided essential background knowledge of the technical organization involved. These experiences, however, were prior to and supplementary to cross-checked information from informants.

THE ORGANIZATION OF HOTEL PILFERAGE

Hotel restaurant organization is basically universal. Food, prepared behind the scenes in kitchens and stillrooms, is taken to dining-rooms and lounges where it is consumed and paid for. The problem for the fiddler is to obtain goods from their source, direct it to his own account, and obtain and pocket the payment at its destination. This means that if three meals are booked out of the kitchen and he receives payment for four he can then pocket the difference. His difficulties in this matter arise partly from the systems of accounting adopted by hotels, partly from the vigilance of higher management and partly because, though a level of pilferage is tolerated by management this varies at different times and for different people. There is thus a large element of ambiguity and insecurity concerning management's acceptable level at any one time.

Dining-rooms, and restaurants where their scale of operations is large enough, attempt to limit fiddles by the employment of a checker, sometimes called a control clerk. It is the checker's primary job to sit at a desk between the kitchen and the dining-room, account for food passing from one to the other, and see this tallies with the waiters' cash receipts. A secondary aspect of his job is to ensure that correct-sized portions are served – Whyte's classic study of restaurants[3] refers only to this secondary task of the checker: he ignores the likelihood of pilferage in his treatment of the role.

Most accounting systems simply involve the waiter's exchange of dockets for food. A waiter takes an order for, say, two meals, writes out a docket, and exchanges this at the kitchen for his meals which he then takes to his customer and for which he receives payment. At the end of the day his cash receipts should tally with his exchange of dockets. The fiddles system hinges on tactics employed by the waiter to get unrecorded food past the checker. How does a waiter beat the checker? In essence the method can be understood by describing its simplest form, which occurs in hotel lounges.

In lounges serving coffee and tea, fiddling is often extremely simple. A waiter receives an order for, say, two coffees. He goes to the kitchen, orders a single coffee, fills in a docket and passes it to the checker. In return he obtains a standard coffee pot, a standard milk jug and one cup and saucer. The problem is to convert this single coffee to two coffees and his first requirement is for extra cups and saucers. These are frequently hidden in strategic areas in or near the lounge. Crockery may be kept behind a flower display, behind curtains, even carried in pockets – anywhere out of direct contact with authority. A waiter's second requirement is for strong enough beverages; coffee and tea ordered for two may be too weak if served to three. This often requires a 'bent' helper in the kitchen who can supply larger quantities than the lesser order would merit or stronger beverages that can more readily be watered. Supplies of extra hot water do not usually cause problems. Bent helpers are usually repaid in beer, rarely in cash.

A third difficulty concerns the dockets. Those a waiter issues to a customer (known as a 'punter') and those he passes to the checker are often carbon duplicates so they may more readily tally. There are various ways round this problem:

(a) Writing can be made deliberately ambiguous. For example, fives can be made to look like threes; the customer accepts the five; the clerk accepts the three.
(b) Waiters often have a 'spare' docket book.
(c) If the waiter can retrieve the copy docket passed to the checker's desk after she has received it, this can then be re-used. One method involves the use of a wet tray placed on top of the docket which then sticks to its underside when the tray is moved. Another is to distract the clerk; an accomplice waiter, for instance, can cause an argument. A third involves different varieties of 'bending' the checker, ranging from bribery and flattery to subtle deception.

One very experienced middle-aged waitress with a whimsical turn of humour recounted what happened when she moved to a new job in a coffee lounge. 'I said "six coffees". That shook them. They all looked at me as if I was bloody daft! That way everyone thought I was the most innocent one there was. No one [waiter] had ever ordered more than two coffees in that place.' They thought her innocent because a group of six could very easily have been 'knocked' – whereas groups of two or three are more difficult, it being easier to convert four coffees to six than to convert one coffee to three – yet the gain, two coffees, is the same in each case. Her reputation for naïveté established with the checker, she was then able to fiddle without being suspected.

The more lucrative dining-room fiddles, though following the same basic procedure as to dockets and crockery, are much more complex than are lounge fiddles. These complexities derive from three main sources. In the first place, whereas in lounges most people pay cash, in dining-rooms only non-residents do so; residents have accounts linked to their room number and pay at the end of their stay. It is therefore only through non-residents that fiddles can be obtained. There are two classes of non-residents – those that book meals in advance and those who enter the hotel without prior notice. Tables booked in advance are useless to fiddlers since such bookings are known to the hotel management via the receptionist; it is, therefore, only casual non-resident punters who are good for fiddles. Such punters are called by the generic term 'chance'. Whereas in hotel dining-rooms chance punters are a minority, in restaurants nearly all customers are, of course, chance.

A second distinction between dining-rooms and lounges concerns the systems of accounting which make dining-room fiddling easier. The office of checker exists in both, but the job in dining-rooms would be so complex if all courses of all meals were checked that checking usually applies only to the main courses of meals. If a waiter can 'knock' the main course of a meal he is, therefore, easily able to fiddle the *entire* cost of that meal. Sometimes it is necessary or customary with certain main-course dishes that these be kept in the dining-room if they are to tempt the punter: they therefore bypass the checker. Roast beef on the joint is, for instance, often so displayed. If you are a chance punter where this dish appears on the menu the odds are high that the waiter will feel he 'can certainly recommend the roast beef tonight, sir'!

A third, and the most significant, complication in dining-rooms that is absent from lounges concerns the office of Head Waiter. He is formally responsible for hiring and firing his waiters, overseeing the dining-room and booking in chance punters. These he allocates to their tables and therefore to the waiters who will serve them. The power of a Head Waiter in relation to his waiters is, therefore, considerable and an understanding of his role central to any consideration of dining-room fiddles.

Head Waiters vary as to their 'hardness' or 'softness'. A 'hard' Head Waiter asks for and obtains an accepted upper maximum of 50 per cent of fiddles; a 'soft' Head Waiter, particularly a second or third (deputy) Head Waiter, may receive much less. In return for his kickback a Head Waiter is expected to allocate chance punters, provide services facilitating fiddles and 'cover' any waiter to whom he has allocated a chance party that goes wrong. That is, he must use his office to defend subordinates against higher management. He must, for instance, restrain any tendency of an angry chance punter who has been knocked from complaining on any account to the manager. If this happened and the manager were to check the punter's bill the fiddle would be evident. Managers are usually outside the fiddle system.

Since the supply of chance is limited, its allocation to any one waiter is seen as being at the expense of others. This makes a Head Waiter's job extremely complex: he aims to keep all his waiters happy but cannot do this by a simple rotation of chance among them. Some waiters are cleverer than others at dealing with chance; others are more skilled, have wider experience or longer service, and all these categories merit, or believe they merit, extra increments.

It is this zero sum characteristic of chance, together with the absence of an unambiguous criterion for its allocation, that goes some way to explain why inter-staff squabbles are frequent and why they appear to be an institutionalized characteristic of hotel dining-rooms. This is one reason also why alliances between waiters are uncommon. Though the distracting of checkers is best effected by two waiters operating together, and the sharing of crockery stacks is obviously of mutual benefit, such alliances are relatively uncommon and when they occur are frequently short lived.

Hotel managements are well aware of the institutionalization of much, at least, of what has been described. On the rare occasions a new and ignorant management has attempted to stop fiddling it has quickly found that staff protest with their feet; this is scarcely surprising when the low level of hotel wages is appreciated.

What managements usually do is to structure hotel situations to *limit* fiddle opportunities rather than aim to eradicate them. One of the ways they do this is by employing checkers, as described above. Another is to structure an opposition of the interests of Head Waiters and Chefs. Chefs are responsible for buying as well as cooking the food consumed in a hotel, and for accounting. Frequently they are given a 'percentage' for extra production out of a given stock and this, therefore, gives them a strong incentive to work closely with the checker to limit fiddles. These controls can on occasion, however, provide a two-edged weapon for management. In one hotel the Chef who received a 'percentage' and the female checker were believed to be in alliance for their own benefit, and were accordingly known as 'Bonnie and Clyde'. In spite of their benefits from this alliance the overall level of fiddles was drastically reduced. The staff, however, including the Head Waiter, left to work elsewhere. More serious for a hotel are situations where a bent Chef and a Head Waiter work in unison. As one waitress explained, 'When that happens it's really diabolical.' Another waitress, after describing the expostulations of a very experienced hotel owner/manager, said, 'Well, you couldn't blame him really – some of them were really diabolical.'

This use of the word 'diabolical', frequently uttered by waiters, refers to a level – whether of money fiddle, bar or knockoff – that is considered too high for safety and likely, therefore, to disturb the *status quo*. There are, however, no group sanctions applied against such 'diabolical' waiters.

It is interesting in this respect to quote the manager concerned in this case as an indication of his acceptance of an institutionalized level of pilferage. He said, 'You wouldn't be worth your weight in salt if you couldn't make a wage for yourself – but Christ! leave me a bit!'

DISCUSSION AND IMPLICATIONS

Two facilities are found necessary for pilferage to occur. First, and self evidently, men must have or be granted *access* to goods. Second, access alone is rarely sufficient to ensure security in pilferage: for this to be achieved it frequently needs to be backed by the *support* of others. It is in the distribution of these two facilities and the alliances which follow such distribution that a system can be seen.

In the docks, group interests are paramount and individual interests correspondingly minimal. This is, of course, to large extent derived from the interrelated nature of work tasks that are technically determined. Men inducted into the dock work-gang have to prove – often over considerable periods of time – that they are in all respects 'trustworthy'. Trust in this context means both an assured technical and a social competence as

207

these apply both to legitimate and to illegitimate tasks. It was found that, in their organization of pilferage, access and support functions in the dock work gang are differentially allocated *within* the group such that no one individual can exert a monopoly over either feature. Control is internal and dispersed; autonomy lies with the group and no one man can act individually without incurring effective group sanctions. In effect it is the group which is seen to exercise social controls. Pilferage is not only organized and effected by the group, but its limits – both of type and of quantity also – are determined and controlled by the group as are also questions concerning output and, to a large extent, recruitment, though this, as in the hotel, is formally the foreman's responsibility.

In hotels the situation is very different. The solidary work group is absent, turnover high, individualism paramount and workers' orientation to their jobs seen as individually instru-mental[9]. Yet fiddlers in hotels, as in docks, still require combinations of access and support if fiddling is to be secure. In hotels both access and support, however, are mediated through and monopolised in one role – that of the Head Waiter. Instead of control over both functions being vested in the workers themselves, as in docks, the monopoly of access and support in hotels, located as it is in a single external source, means that control is vested in that source.

We have thus in both situations systems of pilferage facilities that are linked to systems of legitimate work roles. These run in parallel and act in alliance so that access and support roles derived from legitimate tasks work in harness to facilitate non-legitimate tasks. The granting, possession and possibility of the withdrawal of access and support – in a word, the *control* – over essential components in the covert system, however, necessarily involves relationships of power. Thus it is that we are enabled, by appreciating the covert pilferage system, to examine power relationships on a different dimension and with new insights,* and to account for factors affecting its incidence that might otherwise be ignored. We can see how

* The use of the categories covert/overt, legitimate/illegitimate is not to suggest that the actors themselves see their behaviour in these terms. Indeed, their ideology can be understood as legitimising the illegitimate whilst what is termed 'covert' is only made so to outsiders. The categories as used here are abstractions for explanation.

power derived from legitimate office, the office of foreman, for instance, may be buttressed or negatived by that office's position relative to a covert socio-technical system. We are particularly able, therefore, to throw a new light on inter-worker relations and on the perennial problems of first-line supervisors in situations where pilferage is institutionalized.

Using this analysis we can appreciate that a waiter is parti-cularly vulnerable to the power of his Head Waiter, *not only* because a Head Waiter has control of hiring and firing but also in that he is able to apply a brake on access or to withdraw essential support in ways quite impossible for a dock foreman. This is so since a Head Waiter's legitimate power derived from his monopoly of access/support both act together to determine his *total* power position *vis-à-vis* subordinates.

Dock foremen, on the other hand, who are also formally responsible for hiring and firing but who find themselves external to the covert socio-technical system, are able only to operate control derived from their (overt) office. In doing this, however, they face a solidary work group whose legitimately derived solidarity is further enhanced by non-legitimate access/support solidarity. In contrast to dock foremen, however, hotel Head Waiters find themselves in a situation where solidaristic tendencies of their subordinates are negatives on both covert *and* on overt levels. The presence of institutionalized pilferage is thus seen to have very different effects on the role of first-line supervisor in the two situations. For the Head Waiter, pilferage buttresses his authority, whilst for the dock foreman its institutionalized presence can only be understood as detracting from his.

In advocating the importance of covert social organization it is not suggested that the place of institutionalized pilferage in determining work relationships is greater than the place played by other factors (such as class, age, sex or ethnic category) which also contribute to the articulation of roles at work. What is suggested, however, is that the study of covert social organization based on pilferage is relevant to the interests of industrial sociologists because it *parallels* in the workplace what I have called the overt social organization. In this the systematic study of pilferage can be rated with studies of work restriction.

What is required in studies of work relationships, it is suggested, is awareness of the importance of the covert and the

O

illegitimate where these appear to be institutionalized. Indeed, we must look with suspicion on studies that ignore or underplay these factors. Whereas this paper has only considered them in brief outline as they influence work groups relations and the role of supervisors, it is considered that the analysis could usefully be extended, particularly to illumine aspects of work socialization, the control of recruitment by workers, and the linkage of work and non-work. There is thus scope for examining the influence of covert work roles as these articulate with occupational career, life and family cycles.

An understanding of these factors and of changes (and proposed changes) in the workplace which are perceived as disturbing to covert relativities can prove useful in suggesting reasons for unrest in specific situations, particularly where changes to the overt system bring unknown and often unanticipated changes in the covert system.

NOTES

1 D. C. Miller and W. H. Form. 1963. *Industrial Sociology*. New York: Harper & Row.
   E. V. Schneider. 1969. *Industrial Sociology*. New York: McGraw-Hill.
   S. R. Parker, *et al.* 1968. *The Sociology of Industry*. London: George Allen & Unwin.
2 T. S. Simey. 1955. *Dock Worker*. Liverpool University Press.
3 W. F. Whyte. 1948. *Human Relations in the Restaurant Industry*. New York: McGraw-Hill.
4 M. Dalton. 1959. *Men Who Manage*. New York: Wiley.
5 E. O. Smigel, and H. L. Ross. 1970. *Crimes against Bureacracy*. New York: Van Nostrand Reinhold.
6 G. J. McCall, and J. L. Simmons, 1969. *Issues in Particpant Observation*. Reading, Mass.: Addison-Wesley.
7 G. Mars. 1972. *An Anthropological Study of Longshoremen and of Industrial Relations in the Port of St. John's, Newfoundland, Canada.* Ph.D. Thesis: London University.
   —— 1973. In Press. Dock Pilferage: A Case Study in Occupational Theft, in *Explorations in Sociology* Series No. 3. Social Control and Deviance (Provisional Title). Ed. Rock, P. and McIntosh, M.: London: Tavistock.
8 Goldthorpe, *et al.* 1968. 'The Affluent Worker: Industrial Attitudes and Behaviour', *Cambridge Studies in Sociology* No. 1, Cambridge University Press.
9 Goldthorpe, *et al., op. cit.*

9 Relative Deprivation, Occupational Status, and Occupational 'Situs': the Theoretical and Empirical Application of a Neglected Concept

EARL HOPPER AND ADAM PEARCE

INTRODUCTION

The purpose of this article is three-fold: to call attention to the little-known and much-neglected concept of occupational 'situs' and its empirical referents; to present data which demonstrate how important it is to consider situs classifications in any study which delimits sub-samples in terms of occupations; and to suggest a few reasons why variations in situs have such strong effects on a large number of diverse personal and interpersonal characteristics. The article attempts to summarize a considerable amount of data, and to convey how a complex theory might be applied to the findings. Thus, several of the issues raised are not resolved.

1. *The concept of situs*

The concept of situs is defined as

'a category of occupations which is differentiated from other categories according to any number of criteria other than or in addition to economic and status bestowal values. For example, whereas manual work in a manufacturing industry differs from clerical work in the same industry in terms of economic and status criteria, it also differs from manual work in service or agricultural industries in terms of situs criteria, e.g. "indoor" versus "outdoor", contact with jobs versus contact with people, etc. The occupations within situses can of course be ranked in terms of their economic and status rewards. By definition, some of the occupations in one situs will bestow economic and status rewards which are identical to those bestowed by some of the occupations in another situs; but in order that one situs be differentiated from another it is not necessary for all the occupations in one to be identical in this respect to all the occupations in another. One situs might contain a number of occupations which are either higher or lower, or both, in economic and status rewards than the occupations in another situs. And the occupations in one situs might all be either higher or lower in economic and status rewards than the occupations in another, but nonetheless be equivalent to all the occupations in still a third situs. Consequently, situses as such are also ranked with respect to the economic and status hierarchies, but such a ranking is difficult to ascertain, and is likely to be of value only in special circumstances.'[1]

The criteria by which occupations are categorized into situses depend on the purposes of a specific study. For example, 'in studies of stratification and mobility [situses are found to] vary with respect to such [criteria] as opportunities to develop mobility orientations and to become mobile, and to potentials for the formation of comparative reference groups and membership groups based on the occupation'.[2] In so far as the present volume is concerned with personal and inter-personal aspects of participation in a job and occupation, the criterion used here is 'economic function', in general. This gives rise to the following situs classifications: distribution; manufacturing; finance and insurance; agriculture; building and transport; communications; civil service, church, military, and government; education; and medicine and health.

2. *The development of the concept and a brief review of the literature*

The preceding list of situses is similar to the standard industrial classification used in the census of England and Wales. In fact, such classifications were made on a common sense empirical basis long before they were considered theoretically.[3] They were used quite early on, for example, in economic-geography as 'primary, secondary and tertiary industries',[4] and in management studies as 'technical, commercial, financial, security, accounting and managerial activities'.[5]

Attempts to consider such classifications theoretically came much later. In 1944 Benoit-Smullyan used the concept of situs to define 'an aggregate of persons essentially distinguished by any common characteristics except status or locus'.[6] He distinguished situses from strata, which were ranked hierarchically in terms of status, and differentiated, by way of example, in terms of sex and clan. When sociologists began to concentrate on occupations as the basis of social stratification, Lloyd Warner, as well as Hatt, used the concept to help clarify the anomalies of status rankings as bestowed by occupations.[7] These initial attempts to introduce 'situs' into the stratification literature as an empirically grounded concept met with limited success. Although it was the mixture of 'vertical' and 'horizontal' properties of occupations which necessitated the use of the concept, this mixture also made horizontal classifications of occupations extremely difficult.

Hatt applied 'situs' to clarify the ranking scale of occupational prestige. He found that ranks assigned to different occupations did not scale well enough to be represented by a single underlying prestige dimension. Therefore, he grouped his occupational categories into various situses according to 'the criterion of similar relationship between occupation and the consuming public. That is, the selling relation, the client-professional relation, etc., were taken as the criterion for the first rough classifications.[8] In this way he obtained eight situses: political; professional; business; recreation and aesthetics; agriculture; manual work; military; and service. These were further divided into 'occupational families', which 'were not conceived as being families in the sense of possessing relatively equal *amounts* of prestige, but as categories constituting parallel status ladders'.[9] He found that whereas the occupations within each family could be scaled, the broader situs classifications could be so treated in only a very approximate way.[10]. The eight situses were not equivalent in the prestige of their occupations, as indicated by the mean, range, or variation of their prestige rankings. Hence, the situs distinction was essential for the construction of scales of occupational prestige. Through his choice of such distinctions as 'manual' and 'business', however, Hatt continued to conflate the horizontal and vertical dimensions of occupations. This prevented a more widespread use of his concept.

The problem was solved by Morris and Murphy in 1959.[11] They employed the criterion of 'societal function' to obtain sets of occupations with 'equal status evaluations' within each category. In other words, they developed a list of situses each of which contains a large number of occupations which bestow a full range of ranked status positions. For every occupation in any one situs there is at least one occupation in each of the other situses which has an equal prestige rank, although the mean of the distribution of prestige ranks of any one situs is not necessarily equal to the mean of any other. It then made empirical sense to employ 'situs' as a 'horizontal' dimension of occupational classifications, and 'status' as a 'vertical' one. They developed ten situses for civilian occupations: legal authority; finance and records; manufacturing; transportation; extraction, including agriculture; building and maintenance; commerce; arts and entertainment; education and research; and health and welfare.

Following the article by Morris and Murphy, there has been little discussion of the concept or the problem. Miller and Swanson distinguished 'bureaucratic welfare' from 'individuated entrepreneurial' occupational settings in their study of *The changing American parent*.[12]. Many studies have shown that 'professions and professionals' differ from non-professions and their personnel in a variety of ways.[13] Research has indicated that not all bureaucracies are alike, and that categories of bureaucratic organizations are needed.* In general, however, even these kinds of distinctions have been rare, and the situs concept has not been used to explain the differences either between or within these categories. Whereas the literature on social stratification and social mobility has long argued that in principle the situs concept must be employed, especially in comparative studies of rates of social mobility,[14] it has been used empirically only once, in a second article by Morris and Murphy.[15] They found that variations in both subjective

* Some of these studies will be mentioned subsequently.

class identification and voting behaviour could be accounted for by variations in situs. A search of a dozen introductory texts disclosed only one reference,[16] and as late as 1969 Hall wrote: 'the situs concept is . . . a useful, but as yet undeveloped, addition to the understanding of occupational status'.[17]

SELECTED PROPERTIES OF SITUS-CLASSIFIED PERSONNEL

1. *Scope and method*

The data to be presented here are taken from a large study of the personal and inter-personal characteristics of 183 men who in 1965 were between 32 and 40 years of age, and who had various career structures and 'patterns of either social mobility of non-mobility'.[18] The sample lived in various parts of England and Wales, but primarily in large urban centres. They were interviewed during 1965–6. Although certain major public schools were represented, the balance of the sample attended local authority primary schools, grammar schools, and then entered either the labour market, the University of Leicester, or the University of Cambridge. The social class and educational properties of this sample will be considered in more detail below. It is impossible to provide here further information concerning the experimental design, the method of data collection, or the sample itself.* The sample is not random, and the findings should be inferred to a wider population with caution. In other words, this study employs secondary analyses of data which were not collected specifically for a study of situs, but can be examined in terms of the situs concept.

The distribution of the sample by occupational situs, adult social class position, and educational route and amount is shown in Table 1.

To obtain the adult social class positions the sample were classified according to a revised version of the Hall-Jones scale.[19] Social class I, which might be called upper and upper-middle social class, is represented by such occupations as: higher levels of management, university professors, medical consultants, etc. Social class II, which might be called middle-middle social class, is represented by such occupations as:

* Further information is available upon request.

Table 1 SOCIAL CLASS AND EDUCATIONAL ROUTE FOR SELECTED SITUSES

SITUS	Social class	Major public school to Cambridge university	Grammar school to Cambridge University	Grammar school to Leicester University	Grammar school only – 3 or more 'O' levels	Grammar school only – less than 3 'O' levels	ALL N	ALL %	Mean educational amount*	Mean social class†
Distribution	I	1	1	4	1		7	37		
	II			3	2	4	9	47		
	III				2	1	3	16		
	ALL	1	1	7	5	5	19	100	·79	·79
Manufacturing	I	3	7	13			23	62		
	II		1		3	1	5	14		
	III				3	6	9	24		
	ALL	3	8	13	6	7	37	100	·54	·62
Finance	I	3	6				9	56		
	II		1		3	2	6	38		
	III				1		1	6		
	ALL	3	7		4	2	16	100	·50	·50
Government	I	1	11	4			16	76		
	II			1	3		4	19		
	III				1		1	5		
	ALL	1	11	5	4		21	100	·19	·29
Education	I	1	24	24			49	79		
	II		2	9	2		13	21		
	III									
	ALL	1	26	33	2	2	62	100	·03	·21
TOTAL (including other situses with 10 or fewer representatives)	I	21	53	46	4	8	124	68		
	II		4	13	18	9	43	23		
	III				7		16	9		
	ALL	21	57	59	29	17	183	100	·34	·41

Key: *0 = university
1 = grammar school, 3 or more 'O' levels
2 = grammar school, less than 3 'O' levels

†0 = I
1 = II
2 = III

lower management, secondary school teachers, highly skilled technologists, etc. Social class III, which might be called lower-middle and upper-lower social class, is represented by such clerical and highly skilled manual occupations as: supervisory clerks, policemen, mechanics, small shopkeepers, etc. Although this distinction combines manual and non-manual categories in a way which is usually not legitimate, there are only five highly skilled manual workers in the sample, and, thus, attention will be given to comparisons mainly between social classes I and II.

The present situs classifications are very similar to the ones selected by Morris and Murphy, with the exception that military occupations are combined with the government, church, and civil service.[20] Ideally in a study of this kind, situses should contain a fuller range of social class positions; but the present sample does not provide them. No one in the sample attended a secondary modern school, and many of the clerical and manual occupations in the more 'professional' situses, such as 'office workers' and 'porters' in a university, are not represented. Further, adult social class positions, situses, and educational routes and amounts are interrelated; thus, some of the resulting sub-samples are very small.

Nonetheless, the cross-classification of situs by adult social class position produces several sub-samples which warrant attention. When compared, the resulting data show clear, strong patterns. Although educational routes and amounts have an independent effect, as do patterns of social mobility and non-mobility, these do not offset the independent effects of situs and of social class. In order to increase the size of the sub-samples, and to simplify the presentation of findings, the effects of the education and mobility variables will not be examined here.

Several hundred personal and inter-personal properties were considered in terms of the independent variables. Eventually, after more careful inspection, over half of these were examined by situs, adult social class, and situs and adult social class combined. Means, standard deviations, and distributions for each property were obtained for each situs and social class category. Some attempts were made to test *a priori* propositions, but, in general, a curiosity search was made for 'strong' relationships.[21] A measure of strength of association was required, and for various reasons the F-ratio was selected.[22] With respect to the effects of variations in situs overall, an F-ratio $\geqslant 1 \cdot 6$ was used to define a 'strong' relationship. When the effects of variations in situs overall did not meet the criterion for strength, the effects of a particular situs were sometimes compared with those of another. These more limited but specific comparisons often exceeded the criterion.

2. Conceptual and operational definitions selected variables

A few of those variables whose operational and conceptual definitions are not self-evident from the text will now be discussed. A full description of any of the item will be supplied on request. It should be stressed that detailed consideration of the conceptual and operational issues must await a later monograph.

Attitudinal variables were measured by asking the respondents whether they agreed or disagreed with a series of statements. Their responses were ranked from strongly agree to strongly disagree on a numerical scale (usually a ten-point scale). For individual items the scores alone were analysed, but for indices the principal component was usually extracted from groups of individual items, which were also examined to test the validity of the grouping together of items, using either cluster analysis, or further factor analysis in addition to the 'face validity' of the groupings.

Inter-personal or structural characteristics were measured in a more straightforward way. However, validity checks were made on various items by asking the same kinds of question at different places in the questionnaire, and by 'probing' whenever a respondent seemed uncertain of his reply.

a. The work context

The respondents filled out a chart for their occupational history, from their first full-time up to their current job, giving (among other information) the job title and description, department, industry, income, and duration of each job. The number of job changes was the sum of changes to a different position within the same firm and changes to a different firm ('firm changes'). The status of each job was measured on a nine-point scale, from which the number of status reversals was calculated.

218

The ratio of the number of firms to the total number of jobs held was calculated for each situs-social class group, and was defined as (firm changes + 1) ÷ (job changes + 1).

b. The stratification context

Achievement orientations refer to a concern with those specific attitudes, values, and beliefs which encourage an actor to behave in a manner and in a pattern which is necessary in order that he improve or maintain at a high level his socio-economic positions, but which may not be concerned directly with the positions themselves.[23] An achievement orientation may be concerned with the successful performance of job and occupational tasks for their own sake rather than for their stratification rewards, in which case it is called an 'occupational or job esteem orientation'. Alternatively, the orientation may be directed towards the maintenance of positions in the strati-fication hierarchies, in which case it is called a 'stratification orientation'. This should be distinguished from a 'mobility orientation', which refers to the object of raising, as opposed only to maintaining, the positions in the stratification hier-archies. Both stratification and mobility orientations may be analysed further with respect to specific stratification hier-archies, such as the political, economic, or status hierarchies (or to a particular combination of them), in which case it is useful to refer to an economic orientation, a status orientation, a political eminence orientation, etc.[24]

In this study we attempted to measure some of these achieve-ment orientations through a battery of 25 statements in which responses were rated on a ten-point agree/disagree scale. From there we were able to generate scales for the following orienta-tions: economic (A) and (B), occupational esteem, three status orientations (concern with the status of friends, with maintain-ing and raising one's social status, and with respectability), and a political eminence orientation. An 'economic (A)' orientation refers to the occupation in terms of its economic rewards, as indicated by, for example: 'It is best not to take a job with a good income if it means being away from one's wife and children more than three days a week.' An 'economic (B)' orientation is slightly different in that it refers to economic achievement within one's occupational career, for example: 'A

219

man who aims high and is willing to take risks is a more useful member of our society than one who is contented with a moderate but steady income.' An 'occupational esteem' orientation refers to a concern with the instrinsic quality of the job, for example: 'It's more important to do a meaningful job well than to get ahead in my career.' A status orientation towards raising and maintaining one's position refers to, for example: 'Raising and maintaining one's social standing is a worthy aim'; with respect to friends, for example: 'It is important to have friends who can help one to be successful'; and with respect to respectability, for example: 'When in public places people should be extra careful of their behaviour.' And a political eminence orientation refers to a concern for high position in the hierarchy of political power, and was measured by agreement with: 'Becoming well known and influential would be more rewarding than being financially successful.'

Whereas 'achievement orientation' refers to the degree to which an object is cathected as a goal, 'goal orientation' refers to an actor's concern with the reduction or the establishment of his 'goal discrepancy', which refers to the condition denoted by his having a 'level of aspiration' which exceeds his 'level of achievement' with respect to the goal in question. There are many kinds of levels of aspiration. Our research has indicated that for the present purposes the most important is the 'level of normative expectations'. This refers to a goal or to an amount of it which represents what an actor feels and believes to be normatively appropriate for a person in his statuses, with his experiences, and at his stage in the life cycle. It has been defined elsewhere as a goal or its amount which if not reached is likely to generate the self-evaluation of 'failure'.[25] Perhaps it is useful to retain the more general term 'level of aspiration' to refer to a goal or to an amount of it which represents what an actor feels is worth striving towards even though he is unlikely to reach it. In this sense, as aspiration is a guideline or an ideal towards which an actor will orient his feelings and behaviour patterns, but which he need not cathect very strongly; a level of aspiration is likely to reflect his fantasies.

Data were obtained for goal orientations with respect to many goals, particularly status and income. Taking income, for example, a level of achievement was measured by a subject's current annual income from all sources; a level of normative expectations by the responses to the question 'Would you name an amount that you think a man in your position, and with your experience and education, ought to make a year?'; and a level of aspiration by the responses to the question 'Would you name an amount per year which best represents what you would really like to make a year in order to be perfectly satisfied?' Various forms of goal orientation were derived from this information in terms of the relative and absolute discrepancies between the level of achievement and each of the two kinds of levels of aspiration, individually and in combination.

Feelings of relative deprivation refers to feelings of dissatisfaction or discontent with one's present level of achievement with respect to any given goal.[26] It is obvious that 'deprivation' implies the experience of dissatisfaction or discontent. 'Relative' connotes that all feelings of deprivation arise in reference to objects which have been cathected as goals according to a social standard which has been internalized in the form of a self-expectation. This implies that: a person may feel deprived with respect to one goal but not with respect to another; and, hence, with the exception of feelings of deprivation which automatically arise when certain minimum levels of biologically necessary goals are not maintained, all feelings of deprivation are and must be relative. It follows that to measure feelings of relative deprivation, it is necessary only to ascertain the feelings of deprivation; that they are relative can be assumed.*

Feelings of relative deprivation were measured with respect to various goals. For income, it was measured by replies to several questions, for example, 'Does your current annual income represent a satisfactory achievement, a disappointment, or a compromise with respect to the goals you had set for yourself at the age of 25?' and 'Are you "Very Dissatisfied", "Dissatisfied", "Satisfied" or "Very Satisfied" with your current annual income?'

---

* This is not to imply that we are unconcerned with such problems as 'deprivation with respect to whom, what, and when', but that to measure this feeling one need not take these aspects into account. Indeed, we are primarily concerned with the implications of the term 'relative'.

Table 2 SUMMARY OF EMPIRICAL FINDINGS: SITUS RANKINGS

Variable	SITUS: rank order (1 = high, 5 = low)					Social class effect	F-ratio
	Distribution	Manufacturing	Finance	Government	Education		
1. WORK CONTEXT							
Occupational qualities – subjective							
Secure	3	5	4	2	1	weak +	2·1*
Significant	5	3	4	2	1	weak +	1·7
Sociable	2	4	3	5	1	weak +	2·3
Interesting	5	3	2	4	1	moderate +	1·8
Meaningful	5	3	4	2	1	moderate +	2·9
Occupational qualities – objective							
Creative	4	3	5	1	2	moderate +	3·1
Many decisions	5	2	1	4	3	moderate +	1·6
Unsupervised	3	4	1	5	2	strong +	1·5
Job dissatisfaction	1	3	2	4	5	strong –	1·1*
Characteristics of occupational career							
No. of job changes	2	2	1	5	4	non-linear / weak	2·1
No. of skill changes	2	3	1	4	4	strong –	1·3
No. of firm changes	4	5	1	2	3	weak non-linear	1·3
No. of status reversals	1	3	2	5	4	strong –	1·9*
Ratio of no. of firms to total no. of jobs held	3	5	4	2	1	weak +	4·2
Inter-generational mobility	4	4	3	1	2	strong +	3·6
Intra-generational mobility	3	2	1	4	5	strong +	3·2

2. STRATIFICATION CONTEXT

Achievement orientations							
'Esteem'	5	3	4	2	1	strong +	5·4
'Eminence'	4	3	5	2	1	strong +	2·6
Economic (B)	2	1	3	4	5	strong −	2·2*
Economic (A)	1	2	3	4	5	strong −	2·6
Status: friends	4	1	3	2	5	strong −	2·4
Status: maintaining and raising	3	1	2	4	5	strong −	5·3*
Aspects of goal orientations							
Level of achievement (income)	5	2	1	4	3	strong ++	5·8
Level of normative expectations (income)	4	5	1	3	2	strong ++	3·0
Level of aspirations (income)	3	1	2	5	4	strong +	1·1
Discrepancy between n.e. and ach. relative to ach.	2	3	5	1	4	strong −	1·7*
Relative deprivation with respect to:							
Status	1	2	5	3	4	strong −	3·7
Income	1	2	3	5	4	strong −	2·9
Perception of blockage in career	1	3	2	4	5	moderate −	1·8
Status group							
Mean social class of 5 best friends	5	4	2	3	1	strong +	7·3
Difference between subject's social class and mean social class of 5 best friends	3	2	5	4	1	very weak	0·6*
Inter-generational mobility of 5 best friends	5	4	3	2	1	strong +	2·0*
% of visits to friends of same social class	4	3	2	5	1	weak and inconsistent	3·3
'Social exclusivity' of subject's memberships in clubs and societies	2	3	1	4	5	strong +	4·4

223

Table 2 SUMMARY OF EMPIRICAL FINDINGS: SITUS RANKINGS—*continued*

Variable	SITUS: rank order (1 = high, 5 = low)					Social class effect	F-ratio
	Distribution	Manufacturing	Finance	Government	Education		
2. STRATIFICATION CONTEXT—*continued*							
Sponsorship							
% of sponsors in educational system	5	3	4	1	2	strong +	1·4*
Self-description as ambitious:							
Now	2	1	3	5	4	moderate −	3·4*
In the past	3	1	5	4	2	moderate −	2·7
3. COMMUNITY CONTEXT							
Activities in voluntary associations							
No. of memberships	5	4	2	3	1	strong +	2·8*
'Heterogeneity' of participation	5	4	1	3	2	strong +	2·4
Activities with friends							
No. of contacts	1	4	3	5	2	moderate non-linear	2·8
No. of hours spent during past month	1	3	4	5	2	moderate non-linear	2·2
No. of times wives absent	1	3	4	5	2	weak +	2·4
% of times subject was entertained	2	5	1	4	3	strong +	1·0
Geographical mobility							
Average distance of moves (in miles)	5	2	4	2	1	moderate +	1·4*
4. FAMILY CONTEXT							
Indices of amount of contact							
Subject to parents	1	4	5	3	2	weak −	2·4
Parents to subject	1	2	5	3	4	weak −	3·6

	1	2	3	4	5	Social class effects	F-ratio
Subject to in-laws	1	4	5	3	2	weak non-linear	3·3
In-laws to subject	2	1	4	3	5	weak non-linear	3·3
Indices of quality of contact							
Frequency of requests for help and advice, e.g.:							
In-laws asking subject	5	4	1	1	3	moderate non-linear	1·5
Warm and affectionate feelings of subject towards							
his parents	2	3	5	1	4	none	1·6
Subject's number of children	3	5	1	1	4	weak +	1·1
Miscellaneous personal characteristics							
Colour prejudice	3	2	1	4	5	weak −	2·8
Authoritarian personality	2	1	4	3	5	strong −	4·6*
Feelings of: Isolation	1	3	4	2	5	moderate −	1·5
Paranoia	2	1	4	3	5	strong −	2·7
Rigidity	2	1	5	3	4	strong −	5·6
Social powerlessness	4	3	2	1	5	strong −	2·0
Anomia with respect to ends	3	2	4	1	5	moderate −	0·9
Despair (summary)	3	2	4	1	5	strong −	1·6
Voting behaviour							
% voting Conservative in previous election (1964)	1	2	3	4	5	strong +	3·3*

EXPLANATION OF SYMBOLS

'Social class effects': 'strong', 'moderate', and 'weak' indicates the relative level of the F-ratio for the relationship between social class and the variable under consideration. 'Strong' indicates an F-ratio of 3 or more; 'moderate' one of 1 to 3; 'weak' an F-ratio of less than 1.

'+', '−', or 'non-linear' indicates the direction of the relationship. '+' indicates that scores for the variable under consideration *increase* with increasing social class, and vice versa for a '−' sign. If there is no consistent trend, this is indicated by 'non-linear'.

* indicates interaction effects from the combination of social class and situs.

P

c. The community context

A chart of activities in voluntary associations was used to give the number of memberships, offices (official positions held), and hours. The heterogeneity of participation was obtained by examining the different types of voluntary associations listed – so that memberships, for example, in three different athletics clubs gave a heterogeneity of 1, while memberships in a sports club, a bridge club, and a professional association gave a heterogeneity of 3.

Information on 'Activities with friends' came from a list of contacts with friends during the past month, giving the number of contacts, number of times wives present, percentage of times subject was entertained, and hours spent last month.

d. The family context

The amount of contact with relatives was obtained from a chart giving the frequency of contacts and the number of hours of travelling time required to make each contact. An index of contact was calculated by multiplying the number of contacts by the hours of travelling time needed to make each contact, in order to attach greater weight to contact with relatives who lived at a considerable distance from the respondent. The 'warm and affectionate feelings towards parents' variable was made up of the arithmetic sum of ten-point agree/disagree scores for three statements referring to the way the respondent felt about his parents, e.g. 'There are no excuses for a man's not maintaining a warm, loving, and close relationship with his parents.'

e. Miscellaneous personal characteristics

All the attitudinal variables discussed in this section were calculated by the principal component method, from groups of items which were either selected from earlier studies of personal characteristics or constructed for purposes of the larger study on which this article is based. The variables were measured by asking respondents for agreement or disagreement with a statement, or by asking them to choose which of two statements most nearly represented their views. For example,

		1 Perceived job security			2 Job dissatisfaction			3 Number of status reversals			4 Ratio of number of firms to number of jobs		
		M	SD	N	M	SD	N	M	SD	N	M	SD	N
Distribution	I	1·00	1·0	7	·14	·4	7	·29	·5	7	·83	·29	7
	II	·78	·8	9	·56	·5	9	·44	·5	9	·61	·33	9
	III	0·00	0·0	2	·68	·6	3	·67	·6	3	·69	·30	3
	ALL	·78	·9	18	·42	·5	19	·42	·5	19	·70	·31	19
Manufacturing	I	1·05	1·0	22	·25	·4	20	0·4	·2	23	·59	·27	23
	II	2·00	1·6	5	·40	·5	5	·20	·4	5	·65	·25	5
	III	1·33	1·0	9	·56	·5	9	·33	·5	9	·68	·23	9
	ALL	1·25	1·1	36	·35	·5	34	·14	·4	37	·62	·26	37
Finance	I	1·38	1·3	8	·33	·5	9	·11	·3	9	·63	·29	9
	II	1·00	1·2	5	·50	·5	6	·33	·5	6	·66	·27	6
	III	0·00		1	0·0		1	0·0		1	1·00		1
	ALL	1·14	1·2	14	·38	·5	16	·19	·4	16	·67	·28	16
Government	I	·63	·9	16	·13	·4	15	·00	·0	16	·82	·25	16
	II	·50	1·0	4	·75	·5	4	·25	·5	4	·90	·12	4
	III	1·00		1	1·0		1	0·0		1	·50		1
	ALL	·62	·9	21	·30	·5	20	·05	·2	21	·82	·23	21
Education	I	·55	1·1	47	·20	·4	49	·02	·1	49	·84	·20	49
	II	·39	1·1	13	·08	·3	13	·39	·5	13	·85	·23	13
	III			0			0			0			0
	ALL	·52	1·1	60	·18	·4	62	·10	·3	62	·84	·21	62
TOTAL	I	·79	1·0	120	·21	·41	119	·07	·3	124	·76	·26	124
	II	·98	1·3	42	·42	·50	43	·30	·5	43	·73	·26	43
	III	·93	1·0	14	·56	·51	16	·50	·6	16	·70	·23	16
	ALL	·85	1·1	176	·29	·5	178	·16	·4	183	·75	·26	183
F-ratio		2·1			1·1			1·9			4·2		

Table 3—continued

		5			6			7					8		
		Status orientation: maintaining and raising			Friends' average mobility			% Sponsors in educational system			Sponsorship % Sample with sponsors		Average distance of moves in miles		
		M	SD	N	M	SD	N	M	SD	N	%	N	M	SD	N
Distribution	I	13·0	8·0	7	1·1	1·2	7	42	50	4	57	7	25	20	7
	II	18·3	7·0	9	·2	1·7	4	25	38	7	78	9	27	35	8
	III	24·7	2·2	3	-·1	1·3	3	0		1	33	3	25	22	3
	ALL	17·4	7·8	19	·6	1·3	14	29	40	12	63	19	26	26	18
Manufacturing	I	19·9	4·9	23	1·3	1·4	14	53	37	21	91	23	49	61	22
	II	16·2	5·4	5	1·7	·2	2	17	29	3	60	5	14	26	5
	III	18·7	5·7	9	-·2	1·5	4	33	58	3	33	9	29	35	8
	ALL	19·1	5·2	37	1·0	1·4	20	47	39	27	73	37	39	53	35
Finance	I	16·6	6·4	9	1·1	1·7	9	45	46	7	78	9	53	62	8
	II	18·6	2·3	6	1·1	1·1	5	20	45	5	83	6	17	18	6
	III	24·3		1			0	0		1	100	1	0		1
	ALL	17·8	5·2	16	1·1	1·5	14	32	44	13	81	16	35	15	15
Government	I	14·4	5·2	16	1·2	·8	7	57	44	15	94	16	38	32	15
	II	20·5	5·8	4	4·2		1	50	71	2	50	4	35	26	3
	III	16·3		1	1·0		1	100		1	100	1	55		1
	ALL	15·6	5·6	21	1·5	1·2	9	58	45	18	86	21	39	30	19
Education	I	10·8	6·7	49	1·8	1·6	32	56	34	41	84	49	41	66	47
	II	16·2	6·0	13	1·4	1·5	9	35	47	10	77	13	59	61	10
	III			0			0			0		0			0
	ALL	12·0	6·9	62	1·7	1·5	41	52	38	51	82	62	44	65	57
TOTAL	I	13·7	7·1	124	1·3	1·4	84	52	38	101	81	124	44	58	119
	II	17·2	5·9	43	1·3	1·4	25	28	42	31	72	43	29	41	38
	III	20·6	5·6	16	-0·1	1·2	9	29	49	7	44	16	26	29	15
	ALL	15·2	7·0	183	1·2	1·5	118	46	41	139	76	183	39	53	172
ratio		5·2			3·0			1·4					1·4		

		9 Warm and affectionate feelings towards parents			10 Colour prejudice			11 How did you vote in the last election?			
		M	SD	N	M	SD	N	Conservative %	Labour %	Liberal %	N
Distribution	I	15·6	5·0	7	11·0	2·8	7	100			2
	II	16·3	6·7	9	10·5	·7	9	86	14		7
	III	15·7	7·8	3	14·1	3·3	3	67	33		3
	ALL	15·9	5·9	19	11·3	2·4	19	83	17		12
Manufacturing	I	15·0	5·8	23	12·5	2·8	22	80	20		15
	II	20·2	3·8	5	10·2	2·3	5	60	20	20	5
	III	14·4	5·1	9	10·3	3·8	9	60	40		5
	ALL	15·6	5·6	37	11·6	3·1	36	72	24	4	25
Finance	I	12·7	3·1	9	10·4	1·7	9	71		29	7
	II	12·7	4·3	6	14·6	4·8	6	67	17	17	6
	III	17·0		1	12·5		1	100			1
	ALL	13·0	3·6	16	12·1	3·7	16	71	7	22	14
Government	I	18·2	5·0	16	10·7	2·4	16	67	33		12
	II	16·3	5·7	4	10·7	0·9	4	100			1
	III	26·0		1	10·5		1		100		1
	ALL	18·2	5·3	21	10·7	3·0	21	64	36		14
Education	I	15·5	4·9	49	8·7	4·2	49	58	42	10	40
	II	14·8	5·6	13	11·6	1·9	13	50	50		10
	III			0			0				0
	ALL	15·4	5·0	62	9·3	2·1	62	36	56	8	50
TOTAL	I	15·6	5·3	124	10·3	3·7	122	54	38	8	95
	II	15·4	5·4	43	11·3	2·7	42	60	34	6	35
	III	15·9	5·7	16	11·3	3·4	16	67	33		12
	ALL	15·6	5·3	183	10·6	3·5	180	56	37	7	142
F-ratio		1·6			2·8			3·3			

229

one of the colour prejudice items was 'Would you mind having a coloured man work with you at the same job?' (responses ranging from 'very much' to 'I would strongly favour it'). An item for 'authoritarian personality' was 'The most important thing to teach children is absolute obedience to their parents.' An item from the scale for anomia with respect to ends-norms was 'I no longer have meaningful goals in life.' Feelings of personal powerlessness was measured by choosing one of each of a number of paired statements; for example: 'I more strongly believe that: EITHER (a) What happens to me is my own doing. OR (b) Sometimes I feel that I don't have enough control over the direction my life is taking.' Rigidity was measured by agree/disagree responses to a series of statements, for example: 'I am the sort of person who likes to know just where he stands on everything.'

Voting behaviour was examined by asking the respondents how they voted in the last and one before last general elections (if they voted at all), and how they intended to vote in the next election. All the respondents who gave any information had voted Labour, Liberal, or Conservative, and only two men indicated that they had either changed their party allegiance over the two previous elections, or intended to change allegiance in the next one.

3. *Empirical findings*

This section consists of little more than a list of those personal and inter-personal characteristics of the sample which (after the effects of variations in adult social class, educational amount, educational route, and all three combined are controlled) are related independently, either to general variations in situs or to specific situs comparisons. The list itself is presented in Table 2. Some of these characteristics evince interaction effects, in the sense that particular combinations of situs and social class together have effects which are greater or lesser than the sum of the effects of situs and of social class each taken separately. Tabular information is presented for a number of these characteristics in Table 3. All data are described briefly in the text, but not discussed. In the first instance only those situses with more than ten respondents are considered.

230

a. The work context

Men in the sample were asked to rate their occupations on a five-point scale with respect to a long list of qualities, some of which referred to their subjective evaluation of the work situation and some to a more objective description. With respect to subjective evaluations, the following qualities were related to variations in situs: 'secure', 'significant', 'sociable', 'interesting', and 'meaningful'. And with respect to more objective descriptions, the related qualities were 'creative', 'many decisions', and 'unsupervised'. In most cases the situses were ranked from least to most favourable, as follows: distribution, manufacturing, finance, government, and education.[27]

An exception to this pattern was 'perceived job security'. As shown in Table 3, column 1, the situses were ranked from least to most favourable, as follows: manufacturing, finance, distribution, government, and education.[28] This quality reflected several interaction effects. Generally, men in social class II perceived their job as being more secure than did those in social class I, whereas the opposite is true for men in the manufacturing situs. Further, the differences between social classes I and II of the government and education situses are much less than the differences between the same social classes of the other three situses.

Two direct questions about dissatisfaction with job and occupation were asked: 'Do you wish you had got into some other line of work when you were younger?' and 'How satisfied are you with your current job?'. Both questions elicited similar patterns of replies, as illustrated in Table 3, column 2, which refers specifically to the 'line of work' question. The situses were ranked from high to low dissatisfaction, as follows: distribution, finance, manufacturing, government, and education. The lower the social class position, the more were men likely to be dissatisfied. Social class II of the government situs presented an unusually high level of dissatisfaction, but further examination disclosed that three of the four men in this category were in military occupations. An exception to this pattern was that in the education situs men in social class II were less dissatisfied than men in social class I.

Many aspects of occupational career were closely related to situs classifications, especially those which reflect 'disorderliness',

231

such as the number of job changes, skill changes, status reversals, and firm changes.[29] With respect to each of these properties the typical ranking of situses from high to low was as follows: finance, distribution, manufacturing, government, and education.

Status reversals, as shown in Table 3, column 3, evince strong interaction effects. Within the government and education situses, a relatively high number of status reversals occurred among men in social class II compared to those in social class I of the same situses. Further examination disclosed that these reversals took place at an early stage of their work careers, and were associated with a change in firm and a loss of income. After this major change, however, their careers were very orderly. Although in general such disorderliness was higher in the other situses, it was more evenly spread over the work life.

Whereas the number of job changes *decreased* from the distribution through to the education situs, the number of firm changes *increased*. However, as indicated in Table 3, column 4, a different pattern emerged with respect to the ratio of the number of firms by which the subject had been employed to the total number of jobs he had held. A higher ratio was found for the government and education situses, with only slight differences between social classes I and II in each of these situses. Lower ratios were found for the other three situses, but the differences among the social classes in each situs were much more marked. Usually, those in social class II had higher ratios than did those in social class I; but in the distribution situs, the opposite applied.

b. The stratification context

A number of achievement orientations varied with respect to situs: 'occupational esteem', 'eminence', two forms of 'economic', and two forms of 'status'. The two forms of economic orientation decreased from the distribution through to the education situs. However, the 'occupational esteem' and 'eminence' orientations evinced the opposite pattern. This inverse relationship between an orientation to work in terms of its economic rewards and an orientation to work in terms of its more 'intrinsic' qualities was also found with respect to social class: the higher the social class, the higher the 'esteem' and 'eminence' orientations. This is consistent with findings

232

from many studies of various industrial societies, as well as for the urban areas of rapidly industrializing societies.[30]

As indicated in Table 3, column 5, achievement orientations towards maintaining and raising one's social status showed a different pattern. This status orientation was highest in the manufacturing situs and lowest in the education situs, with finance, distribution, and government ranked in order between these extremes. In general, the higher the social class, the lower this status orientation. However, an interesting effect obtained in the manufacturing situs: social class I showed a higher level than did either social classes II or III.

Several other personal characteristics were also found to vary with respect to situs classifications: levels of achievement, normative expectations, and aspirations with respect to annual income; and feelings of relative deprivation with respect to status and to income, as well as with respect to general position in the stratification hierarchy. Also important was the perception that one was or had been blocked in one's career.

With respect to levels of achievement, normative expectations, and aspirations, considerable variation was found among situses, but not in the pattern which has been described so regularly above. However, when the relative discrepancy between the levels of achievement and of normative expectations was considered, the more usual pattern emerged. For the education, government, and finance situses relatively small discrepancies were found, and for the distribution and manufacturing situses relatively large ones. However, the three military men of the four members of social class II in the government situs had extremely large discrepancies.

Variations in feelings of relative deprivation with respect to income, as well as with respect to status, showed a pattern which was almost identical to the one evinced by the size of the relative descrepancy between levels of achievement and of normative expectations. However, the scores in the distribution and manufacturing situses were much greater than those in the finance, government, and education situses. Variations in the perception that one was or had been blocked in one's career were consistent with these data.

The rates of inter- and intra-generational mobility were also related to variations in situs, although, as expected, the former was inversely related to the latter. Whereas upward intra-

233

generational mobility decreased, upward inter-generational mobility increased in terms of the following situs ranking: manufacturing (highest upward intra-generational mobility and lowest upward inter-generational mobility), distribution, finance, government, and education. This pattern reflects the fact that in the government and education situses men with professional qualifications started their careers at relatively high social class positions, and experienced relatively little mobility thereafter. It is natural that adult social class positions should be positively associated with both inter- and intra-generational mobility: it is primarily a matter of what is possible. It is, therefore, all the more interesting that in the finance situs those in social class II had a much higher rate of inter-generational mobility than did those in social class I.

Subjects were also asked many questions about the occupations and occupational backgrounds of their five best friends. In this connection, several characteristics were found to vary with respect to situs: the mean social class of the subject's five best friends, the difference between the subject's social class and the mean social class of the subject's five best friends; the mean amount of the inter-generational occupational mobility of these friends; and the extent to which the subject's visits with members of his entire friendship group were primarily to those who showed his own social class position.

As one would expect, the mean social class of the subject's five best friends was closely associated with the subject's own social class position, for both the sample overall and each situs: the higher the subject's social class, the higher the social class of his five best friends. An exception is that men is social class I tended to have friends in a social class position only slightly lower than their own. Further, variations in situs had a strong effect on the friendship patterns for men in social class II: those in the government and education situses tended to have friends with a higher social status than their own; those in the manufacturing and finance situses tended to have friends of the same social status as their own; and men in the distribution situs tended to have friends with a lower social status than their own.

Variations in situs had strong effects on the average inter-generational mobility of the subject's five friends, as shown in Table 3, column 6. Men in the distribution situses had friends who were only slightly upwardly mobile, whereas men in the

234

education situs had friends who were much more so. Although, in general, compared to men in social classes II and III, men in social class I had friends who were more upwardly mobile, this is not the case within each situs: in finance there is very little difference between social classes, but in manufacturing considerable differences are found. In manufacturing those in social class II had the most highly mobile friends.

The percentage of visits to friends who share the same social class position as the subject was equally important. Men in the education situs were most likely, and men in the government situs least likely, to visit friends within their own social class, and those in the distribution, manufacturing and finance situses were between these extremes. This aspect of visiting patterns was not closely associated with social class.

Subjects were scored with respect to the extent to which their lists of memberships in voluntary societies included those which were 'socially exclusive' and prestigious. A strong situs effect was found, with distribution and finance ranking very high, and the other situses very low.

When the subjects were asked whether they considered themselves to be or to have been ambitious men, very striking differences emerged. In the distribution and manufacturing situses comparatively large numbers considered themselves to be and to have been ambitious; in the finance situs most people considered themselves to be ambitious now, but not to have been so in the past; and in the government and education situses the respondents tended to feel that either they had never been ambitious or, if they had been, that they were not now.

Subjects were asked to recall the extent to which they were befriended and helped early on in their educational and occupational careers by people who might be termed 'sponsors'.[31] In so far as these data were taken from a study which was primarily concerned with social mobility, it is not surprising that many of the respondents had sponsors. Although most of the sponsors named were teachers, members of the finance situs were more likely to name senior men in their business careers. However, there is considerable variation which is accounted for by adult social class, situs, and by both combined, as shown in Table 3, column 7. Education and government situses showed the highest rate of sponsorship by teachers, and distribution and finance the lowest, with manufacturing taking an intermediate rank. About half of those sponsors mentioned by respondents in social class I were teachers; but respondents in social class II, especially if they worked in the educational and government situses, were even more likely to mention them.

c. The community context

Two aspects of participation in voluntary clubs and societies showed strong situs effects: the number of memberships and the 'heterogeneity' of participation.[32] With respect to each of these variables situses were ranked from low to high, as follows: distribution, manufacturing, government, finance, and education.[33] The higher the social class, the higher the number of memberships in clubs and societies. But this was not so marked for respondents in the education situs. Respondents in social class II of the distribution and government situses reported fewer memberships than did their counterparts in the other situses.

The following properties of contacts with friends showed strong situs but weak social class effects: the number of contacts, the number of hours spent last month, whether wives were present or absent, and whether the respondent was entertained or did the entertaining. Three empirical patterns were distinguished. The 'work-centred' pattern was characterized by a high number of brief contacts in which the respondent was usually entertained without his wife. This was found primarily in the distribution situs, but to some extent in the manufacturing situs as well. Two 'family-centred' patterns were found. The first was characterized by a moderate number of visits of moderate duration, in which the wives were usually present, and in which responsibility for the entertaining was shared equally between the respondent and his friends. This was found primarily in the finance and education situses. The second family-centred pattern was characterized by a low number of contacts, but of greater duration than those in the other two patterns, in which the respondent and his wife usually did the entertaining. It was found primarily in the government situs, but to a slight degree in manufacturing as well.

Subjects were asked how often they changed their residence and how far they moved each time. The average distance of moves in miles showed strong situs, social class, and interaction effects, as shown in Table 3, column 8. In general, respondents

236

in the education situs had the highest average distance of moves, and those in the distribution situs the lowest, with finance, manufacturing, and government ranked between these extremes. Similarly, in general, the higher the social class, the greater the average distance of moves. However, in social class I, respondents in the manufacturing and finance situses moved greater distances than did their counterparts in the other situses; and in social class II, government and education respondents showed much higher average distances than did their counterparts in the other situses. In the distribution situs the average distance moved was low for all social classes.

d. The family context

Many variables dealing with both the quality and the amount of contact with the respondents' families showed the effects of variations in situs. Most important among them were the following three: the amount and symmetry of contact with parents and parents-in-law (corrected by time and distance necessary to make the contact); the frequency and symmetry of requests for help and advice from parents and parents-in-law; and warm and affectionate feelings towards their parents. The average number of children also varied with respect to situs.[34]

These data are too complex even to be summarized here. However, the patterns evinced by the expression of warm and affectionate feelings towards parents can be taken as an example, as shown in Table 3, column 9. In the government situs positive feelings were high in all social classes, whereas in the finance situs they were low for all social classes: in general, distribution, manufacturing, and education were ranked in order between these extremes. However, in the manufacturing situs very high positive feelings were found in social class II.

e. Miscellaneous personal characteristics

A number of personality characteristics were found to be strongly related to situs: colour prejudice, authoritarian personality,[35] feelings of isolation, paranoia, social and personal powerlessness, anomia with respect to ends-norms, and a summary index of a syndrome of patterns of anxiety which might be termed 'despair'. The government and education situses tended to have the lowest scores on each of these variables, and the distribution and manufacturing situses tended to have the highest. The finance situs varied between these sets.

To illustrate these patterns variations in colour prejudice can be taken as an example. As shown in Table 3, column 10, the situses were ranked as follows: finance, manufacturing, distribution, government, and education. In the government situs, there was little difference among the social classes; but in the education situs those in social class II showed a relatively high score. In the finance situs colour prejudice was highest in social class II, but in the distribution situs it was highest in social class III.

In view of the findings reported by Morris and Murphy in their second article on situs,[36] the voting behaviour of the respondents was examined. The respondents were asked how they voted in the last election (1964). The percentages who voted Conservative, Liberal, or Labour are presented in Table 3, column 11. As might be expected, within each situs, the higher the social class, the higher the percentage voting Conservative. However, the distribution situs had the highest percentage of those who voted Conservative, and education the lowest, with manufacturing, finance, and government ranked in order midway between these extremes. Interaction effects were slight. The percentage of respondents who voted Liberal or Labour does not show quite such a striking pattern, although taken together they increase from distribution through to education. These findings are very similar to those of Morris and Murphy, with the curious exception of the finance situs which, in the present study, had a relatively lower percentage of Conservative votes.

4. *Summary of empirical findings*

The findings which emerged from this examination of the data can be summarized briefly:

1. With respect to most of the variables considered, as indicated by their average situs rank, the five situses are usually ranked as follows: distribution (lowest, or least favourable), manufacturing, finance, government, and education (highest, or most favourable).
2. This ranking can be treated in terms of two sets of situses: the more 'commercial' ones, i.e. distribution and manu-

facturing; and the more 'professional' ones, i.e. goverment and education. The finance situs is more akin to the professional than to the commercial situses, but this is not always so. The commerical situses evince scores which differ from those for the professional situses with respect to almost every personal and inter-personal property listed above.

3. The effects of variations in social class are greatest in the education and government situs and least in the distribution situs. This applied to variations within social classes as well as to variations between them.

The preceding analysis was confined to the five situses represented by more than ten respondents. Four situses had ten or fewer representatives: agriculture, building and transport, communications, and medicine. A few comments on the findings for these situses might be of interest.

Men in the building and transport situs are similar to those in the distribution situs: for example, they have high career disorder, high levels of 'anxiety', low job satisfaction, and an orientation to the job in terms of its status and economic bestowal values, rather than its 'esteem'. The four in the communications situs evinced extreme variability on many of the properties examined, although in general they too had high career disorder and high levels of 'anxiety'. However, they had an 'esteem' orientation towards their job and higher job satisfaction. All the respondents in the medicine situs were in social class I, and very similar to their counterparts in the education situs. The men in the agricultural situs, nearly all owners of their own farms rather than farm labourers, showed very little career disorder, very low anxiety, extremely high levels of job satisfaction, and an 'intrinsic' orientation to their job, along with almost complete rejection of an orientation in terms of its status bestowal value.

THEORETICAL CONSIDERATIONS

It is difficult to explain such a long list of diverse findings. Parsons discussed some aspects of situs, societal functions, and differential evaluations of work and occupations, but he did not suggest specific, testable hypotheses for the variables mentioned here.[37] Morris and Murphy disclaimed any effort to construct theories about situses or their effects until much more empircal work had accumulated.[38] Neither extreme is justifiable. It is more appropriate to select as problematic a property which reflects the effects of variations in situs, to develop hypotheses which are consistent with the available data, and then to design a further study to test these *a priori* propositions. It is not necessary to concentrate on more than one property at a time, nor to use a given set of propositions to explain the variation in more than one property.

Of special theoretical and practical interest, both in industrial sociology and in sociology generally, is the problem of relative deprivation with respect to income. The data show that variations in situs are related to feelings of relative deprivation with respect to income, as well as to levels of achievement, aspirations, and normative expectations, and to economic orientations. Further, not only does the level of achievement show a weak, negative association with feelings of relative deprivation, but the strength of this association varies in terms of situs classifications. For example, the situs with the highest average income (finance) ranks only third in average feelings of relative deprivation, and the situs with the lowest average income (government) ranks lowest in average feelings of relative deprivation, i.e. the opposite from what one would ordinarily expect. Thus, the problem is to account for the weak, negative relationship between income and feelings of relative deprivation with respect to it, and in so doing to specify intervening variables which are linked to variations in situs. And this set of inter-related propositions must at least be consistent with the available data.

The propositions which follow constitute an attempt to solve this problem. It is necessary to emphasize again that in an article of this kind it is possible to do little more than present a brief outline of the theory, and to order only the minimum of data in its support.

The variables are as follows:

> Dependent: Feelings of relative deprivation with respect to income
> Intervening 1: Goal orientation
> 2: Economic orientation
> 3: Anomogenic factor

     4: Blocking factor
     5: Comparative reference group factor
  Independent: Professional or bureaucratic structure of authority
 Classificatory: Occupational situs: professional or commercial

The propositions are as follows:

Proposition 1

The greater the size of the relative discrepancy between a level of normative expectations and a level of achievement (goal orientation) with respect to an object which has been highly valued as a goal (achievement orientation; with respect to income, an economic orientation), the greater the feelings of relative deprivation with respect to this goal.

The findings which best illustrate this proposition are as follows:

1. The correlation between the size of the relative discrepancy and feelings of relative deprivation for the sample as a whole is ·36.
2. The correlation for those whose economic orientations are ≤ the median economic orientation for the sample as a whole is ·02.
3. The correlation for those economic orientations are > the median is ·50.
4. In contrast, the correlations between feelings of relative deprivation and economic orientations is ·21: the level of normative expectations is ·02; the level of achievement (income itself) is ·25.
5. The discrepancy between the level of normative expectations and the level of achievement is a better predictor of feelings of relative deprivation than is the discrepancy between the level of aspirations and the level of achievement, which produced, in general, lower and more erratic correlations.

Goal orientations are likely to give rise to feelings of relative deprivation according to three related but distinct social-psychological processes. On this basis, three types of goal orientations can be distinguished: the Anomic type, or type A;

Q

the Blocked type, or type B; and the Comparative type, or type C.

A 'type A' goal orientation arises through changes in certain properties of a level of normative expectations, and not through changes in certain properties of a level of achievement. Its primary feature is insatiability, in the sense that no matter what the amount and rate at which a person might raise his level of achievement, his level of normative expectations always rises such as to remain higher and, thus, to maintain the discrepancy.

A 'type B' goal orientation, in contrast to a type A, arises through changes in certain properties of a level of achievement, and not through changes in certain properties of a level of normative expectations. Its main feature is potential satiability, in the sense that if a person's level of normative expectations remains reasonably distinct and relatively stable, then, provided he raises his level of achievement in such an amount and at such a rate as to eliminate the discrepancy between it and his level of normative expectations, he is likely to experience feelings of relative satisfaction.

A 'type C' goal orientation is sufficiently different from both a type A and a type B to justify a separate classification, but it is also sufficiently similar to make such a classification very difficult. A type C goal orientation arises through changes in certain properties of a level of normative expectations which nonetheless remains thereafter sufficiently distinct and stable to permit feelings of relative satisfaction, provided that a person raises his level of achievement in such an amount and at such a rate as to eliminate the discrepancy. Like a type A, a type C arises through changes in certain properties of a level of normative expectations, and not through changes in certain properties of a level of achievement; but, like a type B, it is potentially satiable. Whereas, the *development* of a type C goal orientation is, as with type A, a function of a rise of a level of normative expectations, its *persistence* is, as with a type B, a function of the relative immobility of a level of achievement.

Proposition 2

The greater the number and strength of the anomogenic factors which characterize an actor's inter-personal community, the more is it likely that he will develop an anomic goal orientation.

Proposition 3

The greater the number and strength of the blocking factors which characterize an actor's inter-personal community, the more is he likely to encounter blockages, and, further, the greater the number of the blockages which he is likely to encounter, and the more intense are they likely to be; the greater the number and strength of the blockages which an actor encounters with respect to a goal, the more is he likely to develop a blacked goal orientation.

Proposition 4

The greater the number and strength of the comparative reference group factors which characterize an actor's inter-personal community, the more is it likely that he will take and hold a given group as his positively cathected comparative reference group, and the more intense is his cathexis likely to be; the location of his positively cathected comparative reference group with respect to a given goal will depend on the specific value of the factors in question; the higher the value of such factors, the higher the location of the reference groups with respect to the amount of the goal (this is a dynamic and not a static relationship); the greater the discrepancy between an actor's comparative reference groups and his membership groups with respect to a given goal, the more is he likely to have a discrepancy between his level of normative expectations and his level of achievement with respect to this goal, and the greater is this discrepancy likely to be.

Clearly, Propositions 2 through 4 require considerable discussion, and the argument suffers in so far as space does not permit it. Each set of factors, the anomogenic, the blocking, and the comparative reference group, is infinite in kind and number. Of interest here are only those which are structural rather than personal in origin, and which are not randomly distributed throughout the education and stratification systems. The relationship between each set of factors and the eventual development of a discrepancy between the level of normative expectations and the level of achievement is one of *process*. The three processes, the anomogenic, the blocking, and the comparative reference, each involve several phases, and each process is interdependent with the others at specific phases.

243

For the present purposes we will have to assume the processional aspects of the propositions, and examine only the summary relationship between each factor and the discrepancy in question. However, at least some further explanation is necessary.

To explain the development of any type of goal orientation, it is necessary to consider the factors which are likely to encourage an actor to take and to hold a given group as his positively cathected comparative reference group, and, hence, which are likely to shape and buttress his level of normative expectations. Therefore, it is also necessary to distinguish the effects of such comparative reference group factors on the development of the comparative type of goal orientations from their effect on the development of goal orientations generally. This distinction can be illustrated in connection with the difference between the blocked and the comparative types of goal orientations. A blocked goal orientation can only be explained in terms of blocking factors; but this does not imply that comparative reference group factors did not operate to form, and do not operate to maintain, a positively cathected comparative reference group, and, hence, a level of normative expectations. A comparative goal orientation can only be explained in terms of comparative reference group factors; but this does not imply that blocking factors do not prevent an actor from raising his level of achievement so as to eliminate the discrepancy. In other words, whereas comparative reference group factors contribute to the *maintenance* of the blocked type of goal orientation, variations in them are responsible for the *development* of the comparative type.

1. An 'anomogenic factor' is any property of a situation, of an actor's personality, or of the two combined, which prevents him from experiencing a clear and salient normative guideline concerning what might constitute satisfaction, i.e. any condition which prevents a person from forming a satiable level of normative expectations with respect to a given goal. An example of the kind of structural anomogenic factors for which data are available is a disorderly occupational career, especially one which has involved status reversals. In this connection, the mean feelings of relative deprivation for those who are $\leqslant$ the median status disorderliness is $1 \cdot 18$, and for those who are $>$ the median is $1 \cdot 62$ (the difference being significant at $\cdot 05$ P).

Another example is the degree of participation in clubs and societies, and the heterogeneity of this participation, especially the kinds of participation which are likely to involve positive sanctions concerning one's economic and status achievements. In this connection, the mean feelings of relative deprivation for those who are $\geqslant$ the median degree of participation is ·98, and for those who are $<$ the median is 1·72 (the difference being significant at ·01 P); and for heterogeneity of participation the relevant means are ·73 and 1·61.

2. A 'blocking factor' is any property of a situation, of an actor's personality, or of the two combined which, through its effects on an actor's level of achievement, produces a goal orientation, or which alters it in kind and/or amount. It refers to a demand that an actor possesses certain skills and/or qualities in order that he be enabled to attain a given object or amount of it. A blocking factor differs from a blockage: if an actor does not possess the requisite skills and/or qualities, then he is likely to become blocked; if he does possess them, then he is unlikely to become blocked. In so far as his level of achievement becomes blocked, he is likely to develop a blocked goal orientation. In so far as it is blocked below his level of normative expectation, he is likely to develop a blocked goal orientation which produces feelings of relative deprivation with respect to the goal in question.

It is difficult to measure structural blocking factors because it is essential to obtain information which is independent from the actor's perceptions of his situation. However, one example for which some data are available is the demand for evidence of ability to perform certain tasks which is publicly and officially recognized, in order that promotion or advancement be granted, as opposed to the criterion of 'seniority' or the vague 'necessary experience'. With respect only to the goal of income, a career structure which bestows a steady annual rise which is also corrected for inflation (such as found for university lecturers) can be contrasted to a career structure which bestows sharp rises for evidence of success and either a freeze or even a drop for adequacy or slight inadequacy in the task (such as found for the sales staff of large manufacturing concerns). In the present sample, those whose feelings of relative deprivation are $<$ the median for the sample as a whole are much more likely

245

than those whose feelings are $\geqslant$ the median to work in an organization with the former rather than the latter kind of career structure. Similarly, the number of income reversals and the average size of income changes were lower for those whose feelings of relative deprivation are $<$ the median than for those whose feelings are $\geqslant$ the median. Consistent with these findings is that unusual changes in income are usually related to important review points and phases in the occupational career structures, as perceived by the respondents when questioned about their careers.

3. A 'comparative reference group factor' is any property of a situation, of an actor's personality, or of the two combined, which encourages an actor to cathect a given group in such a way that he compares himself to it with respect to any kind, number, and amount of his qualities. On the basis of this comparison, an actor is able to formulate his level of normative expectations.* It is essential to recognize that this is a dynamic relationship. An actor's comparative reference groups are subject to change, and, hence, so are his levels of normative expectations. But this is not necessarily an anomogenic process. If the new identifications and comparisons become stable and sufficiently meaningful to the actor, then his new level of normative expectations is likely to remain nomic.[39] One example of a 'secular' and incipient comparative reference group factor is the formal sponsorship of students through the educational system into the labour market in a way which helps to form various groups of adults with a collective identity, especially with respect to their location in the status hierarchy. Members of such carefully defined status groups are likely to compare themselves to one another with respect to their incomes. In this connection, the number of reported sponsors, the length of time during which respondents 'kept in touch' with their sponsors, and the degree to which sponsors are felt to have been helpful, are all greater among those whose feelings

* To convey how such factors are likely to operate, a more detailed discussion is necessary, for at least two reasons: unlike anomogenic and blocking factors, which directly affect the level of normative expectations, comparative reference group factors have an indirect effect in that they lead first to the formation of comparative reference groups; and because the formation of comparative reference groups is likely to affect the level of normative expectations of any type of nomic goal orientation, including non-pathogenic ones, it is necessary to distinguish their special relevance for the etiology of the comparative type.

of relative deprivation are < the median for the sample as a whole than they are for those whose feelings are ≥ the median.

Several other comparative reference group factors warrant mention. Those whose feelings of relative deprivation are low tend to make lateral or horizontal comparisons based on 'cosmopolitan' orientations to their careers, whereas those whose feelings of relative deprivation are high tend to make vertical comparisons based on 'local' orientations.[40] In other words, the degree to which respondents compare themselves to men whose career qualifications and career achievements are similar to their own, even if these 'significant others' work in other organizations and in other cities, is greater among those whose feelings of relative deprivation are < the median for the sample as a whole than for those whose feelings of relative deprivation are ≥ the median. Similarly, those with low feelings of relative deprivation are less likely than those with high to have much face to face interaction with either superordinates or subordinates within their work situation. And, further, those with low feelings of relative deprivation are less likely than those with high to be in career situations in which their income and occupational ranks are defined and delimited in terms of official qualifications which were felt by the respondents to be arbitrary and unrelated to the requirements of the task. For example, to be kept in a subordinate grade because one's educational qualifications are low is acceptable in, for example, a medical context, in which the superordinate grade is that of consultant doctor; it is less acceptable when the subordinate grade is supervisory clerk and the superordinate one is office manager.[41]

Still another comparative reference group factor is the style of leisure-time contact with friends. Those whose feelings of relative deprivation were low tend to have a 'family-centred' style, in which the friends were in similar occupations and who had similar incomes and occupational ranks as well. Those whose feelings of relative deprivation were high tend to have a 'work-centred' style, in which the friends were more likely to be 'associates', and who, although in similar occupations, were more often in either higher or lower ranks.

Proposition 5

The greater the degree to which the structure of authority

THE SOCIOLOGY OF THE WORKPLACE

within the work situation is 'bureaucratically' rather than 'professionally' organized, the more is an actor within this situation likely to encounter anomogenic, blocking, and comparative reference group factors.

It is certain that this proposition is insufficient for the present purposes. Variations in the structure of authority is only one of the many possible intervening variables. Further, although the present data are consistent with the proposition, the number of deviant cases is too high to permit the proposition to be accepted without qualification or at least additional corollaries. However, many studies of organizations and authority suggest that the degree of professionalization of the authority structure is highly relevant.

Following Weber's discussion of rationality and rational-legal authority within bureaucratic organizations,* many sociologists have attempted to qualify Weber's propositions by distinguishing between two types of bureaucratic organizations, primarily on the basis of certain properties of their authority structures. For example, consider the work of Udy, Dalton, Gouldner, Etzioni, Burns and Stalker, Clements, Brewer, Blau, and Hopper.[42] In one way or another, each distinguishes what Blau calls a 'professional' structure of authority from a 'bureaucratic' one, and does so in terms of very similar lists of structural properties, such as 'supervisory styles'. They also show that although one type of authority structure is likely to predominate in a particular organization, both types are likely to occur in any one organization. It is possible to consider the

* Implicit in much of Weber's work is a distinction between power and authority: 'authority' refers to 'power', the possession and exercise of which is experienced as legitimate by both the powerful and the powerless. This is most apparent in his discussion of stratification in which certain hierarchies or orders are said to be based on authority, such as the status order, while others to be based on power, such as the economic order. Curiously, Weber does not apply this distinction in an obvious way to his study of organizations. Once an organization is bureaucratized, in the sense that it can be described in terms of his five major properties of bureaucratic organizations, he assumes the existence of 'rational-legal' authority, and the concept of power no longer applies. It is conceivable that, for Weber, in so far as 'rationality' was bound to become the value orientation from which any organizational form would derive its legitimacy, a bureaucracy, which is the manifestation of the rational pursuit of aims, would, by definition, be based on authority rather than on power. However, this assumption and the complex perspective which hinges upon it have stimulated considerable debate.

248

properties which distinguish bureaucratic from professional authority in terms of the degree to which they are likely to function as anomogenic blocking, and comparative reference group factors. Although they express the same point in a variety of terminologies, each of the sociologists mentioned above has shown that situations characterized by bureaucratic authority structures are more likely than those characterized by professional authority structures to generate these factors.

To obtain further evidence concerning this proposition, members of the sample were compared in terms of the two syndromes of structural properties which have been associated with each type of authority structure, e.g. closeness of supervision, autonomy and scope of responsibility, promotion based on merit, etc., with respect to their own personal work situation and their own descriptions of the organizations in which they worked. Of course, those who worked in professional situations tended to be in professional kinds of organizations, and those in bureaucratic situations to be in bureaucratic organizations; however, this relationship depended primarily on the echelon at which they work. The higher the echelon, the stronger the connection. The evidence showed that the more highly bureaucratized the situation and the organization, the higher the number and the greater the intensity of the anomogenic, blocking, and comparative factors. Consistent with this pattern was the finding that those whose feelings of relative deprivation were low tend to work in professional situations and professional organizations, and those whose feelings of relative deprivation were high in bureaucratic situations and bureaucratic organizations.

Proposition 6

Occupations which are classified in the commercial situses (e.g. manufacturing, distribution) are more likely than those which are classified in the professional situses (e.g. government and education) to be characterized by bureaucratic rather than professional structures of authority with respect to work situations and their organizational contexts. Occupations were classified into situses according to the principles outlined in the first section of this article. This was an almost self-evident task. Why commercial situses should contain organizations with bureaucratic authority structures and professional situses those with professional authority structures is an important and interesting sociological question. It is also beyond the scope of the present task. However, as is usually the case, the speculations of Parsons are instructive.[43] In addition to the problems of 'centre and periphery' of the core-value system, and of with what functional tasks a situs is concerned, such variables as organizational size and complexity, the personnel – specific quality of the task, the support systems in the organization's environment, etc., will all have to be taken into account.

Proposition 7

Personnel with high economic orientations are more likely than those with low economic orientations to enter and to be recruited to occupations within commercial as opposed to professional situses; the work ideologies of occupations in commercial situses are more likely to support high economic orientations than are the ideologies within professional situses, which are more likely to support orientations towards occupational esteem and status.

In this connection it is of interest that the mean economic orientation for those in commercial situses is 19·5, and the mean for those in professional situses is 16·9, the difference being significant at ·05. Clearly, people tend not to enter the professions, especially those in the educational situs, if they are oriented primarily towards income as a goal. And, if in the course of their careers, they should discover that they do value money highly, they are likely to enter another situs.

Proposition 8

Therefore, the personnel in 'commercial' situses are more likely than those in 'professional' situses to experience feelings of relative deprivation with respect to income.

CONCLUSIONS

A theory was formulated and evidence adduced to show why feelings of relative deprivation vary with situs classifications. However, 'situs' was used as a classifying or demographic variable, and was not integrated into the etiological chain between feelings of relative deprivation and bureaucratic structures of authority, the independent variable. In this respect it is apparent that research in industrial sociology would profit from making explicit the situs classifications of the organizations under consideration. In so far as authority structures are an important variable in the study of a given problem, research findings should be generalized across situs classifications with extreme caution. It is equally apparent that research in social stratification, especially that concerned with the characteristics of the persons and families at various echelons in the main hierarchies of status and economic power, must try to build situs classifications into their designs. This is essential for international comparisons. As important as classification may be, it is not the main problem. Having seen that classification of this kind is important, the next step is to explain why variations in situs should be related to many structural properties of their member organizations. This is by no means an easy task.

NOTES

1 Earl Hopper, 'Notes on stratification, education and mobility in industrial societies', p. 17, in Earl Hopper (ed.), *Readings in the theory of educational systems*, London: Hutchinson University Library, 1971.
2 *Ibid.*
3 Major shifts of population among these classifications have occurred between specific phases of industrialization processes in almost all industrial societies. However, within these phases the distribution of population is relatively stable. It is possible that in his arguments for the infamous 'selective employment tax', Professor Kaldor did not consider this point. With respect to the case of the United States, see Alba M. Edwards, *A social-economic grouping of the gainful workers of the United States*, Washington, D.C.: Government Printing Office, 1938.
4 For a contemporary example, see N. J. G. Pounds, *An introduction to economic geography*, London: John Murray, 1970, p. 1.
5 See 'Henri Fayol' in D. S. Pugh *et al.*, *Writers on organisations*, London: Penguin Books, 1964, pp. 60–5.
6 Emile Benoit-Smullyan, 'Status, status types and status inter-relations', *American Sociological Review*, vol. 9, April 1944, pp. 151–61.
7 W. Lloyd Warner *et al.*, *Social class in America*, Chicago: Science Research Associates, 1949; Paul K. Hatt, 'Occupation and social stratification', *American Journal of Sociology*, vol. 55, May 1950, pp. 533–43; see also Joseph A. Kahl and Jerome Davies, 'A comparison of indexes of socioeconomic status', *American Journal of Sociology*, vol. 20, June 1955, pp. 317–24.
8 Hatt, *ibid.* p. 539.

9 *Ibid.* p. 539.

10 *Ibid.* pp. 540–2. For example, the business situs had prestige scores which ranged from 58 to 88, whereas the manual work situs ranged from 34 to 83; 8 of the 18 manual occupations ranked as high or higher than the lowest ranked occupation in the business situs; and the median ranks were approximately 72 and 54 for the business and manual work situses, respectively.

11 Richard T. Morris and Raymond J. Murphy, 'The situs dimension and occupational structure', *American Sociological Review*, vol. 24, April 1959, pp. 231–9. This article also gives a very useful summary of the previous literature on situs.

12 Daniel R. Miller and Guy E. Swanson, *The changing American parent*, London: Chapman and Hall, 1958.

13 For example, see E. A. Friedmann and R. J. Hainghurst, *The meaning of work and retirement*, Chicago: University of Chicago Press, 1954, pp. 5 and 6, which looks at steelworkers, coal miners, skilled craftsmen, sales people, and physicians: see also Anne Roe, *The psychology of occupations*, New York: Wiley, 1958; and A. M. Carr Saunders *et al.*, *A survey of social conditions in England and Wales*, Oxford: Clarendon Press, 1958, pp. 113–16. Various studies of the professions employ some aspects of the 'notion' of situs but not the concept itself: the best example is William J. Goode *et al.*, *The professions in modern society*, New York: Russell Sage Foundation, 1957. A good bibliography of such studies can be extracted from Cyril Sofer, *Men in mid-career*, London: Cambridge University Press, 1970, especially pp. 39–84.

14 See for example P. Sorokin, *Social and cultural mobility*, Glencoe,Ill.: Free Press, 1959, p. 7 (first published 1927).

15 Richard T. Morris and Raymond J. Murphy, 'Occupational situs, subjective class identification, and political affiliation', *American Sociological Review*, vol. 26, 1961, pp. 383–92. A chapter on situs appeared in Paul K, Hatt and A. J. Reiss Jr. *et al.*, *Occupations and social status*, Glencoe, Ill.: Free Press, 1961, but this was a reprint of Hatt's earlier article. It is worth commenting that although this book mentions the first article by Morris and Murphy ('The situs dimension and occupational structure') as a source for the concept of situs (see p. 45), in fact Morris and Murphy are critical of Hatt's earlier article ('Occupation and social stratification') in so far as it maintained the confusion between situs and status.

16 Leonard Broom and Philip Selznick, *Sociology: a text with adapted readings*, 3rd edition, New York: Harper and Row, 1963, pp. 204–5.

17 Richard H. Hall, *Occupations and the social structure*, London: Prentice-Hall, 1969, p. 296.

18 For a recent discussion of the concepts of a 'pattern of social mobility', 'career structure', 'educational route', 'channel of mobility', 'life-trajectory', etc., see Hopper, 'Notes on stratification, education and mobility in industrial societies', *op. cit.*

19 John Hall and D. Caradog Jones, 'Social grading of occupations', *British Journal of Sociology*, vol. 1, January 1950, pp. 31–55. For the

purposes of the present article, the Hall-Jones scale has been condensed from five into three categories. 'Social class I' refers to their I and II; 'social class II' refers to their III; and 'social class III' refers to their IV and V. For some of the dependent variables, such as 'friends' mean social class and mean mobility', an *expanded* Hall-Jones scale was used: each of their social classes I through IV was split into a high and low group (this was not done for social class V, as all these men in our sample were highly skilled manual workers), giving a nine-point scale overall.

20 We based this situs combination on the conventional wisdom, such as expressed by Trollope: 'She had an idea that the son of a gentleman, if he intended to maintain his rank as a gentleman, should earn his income as a clergyman, or as a barrister, or as a soldier, or as a sailor. . . There might possibly be a doubt about the Civil Service and Civil Engineering; but she had no doubt whatever that when a man touched trade or commerce in any way he was doing that which was not the work of a gentleman . . . ' Anthony Trollope, *The Vicar of Bullhampton*, 1870, quoted in Robert N. Rapoport *et. al.*, *Mid-career development*, London: Tavistock Publications, 1970, p. 16. An example of the contemporary relevance of this piece of Victoriana is the member of our sample who described his father's occupation as a 'gentleman', but who revealed, eventually, that he owned a brewery.

21 This point is recognized by Udy, who in advocating exploratory studies, rather than attempt at hypothesis testing in the comparative analysis of organizations, makes the following comment: 'Despite the "inappropriate" character of statistical methods in exploratory situations, the researcher confronted with many cases still has to think about a vast amount of material in some way, and, by projecting it all against a random model, eventually present conclusions which allege relationships he believes do not occur by chance. This is exactly what statistical procedures do with large amounts of data.' Stanley G. Udy Jr., 'The comparative analysis of organisations', in James G. March (ed.), *Handbook of organizations*, Chicago: Rand McNally, 1965, p. 684.

22 For a discussion of the F-ratio, see Hubert M. Blalock, *Social statistics*, New York: McGraw-Hill, 1960, esp. pp. 242–72.

23 For example, see Joseph A. Kahl, 'Some measures of achievement orientation', *American Journal of Sociology*, December 1968.

24 For example, see Ralph H. Turner, *The social context of ambition*, San Francisco; Chandler Press, 1968.

25 See Mildred B. Kantor (ed.), *Mobility and mental health*, Springfield, Illinois: Charles C. Thomas, 1965.

26 This is what most sociologists would mean by the term. It was first discussed systematically by Robert K. Merton, *Social theory and social structure*, Glencoe, Ill.: Free Press, 1957; in also W. G. Runciman, *Relative deprivation and social justice*, London: Routledge and Kegan Paul, 1965.

27 See Peter M. Blau, 'The hierarchy of authority in organizations', *American Journal of Sociology*, vol. 73, January 1968, pp. 453–67, who found that men in organizations which could be classified as

having 'professional' rather than 'bureaucratic' authority structures were more likely to perceive their work as having the following properties: 'less supervised', 'more decisions', 'significant', 'sociable', 'interesting', and 'meaningful'.

28 See Miller and Swanson, *The changing American parent*, who found that 'perceived job security' was highest in occupational settings which are similar to those found in the government and education situses.

29 For a discussion of 'career disorderliness', see Harold Wilensky, 'Orderly careers and social participation', *American Sociological Review*, vol. 26, no. 4, (August) 1961.

30 See for example, Joseph A. Kahl, *The measurement of modernism: a study of values in Brazil and Mexico*, Austin, Texas: University of Texas Press, 1968.

31 See discussions of sponsorship by Ralph H. Turner and Earl Hopper in their articles in Hopper, *Readings in the theory of educational systems.*, *op. cit.*

32 See Harold Wilensky, 'Work, careers, and social integration', *International Social Science Journal*, vol. 12, no. 4, 1960, pp. 543–60; and Wilensky, 'Orderly careers and social participation', *op. cit.*

33 See Melvin L. Kohn, 'Bureaucratic man: a portrait and an interpretation', *American Sociological Review*, vol. 36, June 1971, pp. 461–74, who obtained a similar finding.

34 This finding is consistent with that of Miller and Swanson, *The changing American parent*, *op. cit.*, who showed that people in 'welfare bureaucratic' occupations had more children that did those in 'individuated-entreprenuerial' occupations.

35 See Kohn, 'Bureaucratic man', who obtained similar findings, pp. 466–7, *op. cit.*

36 Morris and Murphy, 'Occupational situs, subjective class indentification, and political affiliation', p. 389.

37 Talcot Parsons, 'A revised analytical approach to the theory of social stratification', in his *Essays in sociological theory*, revised edition, Glencoe, Ill.: Free Press, 1954, esp. pp. 428–35, 415–19.

38 Morris and Murphy, 'Occupational situs, subjective class identification, and political affiliation', pp. 391–2, *op. cit.*

39 The term 'nomic' as opposed to 'anomic', or 'nomie' as opposed to 'anomie', is implied in N. Elias and J. L. Scotson, *The established and the outsiders*, London: Frank Cass, 1965.

40 Alvin W. Gouldner, 'Cosmopolitans and locals: towards an analysis of latent social roles', *Administration Science Quarterly*, vol. 2, December 1957 – March 1958, pp. 281–306, 443–80.

41 This is one of the factors discussed in connection with the growth of middle class trade unionism by David Lockwood, *The blackcoated worker*, London: George Allen and Unwin, 1958.

42 Stanley G. Udy Jr., ' "Bureaucracy" and "rationality" in Weber's organization theory: an empirical study', *American Sociological Review*, vol. 24, December 1950, pp. 791–5; Melville Dalton, *Men who manage*, New York: Wiley, 1959; Alvin W. Gouldner, *Patterns of Industrial bureaucracy*, Glencoe, Ill.: Free Press, 1954; Amatai Etzioni,

A comparative analysis of complex organizations, Glencoe, Ill.: Free Press, 1961; Tom Burns and G. M. Stalker, *The management of innovation*, London: Social Science Paperbacks and Tavistock Publications, 1961; R. V. Clements, *Managers: a study of their careers in industry*, London: George Allen and Unwin, 1958; John Brewer, 'Flow of communications, expert qualifications, and organizational authority structures', *American Sociological Review*, vol. 36, June 1971, pp. 475–84; Blau, 'The hierarchy of authority in organizations'; and Earl Hopper, 'Some effects of variations in supervisory styles', *British Journal of Sociology*, vol. 16, September 1965, pp. 189–205.

43 Parsons, 'A revised analytical approach to the theory of social stratification', *op. cit.*

10 Industrial Conflict Revisited

MALCOLM WARNER

General theories of the labour movement may only be valid for a relatively *narrow* range of situations in recent history and current experience. Even a recent sensible attack on the 'social tranquillity' thesis does not quite appreciate the possibility of endemic and continuing conflicts:

'The LANGUAGE [*sic*] of industrial relations has a built-in bias towards the status quo. Strikes are "sauvage" in France, "wild" in Germany and everywhere reported disapprovingly in terms of the supposed cost to the nation; strikes are wild-cats (what about wildcat employers?) without reference to the grievances or objectives, and even the term industrial relations has an abstractness, a university discipline flavour about it which is far removed from the essentially human and emotional realities. So when people talk about a "Crisis in European Industrial Relations", which was the title of a symposium held at the College of Europe in Bruges, Belgium, at the end of March, the immediate assumption is that a static and deliberately planned system is being suddenly convulsed by an attack of irrational disorder. In fact, of course, industrial relations are not a science with once and for all laws but simply a branch of human behaviour, and as such they take on an infinite variety of forms, all in constant evolution. So is it fair to talk of the current European experience as a crisis at all? Is it not rather a manifestation of *growing pains* as outdated working relationships adjust to changes in industry and society – acute now, as technologies advance apace, but basically healthy?'[1] (italics added)

The analogy of 'growing pains' seems to suggest that the

256

author makes assumptions similar to those he is criticizing. But there are *even greater* over-simplifications of the problem, and this paper attempts to develop a critique of some of their characteristics. As so much discussion of industrial relations has been riddled with these 'partial truths', it is all the more necessary to consider them critically.

Most discussions of the problem imply a system where there are visible and formally organized bodies representing workers' interests able to act in an autonomous manner. They imply, in any case, a range of organized interest groups in society, and that these are able to interact and possibly clash with other organized (say, employers') interests, even the state, in a clearly open fashion. The more open the society, we would argue, the more *manifest* the level of conflict between organized interest groups is likely to be. Hence theories of the labour movement which relate to *manifest* economic and/or political strategies of organized workers' interest groups[2] must perforce be limited to conflicts in the particular type of society referred to, possibly only the United States itself, or at best a narrow range of so-called advanced societies. In societies which deny that there are 'conflicts of interests' because by definition these could not exist in a workers' state, theories of the labour movement concerned with either economic or political strategies, or both, would not be applicable. Strictly speaking here, Marxists do not consider conflicts between classes to exist in post-revolutionary situations and therefore organized versions of such conflicts are held by definition to be impossible, although they admit that there might be contradictions between *strata* in society; but this argument is tautologous because *strata* are defined as groups which do not have contradictory interests, whereas classes are defined as those which do have.[3]

We must next examine the relationship between economic variables and levels of conflict. We must, of course, note that the level of *manifest* conflict depends on the nature of the system because the latter may rule that strikes for example are 'out of court', such that formal autonomy for trade unions is impossible. Economic variables cannot predict the level of *manifest* organized conflict, because they cannot tell us to what degree formal organization exists concerning any level of manifest conflict in the society, let alone that involved in industrial relations. This depends on the political orientation of the system. In the realm of prediction, a recent paper has suggested that the three best predictors of most of the other variables in a society are its size of population, its level of GNP per capita, and its political orientation.[4] If the last of these is so important, it very much undermines the 'convergence' thesis which argues that the dichotomy between pluralistic and non-pluralistic systems is becoming increasingly less valid. We must also note that in fact the level of GNP per capita, and the political orientation of the society, are practically uncorrelated. There may be a level of industrial conflict (at least latent) which can be predicted by the economic variables, but the degree to which it becomes manifest and organized depends on the nature of the society, and more particularly its political orientation.

The degree of meaningful 'organization' or unionization of the labour force may vary proportionately with economic development, but only with certain given political preconditions. We must now ascertain the *necessary conditions* for either economic or political activity of unions, as a primary strategy of labour, as it reflects the expression of manifest conflict. The level of economic development should tell us the degree of industrialization, and hence 'organization' or 'unionization', by and large. But we need to know the nature of the political system, as we have stated, to say how far this is 'meaningful' in relation to the expression, organization, and management of manifest conflict. This must be ascertained prior to stating how far it will take the form of primarily economic or non-economic activity.

Having come thus far, what do we need to know in order to predict whether it will be primarily one or the other? To argue that unions will choose to pursue economic goals where labour has achieved its political and social aims is not quite satisfactory, because these conditions when satisfied in, say, advanced countries outside the USA failed to cause the emergence of the model predicted by Perlman,[5] although we do concede that in Leninist terms all 'non-socialist' union strategies may be dubbed 'economism'. Union strategies and goals will reflect members' demands to some degree, and this will reflect in turn their *relative deprivation* in the context of the economic and political system.[6] Thus, given the nature of the political system (and that unions are not bound within the organizational strait-jacket which the elite might think necessary for industrialization) which is, in part, dependent on the political culture and its tradition, the unions may *still* choose political strategies in certain situations.

Knowing that labour demands of varying kinds are satisfied will not, *in themselves*, allow us to predict the choice of strategy to be followed by the unions. Indeed, strategy may be a dependent variable, and 'chosen' by the dominant elite if we concede the argument of Kerr *et al.*, if only in outline.[7] Each pattern will relate to relative deprivation of trade union members with respect to class or status or power, or combinations of such, in each context. Except for the time-lag in gaining basic social and political goals, there is little difference between the American and European experiences cited in Sturmthal's model,[8] as Europe *eventually* 'caught-up' with the United States. Indeed, it may be asserted, as a matter of *historical fact*, that several European countries gained basic trade union rights before the American workers, that is *before* the New Deal legislation, although the latter may have had the edge concerning formal political rights, like the vote. It may also be argued that certain political and social demands are preconditions of strategy, and once won, are regarded as essential *minima*, and less crucial in the determination of organized labour's policies. It can even be argued that unions may indulge in collective bargaining as a primary strategy, before political and social gains are won, as for example in the essential period of the British trade union movement's development in the latter half of the nineteenth century.[9] This was true before universal male suffrage was established, for example, in the British case at least. The second pattern outlined by Sturmthal,[10] involving unions in newly emerging nations switching from political roles, may not necessarily tend to develop, as the colonial states become independent. Political trends early may lead to even more extreme political strategies later as the countries become run by either revolutionary intellectuals or the military (or both in some sort of working coalition, a pattern currently emerging in Latin America).

Any general theory tends to simplify. Guiltier than most is the view that labour protest is negatively correlated with economic development. For example, Kerr *et al.* observe that

'Labour protest, on a closer look, is on the decline as industrialization around the world proceeds at an ever faster pace. In the mid-twentieth century, workers do not destroy machines. The protest of today is more in favour of industrialization than against it.'[11] This may be the case, but we cannot fully accommodate this view with the 'alienation' thesis. In addition, although Kerr *et al.* point out that 'Labour protest in some situations may still be a potent force, however, particularly in times of crisis',[12] they feel that 'There is likely to be a "peaking of protest" in any individual case of industrialization, but it may not be a very high peak or not difficult to control.'[13] This is a facile view and sees protest as a once-for-all 'residue' which peaks, and can be managed thereafter. While this is true in the sense that it does not continue *vis-à-vis* the process of industrialization in general, it may re-emerge on specific points in a pattern of continuing frequency. There may, for example, be a contrapuntal relationship in some cases of official with unofficial strikes. In addition, the general strike, the political weapon *par excellence* of organized labour, does not seem to have disappeared once industrialization has reached a high state of development. This is clearly the case in post-war Western Europe.

If we take the Kerr *et al.* typology seriously, the outcome of moving towards essentially economic demands may not result, except as an *a-typical* development. It is unfortunate that American (and possibly also the British) experience had been extrapolated by so many writers on industrial relations in the past as a future for general development. In the Kerr *et al.* schema, the 'bourgeois' pattern would seem to be given a very limited weighting as only *one* of five possible types, although the future 'convergence' implies a path towards several of its characteristics, particularly the decline of labour protest. Their overall view on the 'Decline of overt protest'[14] – by which they mean open revolt against factory, falling off as industrialization reaches its late stage, is true only if protest means *absolute* hostility to a machine-dominated economy, but the empirical evidence does not suggest that the worker is less prone to 'absenteeism, prolonged and sporadic withdrawal from work, wildcat stoppages', etc.[15] We can *disagree* with the point that 'protest peaks early'[16] without *necessarily* accepting the Marxist view.

To sum up the argument thus far, the conditions which are necessary for either manifest economic or political activity of unions would seem to be related to the nature of the political system, and the factors determining it. The attitude of the elites towards conflict would be an important variable, to be sure, but the question of how far this is an independent variable is an unsettled question. The attitude may be partly determined by the level of economic development, the elite being more tolerant of conflict as societies become more developed, because they can afford to be. This has been even suggested as a factor affecting the Soviet Union, as well as the other 'advanced' socialist states, such as Hungary. Economic variables, it must be admitted, play a very important role in the process of organized labour's development of strategies, but it is difficult to decide if they are both necessary *and* sufficient determinants of policy choices.[17] Behind all this, the economic factors outlined by Sturmthal may still be very relevant, although the variables may be less independent than supposed at some stages of development and in some societies. They may only be independent under certain conditions. Labour demands may also not move necessarily from political to economic with the onset of the advanced society – and with the emergency of 'planning' may move back to the political.[18] Both the supply and demand variables may be dependent, given the increasing role of the state in developed and developing societies. In the former, the labour market may be controlled by the elites concerned, whether revolutionary or nationalist (assuming that dynastic and colonial types noted by Kerr *et al.* have by now been eclipsed).[19] The move to manpower planning in developing societies by large government and private organizations increasingly helps to make labour supply a dependent variable. This view is not inconsistent with the power of labour to refuse to supply itself in the short term, by way of absenteeism, etc. In societies where migration is permitted, this may also balance the dependence of the variable, but it may be restricted by either economic or political limitations, or both (as in the case of mainland China). The long-term situation in the labour market may also relate to the reasons why even in similar shortage situations, *different* patterns of organization develop and persist; also why with different market phenomena, *similar* forms of organization develop. In addition, organizational patterns may be transmitted and disseminated, rather like ideas, producing considerable incongruous structures in unsuitable environments which may not be able to support them.[20] If the shortage situations determine the organizational variables, it would be expected that the latter change, but there is little evidence to demonstrate this. In conditions of full employment, different patterns of organization continue to exist. Similarly, the development of the early craft form of unionism occurred in varying circumstances of labour supply. The positive correlation between types of organization and conditions in the labour market is by and large quite weak. These craft unions did not necessarily stress collective bargaining. At one period they even provided the support for the First International, before the general unions developed, at least in the British case. The rise of classic Marxism coincides with the period of craft unionism. In addition the argument concerning the pursuit of political strategies for purely economic ends, for example raising labour standards at the price of maintaining an unbalanced labour market, does not adequately fit the case, unless one assumes in the first place the pursuit of narrow sectional interest.

It is difficult to say whether the choice of strategies is determined by the degree to which the labour movement serves as an instrument for the attainment of non-economic objectives, as well as economic goals common to all workers.[21] This is because where it is true to a high degree, we do not always find the choice of a political strategy, although possibly vice versa. The former is probably not true of the British case, where the degree was high, and the strategy became highly economic from the late 1840s to the late 1860s at least. Where the degree was low, however, as in the case of the United States, it may explain the choice of economic strategy, but not such a choice where in fact the movement *was* to a high degree a major instrument for the pursuit of non-economic objectives, at early stages of trade union development, although collective bargaining eventually emerged as a recognizable central characteristic of the industrial relations system. The effect on changes in the structure of the labour force may be indeterminate, although there is some evidence in Western Europe that the rise of white-collar unionism does *not* diminish the pursuit of political strategies.

Indeed, while much of the speculation in the 'fifties about

future trends of the labour movement extrapolated the quiescence of the period, the experience of the 'sixties, especially the later years when the changes in the structure of the labour force were more advanced, suggested that 'militancy' was more likely than 'maturity'. Again, this may be no more than a response to 'la societé bloquée', to use Crozier's phrase, in the French context, and once more relative deprivation may be involved, but the wave of labour unrest is now sweeping Western Europe and North America. The most successful white-collar unions are often considered the most militant these days, and sometimes the most politicized. Social and economic change may cause the conditions of change in the structure of the labour force, and the latter may only be an intervening variable.[22] The upshot may be essentially political in emphasis. But in some cases, labour demands may have become dependent variables, where the elites increasingly control the media in not only the developing (and/or non-pluralistic societies), but also in the 'West'.[23] But whether this is the case or not, the strategy of organized labour in the context of the planning process, whatever its guise, has moved in many cases to a greater emphasis on the political, and is increasingly doing so.[24] If this does not occur, the national union may have little to do, if, as is the case in Britain, the focal point of bargaining moves increasingly to the plant level. The participation of unions in consultative relationships with government is now quite general in Western Europe, and fairly common in some developing countries.

We must note that economic and political strategies may in most cases proceed in harness, especially in advanced societies because as social structure becomes more complex, a higher degree of interaction occurs between all the sub-systems. Similarly, little choice of either strategies may occur outside pluralistic societies. This view would be quite consistent with the Kerr *et al.* typology, although one would place greater weights on some of the ideal types involved, as opposed to others. The crude choice between an 'economic' or a 'political' strategy respectively may simply not occur. There are further analytical simplifications in the Kerr *et al.* model. We would also argue that the distinction in reality between Kerr *et al.*'s ideal types of 'dynastic' and 'middle class' is in fact blurred (see Table 1); similarly in the case of 'nationalist' and 'revolu-

Table 1 WORKER PROTEST AND THE ELITES*

Industrializing elite	*Dynastic*	*Middle class*	*Revolutionary-intellectuals*	*Colonial administrators*	*Nationalist leaders*
Organizing principle of group protest	Class consciousness	Job control	Self-criticism	Anti-colonialism	Nationalism
Forms of group protest	Demonstrations and political strikes	Organized economic strikes	Diffused and suppressed, except for occasional outburst	Demonstrations for independence, often violent	Demonstrations, ordinarily peaceful
Attitudes of elites towards conflict	Inconsistent with paternal society	Affirmative role for limited conflict	Inconsistent with ideology and rapid industrialization	Inconsistent with role of mother country	Inconsistent with nationalist and economic development

*See Kerr et al., *Industrialism and industrial man*, p. 216.

tionary-intellectuals', on all three dimensions of organizing principle of group protest, its forms, and the attitudes of elites towards conflict. This may even be true for the American case, except if the observer shares the Kerr *et al.* assumptions. The modes of protest of columns three and five may merge, assuming the colonial type to have now almost completely vanished with the degree of national independence now achieved. Except for the moot question of how far 'demonstrations, ordinarily peaceful' occur or are allowed to occur in the 'revolutionary-intellectuals' part of the typology, in reality there is convergence of the two columns in good part. In some cases, demonstrations may occur but may be suppressed as was the case in East Germany, in Poland, and Hungary in the mid-'fifties. We must also note the behaviour of the Czech workers in the Dubcek period. But outside these qualifications, the degree of conflict is latent, and only expressed in absenteeism, etc. in, say, recent Soviet experience.[25]

It should be pointed out, however, that even in the pluralistic case, the same response may occur where the state tries to legislate for organized conflict. Currently, for example, the Conservative government in Britain hoped to 'outlaw the unofficial strike' but one critic of their legislation points out the difficulties:

'The legalist approach to industrial relations – briefly, bringing collective bargaining and the unions "within the framework of the law" – can take two forms. There is the simple, sweeping approach traditionally favoured by the right wing which would simply subject all collective bargaining agreements to the normal laws of contract ("outlaw the unofficial strike")'.

The reasons why this approach is impractical were definitively stated in the *Donovan Report*. First, very few agreements as currently drafted would stand up in a court of law. Secondly, the problems of enforcement would be very great. Thirdly, even if one succeeded in making a strike as such illegal, there are many other ways of exercising industrial pressure, which are much harder to pin down – such as "planned absenteeism", "working without enthusiasm", "strict attention to rules" and other euphemisms for refusal to co-operate with management. It is no doubt because they

recognize these problems that whatever their public pro-
testations, employers do not (as Donovan pointed out) use
their present powers of prosecuting strikers.[26]

Indeed, even the legalistic labour-relations system in the
United States has not quite disciplined the workers, and the
term 'wild-cat strike' in fact originated there, and still occurs
on a not inconsiderable scale.

An essential point to make is that the organized labour
movement is *not* homogenous, even within the boundaries of
the nation-state, let alone within the boxes of industrial
relations systems typologists. It may even be the case that
different parts of the same union may act differently from the
official leadership, either unofficially, or quasi-officially. This
is a consequence of the bureaucratization of the labour movement, anticipated by Michels.[27] It may not always be possible
to achieve this harmonization of common objectives in trade
unions and there is much evidence to suggest that there is
frequently considerable manifest conflict, which takes the form
of action directed against both employers and union leaders,
and even the government involved. This may involve 'political'
strategies, or if directed towards economic goals, may take
directions other than those predicted by Perlman, or more
recently, Kerr *et al.*

The defect of much theorizing on the labour movement is that
it encapsulates a model of organizational maturity over time,
and that, as organizations increase in size, they become more
conservative.[28] Michels argues that the 'iron law of oligarchy'
would lead to ostensibly democratic organizations – such as
socialist parties and trade unions – becoming increasingly
controlled by those at the top. (It is of minor interest to note
that Michels himself used the term in German for a '*tendency*' to
oligarchy, rather than being as dogmatic as later writers.)
Michels's view was that the union leaders would be concerned
with sustaining size and would give this priority over its manifest
radical aims and that there was a direct relationship between
the complexity and size of organizations and their 'tendency'
to oligarchy. No matter what the radical or democratic aims
of the organization, his so-called 'iron-law' implied the necessary
development of an oligarchic ruling group in all large organizations, *even* labour organizations. While this view has a certain

prima facie attractiveness, it is sociologically naive, and is empirically deficient. This view is also assumed in the approach of Kerr *et al.*, as it is developed in its organization maturity version which we will discuss shortly. One basic criticism which can be immediately made is that such an approach has a crude *linearity* built into it, and this in itself detracts from its usefulness. If indeed a model of oligarchy can be developed for trade unions, it will have to be more sophisticated, and *at least* an empirical taxonomy. The simple Michels thesis is a theory of organizational growth which further assumes that as the leader becomes part of the hierarchy, his attitude to his position will alter. He constructs an ideology of staying in power, and this overshadows, and may even determine, the goals of the organization. Michels argues that the leader will seek to be free of the control of the membership and independent of it. The Michels position is at best a simplification, and only looks at a limited number of variables. The notion that 'he who says non-oligarchy, [i.e. democracy] says organization' might make better sense in so far as the need for representation requires greater constitutional procedures, etc.

The maturity hypothesis argued by other writers is that unions are like people (or plants for that matter).[29] They have a rapid period of lively growth in their early years; in later stages they 'mature' – and presumably, in a last stage, become moribund. Militancy and factionalism characterize the early stages; common sense, cooperation, and cohesion characterize the so-called mature years. As unions mature, they are supposed to 'grow up', cultivate their garden of sober economic interest, and so on. They will 'settle down' and managers will replace agitators. This would result in the benefits of the 'law of increasing social tranquility', as described earlier. While there is some superficial evidence to suggest this has been the case in the American case, it has strong *normative* overtones. The unions ought to realize – if this line of reasoning is carried to its logical conclusion – that they should act in the 'public interest', cooperate with a voluntary incomes policy, discipline wildcat strikers, and keep their wage claims in line with what the nation can afford. They 'ought' to work with both the trade union and employers' federations, and keep good relations with governments. They 'ought' to avoid political strikes, indeed any major strikes. Conflict, even organized, and according to the 'the web of rules', is to be avoided, and has little place in this schema. A recent analysis has commendably tried to discuss critically the complexities of such conflict regulation, at least for developing economies.[30] Even the structural functionalist approach which encompasses the utility of conflict, at least in the work of writers like Coser and Dahrendorf, is wiser. But unions do not exist to 'satisfy' the public in the way that such local authority bodies do. In analysing organizations, we might ask: who is prime beneficiary? If we do, we find that unions are not basically service organizations. Nor are they quite business organizations. They are mutual benefit associations, and it is argued that they have primarily to satisfy their members, and remain accountable to them.[31] Even in developing economies accommodation to members' interests must be pursued, leading at best to the 'isolation of conflicts inherent in the development process'.[32]

Membership must be considered to some degree an *independent* variable. In systems where trade union membership is 'voluntary' (*pace* the closed shop), union leaders are nearly always worried about keeping up the size of their organization. They tend to be concerned with the maintenance, or if possible the expansion, of their membership, either in the short or long term. This is not *always* the case, nor is the converse *necessarily* true, but a voluntary organization tends to store power through its members and the resources (dues, for example) which they bring to it, and the actions it can influence its members to perform. The more members the better is not, of course, true where there are advantages from having a closed organization, like a small craft union; but even here it is necessary to organize as many of the craft group as possible. Indeed many of the biggest unions today in Britain were craft unions that have opened their ranks to the less skilled like the A U E W. Leaving aside other questions of getting involved in union affairs, the *minimum transaction or act of participation* lies in joining the union and keeping up one's membership. The act cannot be taken for granted, and presents organizational cost problems. The problem of membership turnover is particularly worrying for general union. Similarly, members must be given 'value for money' in the provision of union services. A considerable number of union members have a basically *instrumental* orientation towards belonging to the union.

It follows that even in a large union, with the 'closed shop' and 'check-off' in operation, the membership must be kept minimally happy, and never taken for granted. If there is a widespread dissatisfaction about the militancy of the union leaders (both in terms of Perlman's goals, or indeed Marx's), the union rank and file must be satisfied on this score, especially about the union's primary goals. Otherwise membership will drop, and the power of the union and of its leaders will drop with it. The demand curve for union services is always less than infinitely inelastic.[33] In any system where unions have a minimal degree of autonomy, the strategy the union leaders adopt will not be necessarily determined by the *absolute* level of economic development, although this of course may limit the range of tactics to be adapted. It will more likely to be influenced by organizational necessities.

The line of reasoning employed by most American industrial relations theorists since Perlman has incorporated 'the end of ideology' world-view of Bell, for example.[34] But is it of general applicability, other than in the American context, where it may or may not be quite as true as some believe?[35] If anything, the 1960s was a decade of increasing ideological rhetoric at least, although strikes in several countries rose considerably in number and duration. This leads one to ask whether maturity and conflict are not separate dimensions? The use of the term 'mature' is in fact value-laden, and the degree to which behaviour can be so labelled is clearly a matter of perspective. Certain goals, or courses of action to achieve them, may be called 'mature' by an outside observer, but may appear unwise to members of the organization. It must also be noted that 'militancy' is a relative term too. Large trade unions may not only pursue militant goals if these are organizational necessities, like competing with their rivals, but also generate internal oppositions. The bigger unions become and the more heterogenous their membership, the greater the organizational stresses. Writers like Lester have seen severe competition for top office as a characteristic of the early, radical days of a union; but recent research has found that opposition in British unions has not significantly dwindled over time, with size. American unions have also seen a revival of opposition.[36] Similarly, size and militancy seem to have coincided, at least in the case of the two largest British unions.[37]

The limitations of any theory of the labour movement which stressed organizational maturity, and a move to an 'economic' strategy of relying primarily on collective bargaining as a weapon, is that it cannot essentially convince us that choice of strategy is a function of economic development or selected variables associated with it. We would argue that the 'economic' strategy would not necessarily be associated with a high level of economic development. Militancy now seems to be wide-spread in developed societies once again. How can we explain the non-selection of strategies which certain theories might have led one to expect to be selected? What we *can* say is that these theories are now untenable, without very severe quali-fications on the thesis being introduced.

We have to decide whether we *can* have *general* theories of the labour movement. In any event, they must take into account organizational variables. To survive, union leaders must be extremely adept 'politically'. It would not be in the interest of the large union, or their town, if they allowed rank-and-file dissatisfaction to weaken the union via members' defections, lapses, or abandonment of the national trade union member-ship. Organizations have to adapt to a wide range of forces, and large unions are no exception. At the very least, 'dynamic conservatism', to use Donald Schon's term, must operate. If trace unions sometimes surprise the economist or sociologist, it may be due to the immaturity of the theories to which the latter professions subscribe, rather than to the unions' im-maturity. The trouble with many theories is that they try to generalize from a particular period. The maturity thesis may have fitted the labour movements only at certain times and contexts.

Unions are a great deal more diverse and complex organiza-tionally than typologies usually allow. Unions are still faced with many serious organizational problems. These may consist of holding membership in declining economic sectors, or increasing it either where unionization has in the past been relatively low, say in France and Italy, or where there has been a change in the structure of the labour force, and white-collar unionism has spread rapidly. The power of unions, it has been argued, is in any case often overstated; even in Britain collective bargaining, Turner suggests, only *directly* affects less than 20 per cent of the labour force.[38]

270

CONCLUSIONS

While many union responses may be seen partly due to in-dustrialization and economic change, we cannot see the choice of the prime strategy of the organized labour movement as being determinate. It seems *prima facie* improbable that there will be one model towards which all labour movements will evolve; there might be a diversity of possible models given the dissemination of ideas and organizational patterns, there may be major divergences from what one might expect from an examination of economic factors alone, and although there is considerable adaption it is more likely in our view that the economic adapts to the political and social necessities, than the other way round. This might hold even for the long period lags, because economic rationality goal-optimization cannot be assumed in the real world to the extent that many would like. Theories which claim to be 'a set of interrelated propositions *free of normative aspects*'[39] (italics added) understate pot-ential conflict, fall short of the mark, and insufficiently take into account the complex interplay of non-economic with directly economic variables. In order to produce better theory, we need more research on industrial conflict, comparative strike behaviour, and the organizational behaviour of labour organizations. This research must be interdisciplinary and relate the work carried out in the industrial relations area to industrial sociology and applied economics, to cite just two fields whose utility would be considerable.

NOTES

1 Anon, 'Crisis in European industrial relations', *Free Labour World* (*I.C.F.T.U.*) 251, May 1971, p. 17. Even a sophisticated observer like Dubin has recently speculated 'that in advanced capitalist economies, and in economically developed socialist societies the militancy of labour unions will decline. Unions' expanding involvement in bar-gaining over sources of attachment to work will draw them into higher levels of commitment to the objects of work attachment – the work of organization and its working environment'. See R. Dubin, 'Organiza-tional bonds and union militancy', paper given to the International Conference on Trends in Industrial and Labour Relations, Tel Aviv, January 1972, p. 15.

2 See Adolf Sturmthal, 'Economic development and the labour movement', in A. M. Ross (ed.), *Industrial relations and economic development*, London, 1966, pp. 165–81.
3 Mao's view is in fact more ambiguous – see his essay 'On contradictions' in the *Collected Works*, Peking, n.d.
4 See Jack Sawyer, 'Dimensions of nations: size, wealth, and politics', *American Journal of Sociology*, vol. 73, 1967, pp. 145–72. These three variables are practically uncorrelated with each other, but together highly predict a large number of other national characteristics. The study is based on 236 characteristics of 82 independent nations of more than 8,000,000 population.
5 See for example, Perlman's *Theory of the labor movement*, New York, 1928; also G. Gulick and M. Bers, 'Insight and illusion in Perlman's theory of the labor movement', *Industrial and Labor Relations Review*, vol. 6, July 1953, pp. 510–31.
6 See W. G. Runciman, *Relative deprivation and social justice*, London, 1966.
7 See Clark Kerr et al., *Industrialism and industrial man*, London, 1962.
8 See Sturmthal, 'Economic development and the labour movement', pp. 169–70.
9 See Sidney and Beatrice Webb, *The History of trade unionism*, London, 1894, chs. 4–7.
10 Sturmthal, 'Economic development and the labour movement', p. 170.
11 Kerr et al., *Industrialism and industrial man*, p. 7.
12 *Loc. cit.*
13 *Loc. cit.*
14 Ker et al., *Industrialism and industrial man*, p. 30.
15 *Loc. cit.*
16 *Loc. cit.*
17 cf. Sturmthal, 'Economic development and the labour movement', p. 169.
18 See A. Shonfield, *Modern capitalism*, Oxford, 1965, for example.
19 cf. Sturmthal, 'Economic development and the labour movement', p. 172.
20 These unions may not be able to bargain independently, for example. See R. H. Bates, 'Approaches to the study of unions and development', *Industrial Relations* (Berkeley), vol. 9, October 1970, p. 367.
21 cf. Sturmthal, 'Economic development and the labour movement', pp. 170–1, 174.
22 See *ibid.* p. 177.
23 See C. Wright Mills, *The power elite*, New York, 1956, and subsequent critiques of his work, for example R. A. Dahl, 'A critique of the ruling elite model', *American Political Science Review*, vol. 52, 1958, pp. 463–9.
24 cf. Sturmthal, 'Economic development and the labour movement', p. 179. The 'politicization' of the white collar unions has certainly increased of late, in the British case at least; also one may note in the United States.
25 Dahrendorf suggests that conflicts of interest are at least recognized

272

under the 'subtle' form of totalitarianism, and violent conflicts may simmer just under the surface, with some changes being introduced: see R. Dahrendorf, *Class and class conflicts in an industrial society*, London, 1959, p. 225.

26 Michael Shanks, 'A good bill, but management holds the real key', *The Times*, 15 October 1970, p. 31. cf. Kerr *et al.*, *Industrialism and industrial man*, pp. 256-7. The latter's points are thus only relatively applicable: the established procedures are only *partially* a 'substitute for open conflict' (p. 257).

27 See Robert Michels, *Political parties*, Glencoe, Ill., 1949.

28 This section consists of further reflections on the theme of an earlier article: M. Warner, 'The big trade unions: militancy of maturity?', *New Society*, 11 December 1969.

29 See e.g. R. A. Lester, *As unions mature*, Princeton, 1966.

30 See Bates 'Approaches to the study of unions and development', p. 371.

31 See P. M. Blau and W. R. Scott, *Formal organizations*, London: Routledge, 1963, pp. 45 ff. Although ongoing research by Warner and Donaldson has argued that occupational interest associations, like trade unions, are similar to other kinds of organizations studied, like firms. The differences on several dimensions however may be due to the lay control of members. See M. Warner and L. Donaldson, 'Dimensions of organization in occupational interest associations', *Third Joint Conference on the Behavioural Sciences and Operations Research*, London, December 1971. See also the next chapter (eleven), p. 285, note 8.

32 See Bates, 'Approaches to the study of unions and development', p. 372.

33 It may, however, be more inelastic than many union leaders believed, especially concerning raising members' dues: see J. H. Pencavel, 'The demand for union services', *Industrial and Labour Relations Review*, vol. 24, January 1971, pp. 180-90.

34 See D. Bell, *The End of Ideology*, Glencoe, Ill., 1960.

35 See for example, P. Henle, 'Some reflections on organized labor and the new militants', *Monthly Labor Review*, July 1969, p. 24.

36 See J. D. Edelstein and M. Warner (with W. F. Cooke), 'Patterns of opposition in British and American unions', *Sociology*, vol. 4, no. 3, May 1970, pp. 135-63.

37 The AUEW and the T & GWU, each with over a million members. This correlation will be strengthened if the large white collar unions increase their memberships, and at the same time grow in militancy. The recent miners' strike has tended to strengthen the above argument.

38 See H. A. Turner, 'The Donovan Report', *The Economic Journal*, vol. 79, March 1969, p. 6.

39 See Sturmthal, 'Economic Development and the labour movement. p. 181.

11 Sociological Imagination and Industrial Life

J. E. T. ELDRIDGE

In *The sociological imagination*, C. Wright Mills did more than call a plague on the houses of the grand theorists and the abstract empiricists in an energetic and sometimes almost slapstick way.[1] He did offer some suggestions as to how sociological imagination (which he defines in cryptic phrases such as 'a fruitful form of self-consciousness' and 'a capacity for astonishment') may be stimulated. These suggestions are mainly put forward in the interesting Appendix 'On intellectual craftsmanship'.[2] I should like in this paper to take up some of them with reference to industrial sociology.

CROSS-CLASSIFICATION

'For the working sociologist, cross-classification is what diagramming a sentence is for a diligent grammarian. In many ways, cross-classification is the very grammar of the sociological imagination'.[3]

Mills argues that cross-classification may be employed not only in the treatment of quantitative data – that is, cross-tabulation – but in the handling of qualitative material. He was himself much interested in industrial sociology and elsewhere in his work an example of a qualitative cross-classification is to be found.[4] It has to do with an attempt to clarify the relationship between subjective feelings of work satisfaction or dissatisfaction, and the structure of power within which work is actually carried out (Figure 1). This example is an instructive one. Mills was concerned to articulate the basis

Subjective condition of individual	Objective structure of power	
	Participates	*Does not participate*
Cheerful and willing	1. The unalienated worker	2. Manipulated pseudo-morale: management's goal to gather workers here
Uncheerful and unwilling	3. Malcontent: the unadjusted worker	4. The alienated worker

Figure 1

upon which the Mayo school of industrial sociology operated. He argued that it was essentially a tool of management because, while it was concerned with promoting job satisfaction, it accepted the existing power structure within and surrounding the industrial enterprise. The object of the exercise was therefore to move workers by various therapeutic techniques from the 'alienated' to the 'manipulated' category. Although it is fair to say that the human relations school certainly envisaged a greater means of control by work groups over the immediate conditions of their work and in that sense greater participation, Mills's argument is that, perhaps in part because of its ideological orientation, questions of control are ignored and consequently categories 1 and 3 in the constructed table provide new ways of thinking about the position of the worker in industry. This was later, we may recall, to inform much of his discussion of the white collar worker in the USA.[5] He was, of course, himself concerned that social conditions be realized in which position 1 in the table be approximated by workers. That, one may presume, was a stimulus to his thinking. This in no sense detracts from his contention that cross-classification as a technique 'is the best way to imagine and to get hold of *new* types as well as to criticise and clarify old ones'.[6] In this particular case, new categories are constructed as a product of reflecting on a contemporary orthodoxy in industrial sociology. This would, in its turn, affect the way empirical data was handled and interpreted. To make such cross-classifications explicit is also to point to the conceptual basis from which 'objective' indices (say of job satisfaction or 'alienation') ultimately derive.

One of the mixed blessings of a researcher's life, one may

275

suppose, is the discovery that the original cross-classificatory devices from which one began eventually come to seem rather crude and inadequate. Bernstein, in a discussion of his research in language and socialization, recently made the point very frankly:

'The greatest sadness is that after twelve years I think the theory is sufficiently explicit to stand exploration at both conceptual and empirical levels, but this is now too late for our own research. *For the research was predicated on a much coarser theoretical position and this affected the nature of the data we collected, the methods of analysis and the interpretative principles'.*[7] (my italics)

Let us take a more recent example of cross-classification. In their paper 'Towards an organisational study of trade unions', Child, Loveridge, and Warner explore the issue of membership attachment.[8] This is of course an important element in any discussion of participation in union organizations, and eventually for considering the appropriateness, for example, of oligarchical theories of organizations. The writers argue that one cannot understand membership behaviour as expressed by participation rates without gaining knowledge of what meaning the union has for its members in particular times and circumstances. To facilitate this they construct a typology of membership attachment based on the cross-classification of two variables – the degree of active involvement which a member has in union affairs, and the degree to which union policies appear to him to be congruent with his expectations of the union (Figure 2). The value of doing this, as they point out, is

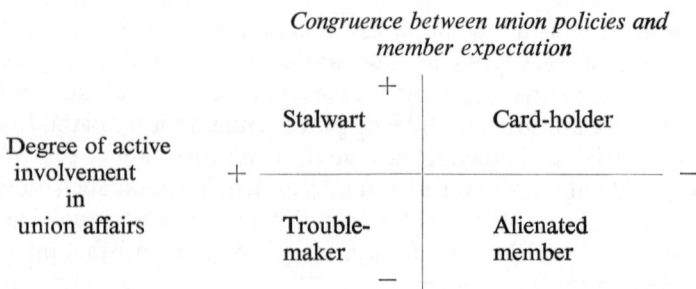

Congruence between union policies and member expectation

	+	
	Stalwart	Card-holder
Degree of active involvement in union affairs $+$		$-$
	Trouble-maker	Alienated member
	$-$	

Figure 2

that it 'creates a framework within which changes in the nature of . . . attachment can be specified and the search for an explanation of such changes be more clearly focussed'.[9] They make clear that even the relationship between the two variables assumed by the cross-classification must be open to empirical investigation but nevertheless 'a prior analytical framework should facilitate the design of such an investigation'.[10] Hence we see the sociological imagination in action and see it as a guide to further discovery. And again we would emphasize that the use of indices and measurements will at least initially be constrained by this prior act of cross-classification.

PRACTISING THE CRAFT

'Let every man be his own methodologist; let every man be his own theorist: let theory and method again become part of the practice of the craft.'[11]

This remark was designed to discourage researchers getting into an intellectual straitjacket, whether in terms of slavishly following certain established procedures of investigation or of following unreflectively a received theory without proper regarded to the problem in hand.

There are not all that many studies in industrial sociology in which the researchers are really explicit in describing the way they approached their problems. But there are one or two which are worth citing. There is, for example, a fairly extended Appendix to Gouldner's well-known study *Patterns of industrial bureaucracy* which discusses fieldwork procedures in a very open way.[12] I will mention two points which arise from this account. First, that norms about how to interview, which abound in well-intentioned textbooks, sometimes need to be abandoned in the interests of the research. In this sense a difference was found in the appropriate stance for interviewing miners as compared to surface workers at the gypsum plant. The notion of the interviewer as an impersonal collector of information and opinion seemed to work with the surface workers. With the miners, however, the interview took on more of the character of an exchange of views and feelings. Gouldner comments:

S 277

'The ideal role of the impersonal interviewer could be approximated on the surface, but it fell flat in the mine. We tentatively conclude from the experience that the danger of interviewer's "over-identification" or "over-rapport" can be much exaggerated and that it is sometimes indispensable to develop friendly ties with certain kinds of respondents in order to obtain their co-operation . . . Deep rapport has its perils but to treat the norm of impersonality as sacred, even if it impairs the informant's co-operation would seem to be an inexcusable form of scientific ritualism.'[13]

It is precisely this ability to make adjustments of this order, in the pursuit of a deeper level of understanding, that is in the spirit of the injunction 'every man . . . his own methodologist'.

The second point relates to the group discussions of the research team. The links between observation, data collection, hypotheses, interpretative hunches, and available theory were forged in an on-going and sometimes groping and untidy way. Gouldner indicates how disparate observations could be and were brought together in ways which suggested increasing bureaucratization in the mine – for example the construction of offices which made closer supervision possible, the introduction of stricter instructions concerning time clocks and of rules forbidding the use of Company equipment for use outside the plant. This encouraged the research team to look more closely at the relationships between supervision and the plant manager where confirmatory evidence was forthcoming about the growth of formal rules characterizing the relationships. Furthermore, the well-known typology of bureaucracy, which is used as an ordering device in the book, was triggered off as a result of obtaining concrete data about safety regulations. Hence, existing theories of bureaucracy with which Gouldner and his associates were familiar could be developed and reformulated as a result of the field experience. It is for reasons such as these that Gouldner refers to 'the intricate interplay between theorizing and data collection'.[14] It is the working through of these intricacies which marks out the craftsman.[15]

Another writer who offers an illuminating appendix on method is Melville Dalton in his excellent study *Men who manage*.[16] Dalton says:

'When treated as a fixed set of procedures, method ignores

278

or obscures the researcher's frequent groping, stumbling and set-backs. In current practice, the listing of fears, mistakes and interpersonal problems in collecting data is likely to seem unorthodox and to be treated as a mark of ineptness. Yet these are accompaniments, and they may greatly influence what is seen and how it is handled.'[17]

Dalton describes how he did not begin with explicit hypotheses but puzzled over a number of observations like the conflict existing between maintenance and operative personnel, the ambiguities surrounding the use of Company materials and services, moving gradually towards his overall guiding question, namely, 'what orders the schisms and ties between official and unofficial action?' So far as possible, he disciplined his observations and hunches as they moved towards tentative conclusions by getting comparative data from other available plants. The interlocking techniques of interviewing, work diaries, participant observation are helpfully described and the way in which he learned of sensitive areas of discussion – notably the Catholic-Mason cleavage and the fact that a number of Catholics had become Masons in the Company, which emerged as a significant factor in evaluating the management power struggle. The realistic flexibility of method is well reflected in the following comment:

'Usually expecting guarded talk, I sought when possible to catch men in near critical situations, and to learn in advance when important meetings were coming up and what bearing they would have on unofficial aspects of various issues. Experience with reneging informants prompted me to get comments or gestures of some kind from certain people before their feelings cooled or they became wary. In interviewing I usually had in mind a schedule of points to follow. But when the respondent's talk covered events of seeming greater importance, I omitted or adapted my prepared questions.'[18]

Much of the discussion in this section bears upon a point made elsewhere by Burns. In reflecting on the study *The management of innovation*[19] he recalled the rather defensive attitude of the author towards their interviewing procedure because they were worried that it was 'unscientific'. However,

279

he now takes the view that complex problems demand all the help the subject can give the researcher:

'Research becomes, in fact, a true search process among the experience of individual members of the social system, in which hypotheses and deduction become a social process. There is a sense in which in their eagerness to achieve "scientific detachment" social scientists have cut themselves off from their main resource – the ability of human beings to memorise and report their own experiences.'[20]

Most of the discussion in this section has to do with the use and handling of appropriate methods in relation to the research problem. The ways in which several methods might be employed in an interlocking way has also been noted. It is one form of what has come to be termed 'triangulation'. It is advocated by those who believe that social scientists who adhere to one method of research and parade its virtues against all the defects of other methods miss the chance of gaining, at best, confirmatory evidence from the application of different methods. Sometimes, of course, the somewhat more confusing effect of contradictions may occur – as in say the differences between attitudes as revealed by interviewing and behaviour as revealed by direct observation. This in itself is a challenge and an antidote to over-firm conclusions based on one method.

Denzin has suggested that there are various forms of triangulation, the whole constituting a process of 'multiple triangulation'.[21] These, for our purposes we may cross-classify as in Table 1. Denzin contends that one's confidence

Table 1

	Data triangulation	Investigator triangulation	Methodological triangulation	Theoretical triangulation
Data triangulation	X	1	2	3
Investigator triangulation	4	X	5	6
Methodological triangulation	7	8	X	9
Theoretical triangulation	10	11	12	X

in the investigation will increase as one achieves a greater measure of multiple triangulation – so, putting it somewhat mechanically, the more cells that are covered in an investigation the greater the reliability of the work. Let us illustrate this briefly with reference to industrial sociology. A good example (cited by Denzin) of data, investigator, and methodological triangulation is Lipset, Trow, and Coleman's *Union democracy*.[2] Clearly there were a number of skilled investigators who were able to counter-act one another's idiosyncratic biases and add to one another's partial insights. We have already seen the usefulness of this in Gouldner's *Patterns of industrial bureaucracy*. Data triangulation was evident in the strategy which recognized that there were various levels of analyses – the union as a whole (ITU), the locals, the shop floor, and the individuals engaged in union activity. This involved the collection of a range of data including union laws, policies, and convention reports, histories of locals, the voting records of shops and locals, and opinions from the men, and their union leaders. The methods entailed included interviewing, historical reconstruction, qualitative and quantitative analyses of documents to ascertain, for example, voting patterns and hopefully to infer the significance of the issues at stake.

Theoretical triangulation involves the researcher in the analysis of the same set of data from different theoretical perspectives. We may take two examples, the first somewhat more straightforward than the second. In the study of *Labour relations in the motor industry*, Turner, Clack, and Roberts[23] examine a number of theories of strike-proneness to see how far the data they had collected 'fitted' with the existing general explanations available about strike causation. In the process they claim to have grounds for missing theories which stress 'technology', 'geographical location', 'tensions of the track', 'political agitation' as dominant. On the other hand, an explanation which emphasizes wages issues (especially relativity questions) and the attempt to maintain job security, they find to be consistent with their data.

The second example relates to the work of Goldthorpe, Lockwood, Bechofer, and Platt, *The affluent worker in the class structure*.[24] This is a good illustration of multiple triangulation except perhaps at the methodological level where the major research instrument was the interview. At the theoretical level, the embourgeoisoment thesis is considered in relation to the data – the idea of assimilation of the working class into the middle class is found not proven (and for that matter suspect on logical grounds). Alternative theories concerning the alienation of the industrial worker are then examined. The various interpretations of the alienation theme are found wanting by the investigators either because they believe some interpretations are dogmatic matters of faith not open to empirical refutation, or because where an empirical position is taken the data do not support it. In particular, the contention of writers such as Mallet that the explanation of worker behaviour is to be seen as a product of the technological environment and the productive relations which ensue, is rejected since it neglects the influence of life outside the factory as an explanatory factor. It is accepted however that Marx's original characterization of alienated labour is broadly in line with the picture of the instrumental worker who finds satisfaction outside the factory but not in work itself, which is only a means for satisfying other needs. But more specifically, although the perspective is not developed in the same way as Marxist or liberal perspectives, a social democratic perspective is put forward which is intended to have some explanatory value. The relevant passage is as follows:

'in our perspective on the new working class and on the question of what its political significance will be, the "degree of freedom" that exists becomes a consideration of central importance. To introduce such an emphasis would seem desirable if only to counterbalance the necessitarian tendencies inherent in other interpretations. But, furthermore, we would underline the heuristic value in bringing out in this way the role that must be assigned to political *leadership*: that is, to purposive action on the part of elites and organisations, aimed at giving a specific and politically relevant meaning to grievances, demands and aspirations, which have hitherto been of a sub-political kind, and at thus mobilising mass support for a programme or movement.'[25]

These examples hopefully show the possibilities as well as the limitations of Denzin's argument for theoretical triangulation. It is not always a simple matter to play one theory off against another in the social sciences in the belief that truth will triumph in the encounter. This is reflected in the less ambitious position of Bernstein whom we cited earlier: 'It is probably wrong to use the word "theory". Perhaps in the end the sole criterion is: do these encourage a shift in perspective so that we can see received frames differently or even a little beyond them.'[26] I suspect that behind these two positions lie the, for me, unresolved issue of the realism/nominalism debate in sociology.

IMAGINING ALTERNATIVES

According to Gouldner:

'Social scientists need a quality of mind which habitually leads them to conceive, to play with, to formulate and to entertain various solutions for social problems rather than simply to describe and explain them. They need a constructive quality of the imagination which can serve what might be . . . let them be compared with the shop-soiled social worlds that are presently up for sale.'[27]

This strain was evident in *Patterns of industrial bureaucracy* although in a more muted form. Gouldner then, it will be recalled, in his discussion of punishment-centred and representative bureaucracy indicates that the distinction has policy implications. Even though he obviously prefered the second, the important thing in his view was to have pointed to representative bureaucracy as an available and sometimes used form of social organization. In this sense, the sociologist even if he is not in a direct way politically involved may inform the terms of the debate.

When sociologists publish, their work tends to be scanned for its policy relevance. For example, the report of Touraine and his associates on workers' attitudes to technical change[28] was criticized by some who attended an OECD conference in 1966 as being descriptive but not prescriptive. This, one supposes, had been the primary intention of the writers. Nonetheless two 'practical' suggestions were written in, namely that information should be given to employees about change and employees should participate in the introduction of change.[29] It is but a short step to move on to 'action research' in which ways of implementing these goals are developed, discussed, and evaluated by social scientists in collaboration with those involved in the changes. This certainly is the underlying rationale of consultancy undertaken by the Tavistock Institute in the UK and the Work Research Institute in Oslo. The emphasis is on designing socio-technical systems which will enhance the autonomy, engage the creativity, and enlarge the choices of individuals and work groups. Clearly there is a process of imagining alternatives – but the processes are to emerge within the existing social order without in any sense questioning its legitimacy. Such an approach can function in a gradualist way but perhaps cannot easily accommodate deeper social crises.

The issue raised in the above paragraph has been developed by Willener in his study of the events in France of May 1968.[30] In effect he contrasts those whose imagination for the future of industrial societies is based on one variety or another of a technological solution with those who construct an action-image of society. The first operates on a consciousness of the possible

> 'which amounts to defining the ends to be pursued according to the resources available – human, social and cultural resources defined in statistics . . . The action-image is exactly the opposite mode. It rejects technocrats and balance sheets which it opposes with invective . . . In the new culture envisaged, and for a time lived, the act of creating is as important as, in fact more important than, the product that results. It is, in other words, the inversion of the instrumentalism that is to be observed in the thinking of many modern specialists . . .'[31]

What is raised, albeit mainly in a rhetorical fashion, is the question, how inevitable is industrial society as we know it, and how inevitable are the 'trends' especially as they pertain to bureaucracy and the exercise of power and authority? One is offered a libertarian solution to the question once raised by Weber, namely, is there any escape from the iron cage of bureaucracy?

NOTES

1 C. Wright Mills, *The sociological imagination*, London: Oxford University Press, 1959.
2 *Ibid.* pp. 159–226.
3 *Ibid.* p. 213.
4 C. Wright Mills, 'The contributions of sociology to the studies of industrial relations', in *Proceedings of the first annual meeting of the Industrial Relations Research Society*, 1948, p. 219. Cited in P. Blumberg, *Industrial democracy: the sociology of participation*, London: Constable, 1968, p. 45.
5 C. Wright Mills, *White collar*, London: Oxford University Press, 1956.
6 Wright Mills, *The sociological imagination*, p. 213.
7 B. Bernstein, *Class, codes and control*, vol. 1, London: Routledge and Kegan Paul, 1971, p. 17.
8 J. Child, R. Loveridge, and M. Warner, 'Towards an organizational study of trade unions', mimeo, to appear in *Sociology*, January 1973.
9 *Ibid.* p. 17.
10 *Loc. cit.*
11 Wright Mills, *The sociological imagination*, p. 224.
12 A. Gouldner, *Patterns of industrial bureaucracy*, London: Routledge and Kegan Paul, 1955.
13 *Ibid.* pp. 259–60.
14 *Ibid.* p. 268.
15 J. Bensman and A. Vidich, 'Social theory in field research', in W. J. Filstead (ed.), *Qualitative methodology*, New York: Markham, 1970, pp. 328–39.
16 M. Dalton, *Men who manage*, New York: Wiley, 1959, pp. 273–85.
17 *Ibid.* p. 274.
18 *Ibid.* pp. 280–1.
19 T. Burns and G. Stalker, *The management of innovation*, London: Tavistock, 1966.
20 T. Burns, 'The comparative study of organizations', p. 155, in V. Vroom (ed.), *Methods of organisational research*, Pittsburgh: Universiy of Pittsburgh Press, 1968, pp. 113–69.
21 N. Denzin (ed.), *Sociological methods. A source book*, New York: Butterworth, 1970, p. 472.
22 S. M. Lipset, M. A. Trow, and J. S. Coleman, *Union democracy: the internal politics of the International Typographical Union*, Glencoe, Ill.: Free Press, 1956.
23 H. A. Turner, G. Clack, and G. Roberts, *Labour relations in the motor industry*, London: Allen and Unwin, 1967.
24 J. H. Goldthorpe, D. Lockwood, F. Bechhofer, and J. Platt, *The affluent worker in the class structure*, London: Cambridge University Press, 1969.
25 *Ibid.* p. 189.
26 Bernstein, *Class, codes and control*, p. 20.
27 A. Gouldner, *Enter Plato*, New York: Basic Books, 1965, pp. 295–6.

28 A. Touraine, *Workers' attitudes to technical change*, Paris: OECD, 1965.
29 *Final report*, 1967.
30 A. Willener, *The action-image of society. On cultural politicization*, London: Tavistock, 1970.
31 *Ibid.* pp. 294–5.

Index